I0105430

Snakes in
American Culture

Snakes in American Culture

A Hisstory

JESSE C. DONAHUE *and*
CONOR SHAW-DRAVES

McFarland & Company, Inc., Publishers
Jefferson, North Carolina

ALSO OF INTEREST
BY JESSE C. DONAHUE AND
ERIK K. TRUMP

American Zoos During the Depression:
A New Deal for Animals (2010)

LIBRARY OF CONGRESS CATALOGUING-IN-PUBLICATION DATA

Names: Donahue, Jesse, author.
Title: Snakes in American culture : a hisstory /
Jesse C. Donahue and Conor Shaw-Draves.
Description: Jefferson, NC : McFarland & Company, Inc.,
2019 | Includes bibliographical references and index.
Identifiers: LCCN 2018058333 | ISBN 9781476662657
(softcover : acid free paper) ∞
Subjects: LCSH: Snakes—United States—History. |
Human-animal relationships. | Animals and history.
Classification: LCC QL666.O6 D5974 2019 | DDC 597.96—dc23
LC record available at https://lccn.loc.gov/2018058333

BRITISH LIBRARY CATALOGUING DATA ARE AVAILABLE

ISBN (print) 978-1-4766-6265-7
ISBN (ebook) 978-1-4766-3453-1

© 2019 Jesse C. Donahue and Conor Shaw-Draves. All rights reserved

No part of this book may be reproduced or transmitted in any form
or by any means, electronic or mechanical, including photocopying
or recording, or by any information storage and retrieval system,
without permission in writing from the publisher.

Front cover images © 2019 iStock

Printed in the United States of America

McFarland & Company, Inc., Publishers
Box 611, Jefferson, North Carolina 28640
www.mcfarlandpub.com

Acknowledgments

We wish to acknowledge several people and institutions for their help with this book. Marget Dykens, the archivist at the San Diego Natural History Museum, was a wonderful help during the two trips that one of us made to read through the Laurence Klauber collection. Ellen Alers from the Smithsonian Institution Archives helped us with the William and Lucille Mann papers and Gregory Raml facilitated our use of the Roger Conant Papers at the American Natural History Museum in New York. John Caltabiano, Ellen Palm, and Matt Lanier at the Staten Island Zoo were of help; and we thank Doris Wesley and Kenn Thomas for help with the Western Historical Manuscript Collection at the University of St. Louis, Missouri; Thomas Donahue for his translation of Afranio do Amaral's work; and Thomas Zantow, our interlibrary loan librarian, who cheerfully tracked down hard to find sources that our library did not own. We also wish to thank the anonymous peer reviewers secured by McFarland who pointed out errors in our scientific writing about snakes. Any biological mistakes about these amazing creatures are our own.

Table of Contents

Preface

Dangerous Neighbors

Jesse C. Donahue

As a child in the early 1970s, living on Storm King Mountain near Cornwall-on-Hudson, New York, accidental visits with snakes were common. Rock walls surrounding houses served as homes for snakes. These animals and I sometimes literally ran into one another as I walked or rode my bike by a wall and they darted out from the safety of their small caverns, fearing the approach of a large animal. These were frightening encounters for a small child, so I always ran home after them seeking comfort from a parent. Being good environmental stewards, my parents informed me that I had nothing to fear from snakes and that they were more scared of me than I was of them. But I was not so sure. There were times when the black snakes, in particular, seemed aggressive, rearing up threateningly and darting toward me. The snakes clearly perceived me much the same way I saw them. From their perspective, I was a threatening giant near their shelter and they wanted to defend themselves and seek safety. Other times, large black snakes scaled trees in our yard, making their way to a sturdy limb to sun themselves.

The place we lived was aptly named because of lightning storms in the summer that hit the mountain and sometimes hollowed out trees. We had a couple of these lightning strikes on our property that split trees down the middle, so previous home owners had placed metal rebars inside one of the trees to preserve it, even though much of the center had been gouged out by lightning. The rebars were placed in a step-like manner up the center of the tree, and black snakes used them as a kind of staircase to get to holes near branches and climb out onto limbs to sun themselves. During one summer, we gathered together as a family on one of our lawns

Face of a western black rat snake found in New York State. They have a painful bite and they are excellent tree climbers (courtesy commons.wikimedia.org; https://snappygoat.com).

and watched in amazement as one large black snake suddenly appeared out of a hole in the middle of the tree. He or she had climbed up the center of one of the lightning-stuck trees and made its way out onto a long branch. The snake was as long as the large and substantial branch on which it was enjoying the afternoon sun—easily as tall as our six-foot-tall father. These encounters left a lasting impression and turned me into one of the millions of ophidiophobics around the world.

Some 20 years later, in the late 1980s on the opposite coast, my environmentalist fiancé convinced me to take a backpacking trip to a breath-taking group of mountains called the Trinity Alps, in Northern California. As a child, he had spent many a lovely day there admiring the beauty of the crystal-clear streams, lakes, and redwoods. After reading the map, I expressed concern about hiking alongside "rattlesnake creek," but he assured me that the name of our destination did not signify the fact that large numbers of this particular reptile lived there. He was wrong. Next to rattlesnake creek were large piles of rock made by gold prospectors over a hundred years ago. We were struck by the challenge that these animals must have posed to miners who sought their fortunes in this rugged part of the world. Like the New England walls, these rock piles had effectively created snake condominiums. We saw the snakes sunning themselves on top of the rock mounds, trying to catch the sunlight filtering through the redwood branches. This time, however, they were large, almost emerald green, rattlesnakes. Even in my state of sheer terror, I recognized that they were absolutely stunning. Their vibrant color, size, and inherent dangerousness gave them a kind of beauty that seemed almost magical. On our four-day trip, we saw, and nearly stepped on, three of them. The trip was supposed to last longer, but the sheer number of them started to get worrisome, and we headed home early. As far as we knew, we were prepared if a rattlesnake bit one of us. Although we were both college educated, including one of us with a graduate degree, neither of us came from a medical field and so we had not read the best and most up-to-date literature on snakebites. Instead, like many Americans, we were burdened with the advice of the past. According to hiking and recreational wisdom, we were supposed to have a snakebite kit of some kind with us, which we did. Inside the kit, we had a razor, a rubber tube for a ligature, some antiseptic, and bandaids. If one of us got bitten, we understood that we should tie a ligature around the bitten limb, slice open the bite area, suck out the venom, and then head to the hospital. All of this was highly unpleasant sounding to me. It sounded, in fact, worse than the bite itself, and I suspected that the whole idea made little sense. I had seen a friend try to pierce another person's ears, and even that simple procedure had not gone well. If I got bitten, I could imagine screaming in pain, tears, perhaps a few curses, and then a struggle with my fiancé about who exactly was going to make the cut on my arm. In short, we were typical Americans in that we were the victims of poor medical advice from the past, coping with one of the most interesting, and sometimes dangerous, animals among us.

As readers shall see throughout this book, these encounters capture several of the findings of this book that examines Americans' complicated relationship with snakes. First, and most obviously, I encountered several of them near my home or during an outdoor recreational experience. There was not just one memorable experience, but repeated ones. Second, whether or not snakes are a problem depends upon one's perspective. To someone whose height is half the length of the snakes and who also climbed trees, they were dangerous. To my white, East Coast parents who worked safely inside buildings, snakes were an interesting and crucial part of nature. Third, the kinds of snakes one runs into depends upon where one lives. An obvious point, but one, as we shall see, that was often lost on writers from the East

Coast in the 18th and 19th centuries. Fourth, much of America still remains rugged and remote, which leads to snake encounters, particularly for the pioneers who work, live, or spend recreational time in these places. The miners struggling in the California mountains in the past capture the types of occupations that placed people into accidental contact with snakes historically. Fifth, the snakes entertained us when we watched the black snake scale the tree, and although we did not use the animal for profit, many other Americans have, as we shall see. But the snakes were also opportunists, using the rebar in the tree, and the rocks on the miners' mounds, to their benefit. Sixth, snakes are unmistakably fascinating. As much as I feared the rattlesnakes in California, I couldn't help but marvel at their dangerous beauty. This fear and fascination is woven into the fiber of our beings through systems of culture and faith. And finally, both types of snake were life-threatening under the right circumstances. We considered their venom before we went into their environment, because getting treated for a bite would be painful at best, and life threatening at worst, even in the late 1980s. And the cure still recommended among lay people at the time was itself a barbaric act. We would have had little choice, as far as we knew, however, because snakes were all around us.

My coauthor, Conor, and I are not alone in writing about snakes. The literature about snakes is voluminous, but overwhelmingly it is found in fields outside of popular culture and the history of medicine. Existing literature on snakes is largely found in the natural sciences. Its primary purpose is to scientifically identify snakes and their habitats for amateur collectors and amateur naturalists. We wish to make it abundantly clear, however, that this is not one of those books. This is not a biological guide to snakes in the United States. Another subgenre of the literature that comes a little closer to the purpose of this book involves current collections of stories or field research experiences told either by amateurs or professional herpetologists.[1] There is also a single study about the struggles over enforcing protection for snakes (and other reptiles) through the Convention on the International Trade of Endangered Species.[2] Another subgenre are medical studies that focus broadly on the scientific nature of snake venom, the demographics of snakebites, and sometimes some of the treatment protocols that preceded antivenin.[3] The closest study to this one is a more internationally focused one by Drake Stutesman, entitled *Snake*, that examines some central aspects of the relationship between humans and snakes throughout the world.[4]

Unlike these books, our work examines snakes primarily in American culture and history from the 1800s forward. It is at once a book that we hope will appeal to people interested in snakes, popular culture, history of medicine, and animal studies. Like *History of Consciousness* scholar Donna Haraway, we are interested in how these two species—humans and snakes—have met. They are, in her resonant words, "entangled" with us.[5] Writing about dogs, she (and others) note that they are the "other" who have included "monsters, creepy crawlies, women, servants and slaves, and noncitizens." These "others" have a "capacity to induce panic in the centers of power." They induce "hyperphalia" and "hyperphobias."[6] Snakes, and particularly dangerous ones, are the ultimate other in the animal world. To examine this, we analyze how people encountered snakes, how people tried to save themselves (or not) from interactions that went badly (bites), how snakes have been used in entertainment, and the role of snakes in American religious movements. This book draws on archival papers from the San Diego Historical Society, the American Natural History Museum, the Smithsonian Institution, and circus archives. We make extensive use of newspaper archives to share stories from around the country to illustrate what people experienced in the states that had the most snakes. We also draw from medical journals, textbooks, and first aid manuals from a variety of organizations whose members came into contact with snakes (particularly rattlesnakes) in the United States. Through an analysis of those texts, we show that some people were perceived as disposable just as the snakes were. In this case, snakes did not cause panic at the center of power, instead, we show that powerful voices downplayed their danger to make themselves seem wise. There was a great divide between humans and snakes, but it was primarily between white, privileged writers from the east and snakes. Writers from the cities on the East Coast either intentionally or unintentionally treated rural people, poor people, children, *and* snakes as though they were either nonexistent or disposable. We show that both species (human, and reptiles in the form of snakes), however, have been opportunists and both have suffered dearly for it, although some humans have clearly benefited the most. Through the use of these documents, we show that snakes have taken advantage of our food, our shelter, and our water for their survival. Humans, in turn, have used snakes for economic gain in all kinds of ways, including entertainment. Unlike other animals who also benefited the human species, however, snakes have fought back and inflicted significant damage on humans in the United States and elsewhere.

Chapter 1 examines how Americans came into contact with snakes in the 1800s forward, primarily by focusing on the encounters that went badly. It is true that some people have always owned snakes as pets in the

United States and have had harmonious relationships with them. It is also equally true that most snake encounters are nonviolent, and that both sides leave one another alone and live together in harmony. Newspaper stories in the mid to late 1800s often covered the fact that parts of America were inundated with snakes. Rural Pennsylvania and New York sometimes found their hillsides swarming with black snakes or rattlesnakes. The southwest was famous for its large numbers of particularly venomous rattlesnakes, and the southeast and south had all of these snakes, plus a healthy amount of cottonmouths as well. We are two species living among one another constantly, and many times we can coexist.

However, many of the snake and human interactions did not end well. And we begin by showing that self-appointed experts from the East Coast perpetuated myths about human and rattlesnake interactions to make themselves sound like reasonable, scientific, and fearless men. Contrary to the facts, these authors made a variety of fictitious claims in newspapers and other sources, including, for example, that rattlesnakes never bit people. Americans who lived or worked outside of cities on farms, ranches, railroads, the woods, and plantations, however, really struggled with venomous snakes, particularly rattlesnakes, who bit them. Poor people encountered snakes during the day as they reached down to pick something up from the ground or to work the earth. And they met them at night as both they and the snakes sought shelter in the slightly warmer interiors of poorly constructed cabins or tents. These communities sometimes attracted more snakes than would have been present in the wild. People brought grain for themselves and their livestock, the kernels enticed rodents, and the snakes followed for the mice. Later, in the early 1900s, when recreational hiking and outdoor wilderness sightseeing became a trend, these kinds of Americans also learned about the sheer number of snakes that surround us and they too attracted snakes to their camps through food.[7] Many of these interactions ended in bites that caused dramatic pain and frequently death for humans and sometimes the snakes as well. We review the many ways in which people were bitten and the agonizing ways in which they died.

As a result of the frequent bites, many people needed medical treatment for them, particularly from rattlesnakes and cottonmouth snakes. In Chapter 2, we show that from the beginning, family healers, and later doctors, in the United States had a variety of ways of approaching snakebites, most of which were ineffective. Early on, the treatment was complicated by the fact that family medical providers, and later doctors, were not herpetologists and sometimes struggled to know which snakes were venomous. Most could recognize a rattlesnake, but some venomous snakes have mimics that appear like them. Were these poisonous too? And how should doctors warn people about venomous snakes in the area? Should they make it clear that venomous snakebites were a serious problem that they could not cure or would that call their medical credentials into question? The answer was that they brazened it out. Even though they were not always sure which snakes were venomous and which were not, they assured people that they could tell the difference. While almost all of their cures were ineffective, they highly recommended them to others in medical journals. This is explained, in part, by the fact that venomous snakes do not always inject venom with their bites, so even when people were bitten by a rattlesnake, they were not always envenonmated. Part of the problem, though, was that doctors during the 1800s simply provided advice that was clearly not good. At their most benign, early doctors recommended herbal treatments that they claimed came from Native Americans. Snakeweed wrapped around the wound was a popular option, as was tobacco leaf in the south. Much more commonly, however, doctors recommended extreme measures, and instead of looking to science, they took their inspiration from hunters who recommended violent and generally ineffective methods of ridding venom from the body. They suggested shooting off bitten digits, placing hot irons on bites, injecting people with strychnine or ammonia, and slashing the bite site and sucking out the venom. Everyone should drink whisky, they said, including small children.

Most official group manuals recommended whiskey alongside the other violent and ineffective treatments except two groups: temperance advocates and outdoor organizations for girls. Prohibitionists were particularly unhappy with the idea of prescribing alcohol and waged a long war against its use for snakebites. They argued that alcohol addiction ruined more lives than snakebites and bemoaned the "serpent" of the saloon. They claimed, generally without evidence, that people faked their snakebites to get whiskey at bars. They characterized working-class men as drunkards who came to get some pain relief from alcohol when there was little else around to help them. And they said that people should simply stay away from rattlesnakes, but offered no real way to cure bites. From women's recreational advocates we find no mention of the need to ply bite victims with lots of alcohol and slash their bodies open with razors. Instead, like the prohibitionists, they simply asserted that the girls should just avoid snakes. If girls did not spend time around snakes, there was no need to discuss how to cure bites. This evidence suggests that they believed that, on some level, the people who were bitten must have deserved it because they put themselves into contact with snakes intentionally. This type of advice also showed that girls were not really deserving of any actual information that might save their lives. If they got bitten because they were hiking near snakes, then they should die.

Luckily for Americans, some clear-headed scientists, soldiers, and zoo directors took a more practical approach to the snakebite problem and created an antivenin that finally worked. In Chapter 3, we show that partly because soldiers and zoo workers were bitten, they realized that a better cure was needed. Unlike newspaper writers in cities who could dismiss the problem, these men saw the consequences of venomous snakebites first-hand and experienced it themselves. They were inspired by Albert Calmette's famous experience with massive cobra attacks in Vietnam, which convinced them to seek a cure that used the relatively new medical approach of creating serums to form resistance in patients. This approach required injecting small amounts of pre-collected venom in horses so that they built up an ability to fight the toxic effects of venom. They worked with Brazilian scientists who were already creating antivenin—Vital Brazil and his protégé Afranio do Amaral. Do Amaral, in particular, became the key figure in bringing antivenin to save Americans even though other scientists, such as Hideo Noguchi, were conducting some important primary scientific research on the properties of venom for the Rockefeller Institute. But first, do Amaral, and later antivenin researchers in the early 1900s, had to answer many questions. Was there one kind of antivenin that would work for all snakebites in the United States? Or would they have to give snakebite victims antivenin from that particular snake? Would antivenin from an American rattlesnake work on rattlesnake victims from different countries with different kinds of rattlesnakes? Did the same type of rattlesnake from different regions have the same venom? Were some venoms more potent than others? Were there different venom yields in different size snakes? How should they preserve the venom? Did it have to remain a liquid, or could they dry it and reconstitute it later on? How long would it last? How much venom could they inject into a horse or sheep at one time without killing it? How could they keep getting the venom from snakes when they were working hard in their laboratories and with animals in their stables to make the serum? And who should get the antivenin? How would it get distributed? These were some of the pressing problems that scientists, soldiers, professors, and zoo directors faced in trying to help Americans bitten by venomous snakes.

We show that to get the venom, antivenin researchers partly relied on a network of amateur snake collectors who donated their snake collecting work and venom extraction labor for free. Men like Martin Crimmins, a colonel in the U.S. military stationed in Texas, and Laurence Klauber, a businessman and amateur herpetologist in San Diego, captured and milked thousands of snakes in their spare time. Sometimes they shipped the snakes north, but typically they just sent the venom. Like those who preceded him, do Amaral found a significant source of income in working with snakes at his state-sponsored Butantan Institute in Brazil. He gave the antivenin to Brazilians for free as a public health measure if, for example, a plantation worker traded a venomous snake safely stored in a bag. In this way he created his own free collection network to keep venomous snakes coming to Butantan. He and his associates milked these snakes and created antivenin. The snakes were housed in what he called a snake ranch that consisted of an enclosed area of small snake houses on the grounds of Butantan. His generous public health approach did not apply as fully to the United States, however. Desperate for a cure in the United States, zoo directors and a Harvard University researcher invited do Amaral to bring and distribute the cure to zoos rather than hospitals. Until the mid 1980s, zoos served as the holding places for antivenin because they had workers who were bitten so often by a variety of poisonous snakes, and because herpetology curators were among the very small number of Americans who were publicly reachable and could correctly identify a snake. Significantly, do Amaral became the scientific voice that also discredited the previous scientific dismissals of the snakebite problem in the United States. He helped set up the first laboratory for making antivenin at Mulford Pharmaceuticals, and he relied on his Brazilian connection with American railroads to help create a snake collection process that kept venom flowing to his laboratory at Mulford.

Americans used snakes for other commercial reasons besides antivenin, however. In Chapter 4, we examine the ways that Americans used black snakes, pythons, and rattlesnakes to make money through entertainment as well. Early newspaper articles, many of which come from the East Coast, were often about black snakes. To some extent, this results from the geographic fact that many of the earliest newspapers started in the northeast where large black snakes sometimes outnumbered other kinds of snakes. Like the encounters with the black snakes discussed earlier, Americans who lived in the rural northeast were repeatedly struck by their size (black snakes can grow over six feet long) and their ability to scale trees and other structures. They stressed the terrifying experience, for example, of men working in the forest near their homes looking for firewood only to come upon snakes who were as large as the trees they passed. Given how startling these experiences were, it is perhaps not surprising that a kind of mythology built up around the black snake in early America that made its way into newspaper stories that were fictional, and somewhat erotic. They combined elements of the Biblical story of the snake in Eden and the Red Riding Hood folk tale. The stories served as entertainment much like the horror stories of our day, stressing the perils of loving the long, phallic symbol of the black snake.

The snakes' entertainment potential, however, was best exploited by two other more formal organizations: zoos and circuses. When zoos formed in the late 1880s and beyond, they quickly spawned a new occupation of exotic animal importer that brought all kinds of animals from around the world into the United States. Large snakes were among those animals brought to coastal cities in the northeast and shipped to zoos, particularly after the turn of the century. Boas were the snake of choice because of their size, beauty, and relative safety compared to other animals. Zoos exhibited the animals for scientific education reasons, but also sometimes took them out for entertainment. Circuses, in addition, immediately recognized their potential for theatre and included them in sideshow performances, frequently with women to eroticize them. In this case, we had two outsiders, women snake charmers and the snakes themselves, scaring audiences out of their money. Here, too, their size, phallic symbolism, and controlled danger were the lure of the show. Snakes, in short, entertained a fair number of Americans.

This trend continues to the present day, as we show in Chapter 5, by examining and analyzing selected snake horror movies, reality television shows, and documentaries. Here we again see the way in which snakes, and particularly rattlesnakes and pythons, are exploited for a great deal of money. By reviewing snake eco horror movies, we show that the basic narrative of the movies is recreated in reality television shows and documentaries even when they are supposed to be educational. We also explore the ways in which some of the entertainment methods of circus snake shows are still employed in reality television as well as documentaries. We illustrate how the woman snake charmer has been replaced by the male snake hunter by American media, and we show the unabashed focus on making money from snakes in these reality TV shows. We argue that although most circuses no longer have snake side shows, this kind of entertainment still exists and is broadcast through reality television shows and documentaries. Unlike circuses that had a vested economic interest in keeping the animals alive for multiple performances, the new snake hunters, the stars of reality television and some documentaries, are killing snakes on a massive scale. Snake death has been corporatized and sanitized for television viewers.

In Chapter 6, we take a look at how the southern Pentecostal movement in the late 1800s and early 1900s developed a new, American form of religious expression based on the abundance of snakes found in the wild, mountainous region of Appalachia and other parts of the south. These "serpent-handling" faiths drew inspiration from the Gospels of the New Testament (specifically the Book of Mark), and made the handling of serpents a primary sign of individuals who had received salvation through the baptism of the Holy Spirit. In this chapter, we review three documentaries—1967's *Holy Ghost People*, 1974's *People Who Take Up Serpents*, and 1991's *In Jesus' Name: Taking Up Serpents*—to illustrate how, unlike the reality TV examples in Chapter 5, this manifestation of faith emphasizes a distinct lack of fear in snakes, minimizes the entertainment aspect of their use in a circus-like environment, and shows individuals actively working to preserve snakes rather than kill them for profit (in fact, one of the biggest problems for these churches is keeping snakes alive and on hand). Also, because the majority of the followers of these faiths are from poorer, rural areas of the United States, and the actual practice of these faiths serves to separate the adherents even further from mainstream society, this chapter will examine how the minority nature of the serpent-handling faiths enhances the types of otherness discussed in the first few chapters of this book.

A close, and illustrative, analogy to snakebite victims are wasp or bee sting recipients. Through those experiences, we see a completely different rhetorical and medical approach to both the animals and the victims. Like venomous snakes, bees killed many people in America. People were killed when they were stung in the neck by wasps that they had accidentally ingested while drinking cider. Others were stung on the face while working outside and died within 24 hours. Some Americans were killed attempting to get honey for their families. Bee sting victims, however, were offered much more rational, humane advice, and were never told to suck out the bee venom by slashing the site, cutting out the poison sack, or cauterizing the sting site, even though many people experienced anaphylactic shock that killed them. Even in the 1880s, bee sting victims were told to use tweezers to pull out the stinger and then place a solution of methylated spirits and water over the site. Keeping the victim comfortable was also recommended.[8] So why the significant difference in the approach to treating the two kinds of encounters? Much like the snakebite history, the answers are found in the animals and their relationship with humans. First, bees had their own interest group dedicated to keeping them alive and beloved. Farmers actively cultivated them and had a vested interest in making them seem benign. Honey bees also gave us something tangible that we enjoyed, unlike venomous snakes who at best provided cures for potential illnesses for their own bites or kept some rodent populations down. And finally, bees were democratic in who they bit. There is no escaping insect bites, so there was no one to isolate and marginalize as deserving of their bite. In contrast, from early on, people bitten by snakes were treated as an entirely different class, one that on some level deserved their fate. The snakes themselves were treated as outlaws and biblically condemned animals. To their great peril and ours we have always been entangled with them.

1

Bitten

Poor Americans and Snakes

"Although I have been interested in the subject for many years, I have never met a man who has seen a fatal case of snake bite. More than this, my friend Mr. Stewart Edward White, a noted hunter and explorer of untrodden ground in regions infested by reptiles, has known of but one case terminating in death which he believes to be authentic."[1]

Samual Hopkins Adams, a "sportsman" from the east in 1910, assured Americans in no uncertain terms that the threat of rattlesnakes and other venomous snakes was a figment of their imagination, a bugaboo. People who were concerned about them were child-like, "beguiling [themselves] with ogre tales upon the terrors which lie just beyond [their] ken." He was writing for an urban, white, male audience who mainly went to the countryside to hunt or fish for recreation purposes. Another turn-of-the-century author assured urban readers that Americans shared snake stories that filled "the remoteness of forest and mountains" with venomous snakes that really did not exist there. And still another writer, who claimed to spend a lot of time outdoors in Montana, informed readers of the *New Northwest News,* published in Deer, Montana, that "nobody was ever bitten by a rattlesnake and no one ever will be." It was hard to find an animal, the writer claimed, who was less able to bite. The snake, he claimed, "couldn't bite" because its jaws were not hinged. It had no leverage to close its jaws against one another, and even if it attempted a bite, it could not pierce the skin. Imagine the futility of a man striking a hook into a log, and that captured the biting power of rattlesnakes in the United States.[2]

The authors claimed the moral high ground of rationality, sanity, and masculinity. They were full of bravado because they knew something about the wilderness that their peers did not know. They were men of science, not mythology and fear. And they were learned men who could write and impart their wisdom on those around them the way a parent would tell a child that there were no monsters under the bed. They described people with concerns about snakes as child-like. Adams claimed to interview ranchers and plantation owners who told him that snakebites were not a problem.[3] There were a few children killed, he acknowledged, but they did not seem to count. Adams' purpose seems to both demonstrate his own virile outdoors masculinity and reassure other members of urban areas of the northeast, who had no direct experience with snakes, that it was safe to take up the new recreational pursuits championed by hunting and outdoors groups in the early 1900s. William Hornaday, the director of the Bronx Zoo in the early 1920s, also portrayed venomous snakes in the United States as basically harmless. Rattlesnakes were unlike venomous snakes in other countries in that they politely warned us about impending bites through their tails. He had hiked many miles in Montana and did not suffer a "moment's fear." The rattlesnake was a serpent with a "timid and retiring disposition," he reassured his readers. "If you encounter one at a fair distance, say ten feet, it will either crawl away, slowly and defensively, or coil and warn you to keep off. In its feeding habits, in captivity, it is one of the most timid and nervous of all reptiles, and seldom eats save when safe from observation and interruption. When darkness falls, and the Reptile House is entirely quiet, the Rattler bashfully swallows his freshly killed rat or guinea pig." He described his "first experiment" with a captive rattlesnake in which he placed a rat in its cage. The rat ran over the snake several times and the rattlesnake simply moved away. But then the rat ran over and bit the rattlesnake on the mouth. Finally, like the classic American cowboy, the good-hearted snake was provoked too far so it drew back and bit the body of the rat. Within about 13 minutes the rat was dead.[4] The messages were clear: snakes were not a real problem. They primarily wanted to live in peace and were quite gentle. Hornaday's message was again aimed at an urban, adult male audience, who at best might spend a few days in the wilderness.

The problem with the sportsmen's arguments was that they were only partly true. It was true that Americans were killing venomous snakes whenever they felt even slightly threatened, and sadly sometimes just for sport or their body parts. But it was equally true that Americans and their animals were seriously injured and killed by venomous snakes on a fairly regularly basis, until the invention of antivenin finally cut back on the human and domesticated animal death toll. Not everyone was killed in the same numbers, however. Urban, white, professional men, women, and children were basically safe from the scourge of bites, unless they headed out into the countryside. But everyone who lived and worked in the country—rural children, farmers, farm laborers, plantation workers, soldiers, and livestock—to name a few, were seriously at risk. People who worked directly with snakes because of their jobs, like reptile house curators or snake collectors, were at significant risk as well. And contrary to the puffed-up sportsmen, the toll that rattlesnakes and other venomous snakes took in the United States and abroad was tragic.

Rural Children

Children in the country were particularly at risk because they were frequently outside playing, exploring their surroundings, and less likely to pay close attention to their immediate environment. Local newspapers reported their deaths in brief obituaries, like the one from the *Dodge City Times* that reported two children from the Medicine Creek area of Rooks County in Kansas died from the effects of a rattlesnake bite.[5] Sadly, however, there were many other stories of young children who were bitten. In Montgomery, Alabama, on a Sunday afternoon in September 1886, three children between the ages of two and six year old, "from a respectable family," were playing near their home around a hole in the ground made by the roots of a tree torn out by a storm. The parents missed the children as the evening progressed and went out to call them in for dinner. The property was strangely silent when they found the children lying near the roots of the tree. A rattlesnake had killed all three children sometime during the evening. According to the newspaper report, the "bodies were terribly swollen and looked as if they had been bitten in several places."[6] In another incident, a healthy eleven-year-old boy was bitten by "a viper" on his left foot. Two hours passed before his parents knew that their son was bitten and called the doctor. The doctor cauterized the bite area with nitrate of silver and ordered rest. The boy barely slept, and his foot and leg swelled grotesquely. The skin turned purple and by the next night he was delirious. The following evening he was taken to a local hospital and was unconscious. The attending physician wanted to amputate his foot. When he regained consciousness he screamed in pain. The wound was black at the site and violet and then lead colored as it progressed up the leg. His stomach turned yellow. All of the blood vessels on one side of his knee were swollen. Touching the area was agonizingly painful. He got lucky and recovered, but spent several weeks in a very weak state.[7] John

Moon, a young boy, was killed by a rattlesnake in Washington State. He and his family ate groundhogs, and he was one of the members of the family responsible for bringing them home. He had gone fishing one morning and then headed out to do this chore for his family. He had a sharpened stick that he used to put into the holes in the ground where the groundhogs lived. Unfortunately, he apparently reached into one of the holes and was bitten by a rattlesnake. He wandered around for a while trying to make his way back home. He had set out on a Saturday, but when he did not return that day, the family assumed that he had gone to some of his nearby relatives and did not look for him. Two of his brothers set out on Monday to hunt for groundhogs as well and found his body, which by that point was badly discolored.[8] Murdyum D. Murphy, a nine-year-old girl, was sitting outside in her yard in Arizona with her brothers and sisters. They were chatting as they sat together when she reached her hand back to steady herself. A rattlesnake struck her on the middle finger of her right hand. The family sent for a doctor who tried his best to save her, but she died in great pain.[9]

Children sometimes thought they could handle the snakes and unfortunately were bitten. Thirteen-year-old Norman Wyman, of Lakeland, Florida, went off early to school one morning and on the way there found and caught a rattlesnake. He brought it to school to show the students and teachers before classes started. Sometime during that period, he was bitten, but continued to want to show the snake to his peers and teachers. His teachers sent him and the snake home, pointing out that it was against the school rules to allow them around people, and they urged him to get medical help. In the process, he started to feel pain and by the next day he was dead.[10]

In contrast to the fictional portrayal of an insignificant number of rattlesnake bites by sportsmen, doctors who actually lived and worked with rural people found the opposite. Robert Marshall, a doctor, reported that his county had "quite a number of snake bites" that season in 1885. And "many of the cases" were "fatal." One boy was bitten by a very large rattlesnake, presumably on the foot or leg region. He was unable to stand on the foot, was nauseated and vomiting, had a feeble pulse, and was generally deteriorating. This boy recovered, unlike the others who died in his county.[11] In Volga City, Iowa, a little girl named Nellie Klugman was bitten and killed by a "huge rattlesnake" in her backyard on August 2, 1889. She was walking from her house to the backyard when a rattlesnake "over ten feet long" rose up and bit her.[12] The venom from the large snake killed her. Twelve-year-old Maynard Sheldon, from Sioux Falls, South Dakota, was bitten and killed in the same way. He too was just playing in a field when he stepped on the rattlesnake and it bit him. It was the largest people had seen in years.[13]

Poor Rural People

Rural people lived and worked in areas throughout the country where venomous snakes had not yet been exterminated, as they had in cities in the Northeast. These were poorer people who lived in areas spread throughout the country from rural Pennsylvania to the midwest, and throughout the southwest. They primarily encountered rattlesnakes, but also had dangerous experiences with water moccasins, as they carved out a living for their families, built poorly constructed houses in the relatively uninhabited wooded areas, and hung out laundry to dry on the prairie. Sometimes it was not clear to people on the prairie whether they were listening to the "ominous clicking" of grasshoppers or the rattle of a rattlesnake. To be sure, occasionally the experiences of westward-moving settlers was dramatized for effect. There were too many reports of snakes crawling into tents and into beds for the sake of warmth. Men were supposed to have slept quietly all through the night, perfectly aware that a rattlesnake shared their tent, understanding that at first light it would go on its own way if they left it alone.[14]

Newspaper articles from the mid 1800s forward, however, show that many people were bitten. Frequently there is little to the story because the person died and there is simply a note about his or her passing. Stories generally amounted to a line such as this one (paraphrased): B.F. Whittick of Fort Wingate was killed by a rattlesnake.[15] Or, in their news about people in other places, the *Day Book* paper from Chicago reported that Dr. Von Ossinski was "dying from [the] effects of rattlesnake bite."[16] When the stories were more elaborate, their purpose was often to share "cures" with others in that region who might find themselves in the same predicament. In these cases, the victims often lived, although it is not at all clear that the treatment they received helped them, but the stories give us insight into who was bitten. A rattlesnake bit a 24-year-old young man named E. Madrigal on the back of the hand near the little finger. The man lived in Bibo, Arizona, so the *Holbrook Argus* paper (from Holbrook, Arizona) relayed the story in great detail as part of the work of a Santa Fe surgeon named Dr. O.S. Brown, who made a "super human effort" to save the man's life. He was bitten one day and it took a full day to reach Winslow, Arizona, where the doctor resided. In the meantime, his arm had swollen so much that the skin was bursting.[17]

But we do get longer descriptions of the ways that rural people were bitten. Sometimes they came into contact through their poorly constructed homes. This was the case of a woman from Texas. On May 30, 1927, a Texan woman was sleeping on a pallet with her nine-month-old son and husband on her screened back porch. She awoke with a terrible pain in the middle of her forehead where she had was bitten by a rattlesnake that had come in through a hole in the floor of their newly constructed house. She woke her husband and asked him to look for what had stung her so that it did not get the child. The husband lit a match and saw a rattlesnake near his child's head. He tried to kill the snake with a hammer, but it escaped through the hole in the floor.[18] She was not in a tent, but the story suggests that if she had been, the snakes could easily have gotten in there as well.

Other times poor people were bitten while trying to get food for their families, either through some kind of gathering activity in the woods, hunting, or farming. Some people in the 19th century were "bark peelers," an occupation in which they worked in the woods of West Virginia, harvesting the bark from hemlocks and oaks for leather tanning. Hemlock, for example, had a high tannic acid content that was used to make the leather less water soluble and gave the leather its deep reddish-brown color. Oak was used for the same purpose, but gave the leather a lighter, yellowish color. In the process of gathering the bark in the woods, the peelers came across rattlesnakes and copperheads, who liked the cool, fresh bark and curled up inside small openings at the base of the trees. When the peelers pulled back the bark they were bitten by the snakes.[19] A doctor reported that there was a "fatal case of rattlesnake bite" in his own neighborhood when a man shot a rabbit for dinner and then saw the rabbit try and get away by dragging itself into a hole in the ground. The man placed his hand in the hole to feel for the rabbit, but found a rattlesnake instead who bit him on the bottom of the palm of his had, where the joint joins the wrist, a location where there are significant veins that could carry the venom quickly throughout his body. He died from the bite in about twelve days.[20] Geo Manly was bitten on his ranch in Kingman, Arizona, when he was turning flood water out of his irrigating ditch into the river about 100 yards north of his house. The snake bit him in the throat while he crawled under a bush. His family found him dead less than half an hour after he was bitten. He was swollen grotesquely. The undertaker came for the body, but would not let the family see him because of his swollen state. Even after the undertaker did his best to preserve the body, the family could "never imagine a human being looking so terrible."[21] The family was too poor to pay for the funeral, so they reached out to others to help them cover the costs. Another case was that of Antonio Fernandez, who was cutting johnson grass near Frio City, 12 miles from San Antonio on August 31, 1946, when a rattlesnake "jumped at him and caught him on the left forefinger and hung on until he shook it off." He had to walk about two miles to get a ride to the R.B. Green Hospital.[22]

Professional and amateur fruit pickers were bitten by venomous snakes in the United States, as they were in the rest of the world. Fruit pickers supplied hotels and grocery stores with berries at a time when large farms that grew berries were scarce. Poor people who lived in rural areas earned money in this way. The problem was that the berries that fell off of the bushes attracted mice, and the mice attracted snakes. As a result, patches of berry bushes were rich with snakes of all kinds. Huckleberry pickers in New York, for example, risked bites from copperheads that hid in the bushes waiting to ambush the mice that fed on the berries. People bitten by copperheads sometimes became unmanageable during the subsequent fever. Frank Fritz and a friend were picking blackberries in Pennsylvania on the York County side of the Susquehanna River, in a place on a mountain known as "Devil's Hole," when a copperhead bit him on his finger.[23] Later two men had to hold him down in his bed when he developed a fever. A woman was gathering strawberries, and was crawling along on her hands and knees to do so, when she was bitten in the lower part of the leg by a snake. She saw the creature, and recognized it as a large yellow rattlesnake, common in Iowa. She was more than half a mile from home, but she made it to a creek where she washed the bite and "made a sort of plaster of clay, and tried it on, then walked home." Henry Gravers from Winslow, New Jersey, was in a field in back of his house picking blackberries. While he was picking he found a rattlesnake lying in the bushes a few feet from where he was working. Instead of simply backing away, he found a heavy stick to use to kill the snake. He tried to kill it a few times, but it defended itself and bit him. He went home in severe pain where he tried every kind of cure he knew, but in a short time he was in agonizing pain and he died late that afternoon.[24] Luther King, better known in Florence, Oregon, as the Rattle Snake King, was also bitten while picking blackberries in the mountains of Idaho. He disturbed a rattlesnake which then bit him near the knee. It was extremely painful, but he dragged himself home. He recovered, but was one of many people who claim after being bitten that he suffered other negative health effects for years until he died. He called it the "serpent's curse" and had deep pain in his leg, struggled with his appetite, and had sleeping problems. At the end of his life, he said that he looked forward to dying to be rid of the long-term side effects of the bite.[25]

The story that nicely captures the economic divide of human and snake interaction comes from Pennsylvania in 1880. There was a picturesque little village there called Erwinna that was set among hills that overlooked the Delaware River. The *New York Times* reported that "prominent people" went there to vacation in the summer, including "Judge Woodhull of Camden; Mrs. John Drew of Philadelphia" and Colonel Scovel, the south Philadelphia politician. They stayed in hotels that local people supplied with fresh blackberries. The columnist interviewed a man, nicknamed "Rattlesnake Pete," who the unnamed columnist described as a "tramp naturalist" who had grown up in the Blue Mountains, near Sussex County in New Jersey. He was one of eight children, and they lived in a cabin in the woods. Their house was surrounded by snakes, including at times rattlesnakes, so he got used to fearing them and heading for the house when he heard them rattle. Once he was out playing with the neighbor children, and one of the boys was bitten on the leg by a rattlesnake and died within a day. His father, who "peddled" berries, showed him how to kill them when necessary. There were "millions of berries" near their home, but they had to keep their eyes open because the area was thick with snakes as well. They always carried big sticks, and he had sometimes heard a few of them rattle at the same time. He was almost bitten during a picking day with his family. His sister was picking berries and startled a black snake, who in turn scared her. She took off running, and in the process ran by and surprised a rattlesnake who then wanted to defend itself and started rattling. Pete chased down and killed the rattlesnake with one of the sticks they brought to protect themselves. Later in his life, Pete made money by catching the rattlesnakes and skinning them to sell their hides to the same wealthy tourists who ate the berries in the hotels.

Farmers were also at significant risk. G.E. Martin, a farmer in Lubbock, Texas, was plowing his farm when he hit a rattlesnake den. He reached down to get an object to kill the snake, but the snake bit him on the hand instead.[26] In another case, two brothers, working on different farms, were bitten on the same day. They were in the fields on their respective farms; one was bitten on the ankle and another on the wrist. A third man, located nearby, was building a fence around his farm and was bitten when he stepped on a rattlesnake.[27]

Pennsylvanians were sometimes inundated by snakes. Reading, Pennsylvania, was overrun by snakes during the summer of 1890. The *New York Times* reported that black snakes, copperheads, and rattlesnakes were "creeping into people's houses on farms and in the country towns, crawling into kitchens, coiling themselves up comfortably in cupboards and closets."[28] Mrs. Oscar Boyer was bitten by a copperhead that crawled into a barrel of potatoes in her cellar, leaving her in critical condition.[29]

Even by the 1940s and 1950s people who lived in the country struggled to find ways to protect themselves from rattlesnakes. In 1948, a man by the name of Warren L. Brazelton bought a farm in San Luis Rey in southern California. His farm had lemon trees, but also brush, wild grasses, and small trees. He had come across a number of rattlesnakes and their presence made him concerned for his children. He wrote to the Biology Department's faculty at the University of California at Berkeley asking for advice, and they forwarded the request to Laurence Klauber, the consulting curator of reptiles at the San Diego Zoo and member of the board of directors at the San Diego Zoological Society.[30] Klauber stressed that the usual method of animal control—traps and poison—were virtually useless when it came to controlling rattlesnakes. Although calcium cyanide had been tried in the past, the problem was that rattlesnakes fed at such long, irregular intervals that the cyanide just succeeded in killing rodents and birds quickly and then the snake was free to dine on animals who were not poisoned. He recommended protecting all of the harmless snakes around the property partly because king snakes and racers ate young rattlesnakes, and partly because the more snakes there were on the property, the greater the competition for food. Eliminating food sources for rodents was crucial because that kept down the rattlesnake population by reducing their source of food. Destroying hiding places like bushes, crevices, or mammal holes eliminated their habitat. Not venturing out much at night in southern California was key as well because rattlesnakes are nocturnal in the summer, thus putting children playing outside and farm workers watering plants in the evening at risk. Surrounding a playground with a fence was possible, but it had to be high (about six feet) and smooth. The area around the fence should be bare so that a parent could check for holes rodents had burrowed underneath the fence that could be used as an entrance to the playground by rattlesnakes. Families had to avoid leaving the gates open because snakes could enter at will. Parents should warn the children not to pick up any snake and consider getting a good lively dog that disclosed the impending presence of the snake before it got near the children. Some dogs, particularly larger breeds, killed rattlesnakes fairly regularly, but the downside, according to

Klauber, was that they were "likely to become careless and get bitten."[31] Dogs that killed rattlesnakes also typically killed harmless snakes as well, leading back to the problem of lack of competition for food. He suggested the possibility of other animals like hogs, deer, badgers, red tail hawks, chickens, and turkeys, all of which have warning sounds or will kill the snakes when they are around. The farmer found the advice useful not only for his children, but also for laying plans for "future building and building arrangements" and for nighttime irrigation work.[32]

Farmers and other people who lived or worked in rural areas often had no idea what kind of snakes lived around them. There were no easily available snake guides, National Geographic specials, or other nature documentaries of any kind. It took herpetologists years to study particular localities, let alone the entire United States, to get a sense of the range of a few of the snakes within that area. As a result, how could one know the difference between a rattlesnake or a gopher snake? If they could identify that it was a rattlesnake, they often had no idea what kind of a subspecies it was, where it ranged, or as we can see from the previous examples, how to keep it from setting up residence in one's home. As a result, people captured the snakes that came onto their property and sent them on to herpetologists like Klauber who knew enough to take the problem seriously. Ada Meling, for example, had a ranch in San Jose and sent a snake that she believed was a rattlesnake to Laurence Klauber in San Diego. Upon receiving the snake, Klauber wrote back informing her that it was actually a gopher snake.[33] However, he was also concerned about other rattlesnakes on her property too, so he sent her a .22 rifle and offered to fix her .22 Winchester. She had been bitten when she was three years old by a rattlesnake, and now she was "permanently afraid of them."[34]

Even people we might expect to know more about snakes were often fairly uninformed. Edwin Mckee, who worked at the Grand Canyon Park, wanted to know the range of Arizona rattlesnakes for the sake of the safety of visitors and workers alike. In response, Klauber sent him a map that diagrammed the range of Arizona rattlesnakes. Mckee in return offered to get Klauber critical species from the Grand Canyon.[35]

Most farmers and others who worked outdoors had significant reason to worry about snakes. Farm laborers who did not own their own farms were also at risk, and here we see the ways in which race, class, and money determined whether anyone cared or pursued the problem of snakebites. Indians in India who grappled with the cobra bite problem were treated with great scorn by journalists when they failed to kill cobras. If the snakes threatened a big company's profits by threatening employed laborers, however, then the company demonstrated real concern, and the problem became real.

Farmers who were bitten by snakes shared their stories and appealed for sympathy, but farm laborers who worked for those farmers and were also bitten were sometimes treated differently depending upon the slant of the article. Occasionally they were treated as normal human beings who faced an unfortunate accident, as in the case of a 45-year-old German immigrant farmhand named Joe Speldrich, in Shaniko, Oregon, in 1905. On the day he was bitten he was helping the farmer re-roof his house. The farmer was throwing shingles off his cabin roof and Speldrich reached down to clean them up off the ground and was bitten by a rattlesnake on the hand. Although he made it to a nearby ranch where a doctor was summoned, he died an agonizing death from the bite.[36] Speldrich was treated with respect in the story, but other farm laborers were sometimes the object of derision. They were portrayed as beggars looking for ways to shirk work or get free whiskey. One farm magazine story captures this attitude toward workers. In the story, the writer claims, "During the haying season an honest old farmer" employed three young men from the city to help cut and store his timothy hay. "None of them liked work half as well as whisky," he told his readers, and so the workers found a way to get the drink by faking snakebites. Initially one of them claimed that he had been bitten by a rattlesnake, so the earnest farmer brought out a bottle of whiskey that all three laborers passed around. The next day the second one claimed he was bitten, and the farmer again brought out the whiskey. And then, as in a fairytale, the third one is bitten and the farmer finally realized that he had been duped by his workers for a little time off and some of his whiskey. The farmer wised up, told the workers they would not receive any more whiskey and lo and behold there were no more snakebites that season.[37] The message of this likely fabricated story was clear: one could trust honest farmers, but not their poorer shiftless workers. If one could not trust white farm laborers, then people of color were even more suspect and sometimes treated as deserving their bites.

On the one hand, America never had India's dramatic snakebite problem. In 1891, for example, at least 21,389 people in India were killed by snakebites.[38] Another estimate is that in India in 1893, one out of every 10,424 people died of a snakebite, primarily from the cobra.[39] Even though Indians were grappling with similar snakebite problems, Americans who wrote about snakes, but clearly did not experience them directly, were scornful and racist about Hinduism's reverence for the animal world. One author opined that the Indian government's failure to staunch the problem stemmed from the "heathen Hindoo's reverence for animal life even in its most objectionable forms."[40]

Ethnic minorities in the United States received very little concern even though they too were on the front lines of the interactions between snakes and humans. When it came down to a choice between supporting African Americans or snakes, the snakes won. The *Working Farmer* magazine contained an article in 1858 urging people not to kill snakes because they were good for farms. Snakes, the unnamed author asserted, were "much abused animals" who had never "caused the death of a single human being." The author's first experience with snakes was in Mississippi "where children and especially careless negroes, were occasionally bitten by the 'ground rattlesnake.'"[41] The unnamed author urged his fellow farmers to remember that snakes were insect eaters, and therefore beneficial to humans. "Rip up the stomach of one, and you will find it stuffed with insects or enlarged by bodies of meadow mice." Except in killing an occasional bird or frog, "nearly all of our snakes are as useful to vegetation as they are harmless to mankind."[42] Mankind, however, apparently did not include African Americans or children. Still other racist accounts of human and poisonous snake interactions give us hints that African Americans were present and in a subservient position required to face the animals and take the risks. In one incident we learn about a Texan riding his horse accompanied by his servant, who is African American and described as "Sambo." They come across a rattlesnake, and "as the horse passed, the snake glided into the long grass by the roadside and attracted the attention of the rider." The white Texan directs his servant to kill the snake while he waits in safety on his horse. African Americans who worked in the fields were bitten by venomous snakes, but it is much harder to find any description of them getting help. It is highly likely that they were unable to afford the doctor to receive treatment. When they were bitten by snakes and there was some record of it, they were typically described as a "Negro" rather than noted by name or initials in written accounts (as they would have been if they were white), suggesting that the authors had less respect for them as victims.[43]

Not all people of color, however, were treated completely as if disposable. If they worked for the United Fruit Company or the Panama Canal, where either a big company or the U.S. government had a vested economic interest in their labor, then it mattered whether they lived or died from snakebite. By 1901, America received an estimated $6,550,896 worth of bananas primarily through a series of small companies who shipped their fruit to ports in New York, Boston, and Louisiana.[44] By the mid 1880s, smaller growers, such as the Boston Fruit Company and Minor C. Keith, consolidated their companies into the United Fruit Company. Keith's company was initially a railroad firm working in Central America that shipped the bananas by boat primarily to the Mississippi Valley area. By 1929, the company "imported 65 million bunches valued at 36 million dollars."[45] Once united as a single company, they tackled a variety of problems that limited their productivity, one of which was that workers were frequently the target of venomous snakes. This was an increasing problem as the company moved further into undeveloped jungle territory to satisfy increased demand for bananas.[46] To plant the trees, workers had to clear a large area in a short amount of time. Unfortunately for the workers, however, the jungle housed a variety of venomous snakes, including the fer-de-lance, horned palm viper, the hog nosed viper, rattlesnakes, and coral snakes. Although the snakes lived in the jungle, workers were most at risk after they cleared the land because, as we have seen, snakes are attracted to the rats, mice, and other rodents that find food on farms. Additionally, once jungles were cleared, the possibility of bites *increased* because more people were present. The snakebites were dramatic and significantly slowed down the work of harvesting the bananas. So much so that we shall see that the United Fruit Company was one of the entities that pushed for the eventual creation of antivenin in the United States and Brazil so that they could save workers from death.

To be sure, not everyone injured by a rattlesnake was poor. Occasionally someone from the upper class was envenomated as well. From newspaper descriptions we find more elaborate stories and descriptions of the people involved. These were not just poor farmers no one missed, these were wealthier people from their area and the papers emphasized their accomplishments. Judge M.H. Williams was one such person. He was born in Louisiana to a wealthy family in 1855. Although his family was impoverished by the Civil War, he and his family moved to Texas where he eventually became a Texas Ranger, studied law and became an attorney. He was thrown from a horse at one point and never completely recovered from a back injury. He later moved to Arizona and worked at a law firm, was elected prosecutor, and then appointed District Judge of the First District by President Grover Cleveland. He suffered from mental health problems and found himself unable to continue as a judge. His family placed him in an insane asylum where he seemed to recover. Because he seemed to be getting better, he was allowed to go to Agua Caliente Hot Springs to enjoy some relaxation in the outdoors. While he was there, a sidewinder rattlesnake bit him on the wrist and ankle. Although his family tried to treat him, and he seemed to get better, he died of the bites the next day.[47]

Zoo Employees

Although they were wealthier than poor laborers on farms, either in the United States or many countries around the world, zoo keepers and snake house curators were certainly not wealthy, and they too were on the front lines of the bite problem, both in the Untied States and abroad. Like poor people who worked the land, they knew first-hand how dangerous venomous snakes could be, and like their rural American counterparts, they were frequently bitten by venomous snakes, often rattlesnakes, even though they intentionally placed themselves at risk by keeping a significant number of other poisonous snakes in their collections. To take one example, a Bronx Zoo snake keeper was bitten by a Texas copperhead while he was cleaning the glass on its cage. The snake saw the keeper and slithered toward him. The keeper waved the snake away, whereupon the animal bit him on the finger.[48] A 39-year-old employee at the Philadelphia Zoo was bitten on the back of the right hand by a four-foot-long diamondback rattlesnake. In this case, another zoo employee cut his bite site and applied a tourniquet at his mid arm. The man was rushed to the hospital at the University of Pennsylvania, a drive that took around 30 minutes, during which he attempted to suck the venom out of his wound. By the time he arrived, his arm and hand were extremely swollen and there were patchy areas of hematomas around the bite.

Even when antivenin was available, the struggle with snakebites remained staggering for those unlucky enough to get bitten. The zoo employee was given five ampules of antivenin into the hand and at various points up his arm, whereupon he developed a systemic reaction. He began sweating profusely and complained of mouth numbness, which made it difficult to communicate. Both the large and small muscles in his face and neck began twitching involuntarily and this symptom spread to almost all of the other muscles in his body. His tongue and lips took on a bluish tinge, indicating a lack of oxygen in his blood, and then he began vomiting repeatedly for about eight hours. He was given phenobarbital sodium intravenously to try and calm him down and prevent seizures as well as penicillin to control the infection. The doctors gave him 500 millimeters of whole blood because his wounds were continuously oozing. Over the first 48 hours of his hospitalization, he had periodic fevers of 101 degrees

Fahrenheit. Four days after he was admitted, his hemoglobin level dropped. He developed fevers as high as 104 degrees and his blood suddenly lacked its crucial clotting ability. All of his lymph nodes swelled and he developed a rash over almost his entire body with pale red, itchy bumps. Seven days after admission to the hospital, x-rays suggested that he had an ulcer and later that evening he vomited some "coffee-ground material" as his abdomen became distended. Finally, after 10 days in the hospital, his fever began to go down and he felt better. He was finally discharged on the 14th day.[49]

Both Roger Conant, the reptile curator at the Toledo Zoo, and Laurence Klauber—two of the important herpetologists and zoo curators who worked to bring antivenin to the United States—were bitten. Conant was bitten by a rattlesnake while working at the Toledo Zoo on September 16, 1929. The snake bit his left thumb and initially he did not experience any pain. After about twenty minutes the doctor arrived at the zoo and began medical treatment, which consisted of an ampoule of antivenin injected partly into his left forearm and partly into his stomach. They went to the hospital where, after about an hour, the pain started to increase, and Conant was placed on sedatives. A few hours later, his "fingers took on the size and coloration of small red bananas." Later large "blebs" appeared all over his fingers and wrist. The palm of his hand developed into one enormous blister which looked almost as if he was "holding half a tennis ball in [his] hand."[50] He was discharged a couple of days later, but contracted tetanus as a result of the medical treatment for his bite and had to have his finger removed. In Klauber's case, he said some "kind hearted idiot" had sent him a medium-size rattlesnake with his "mouth tightly sewed closed." Klauber initially failed to notice the stitches, but then realized that the mouth was sewn shut when he tried to milk the animal. He was cutting the stitches with a knife when "the last stitch suddenly let go and the snake stabbed [him] in the thumb with one fang." The wound bled a great deal and was instantly painful so he assumed that the snake injected some venom. He applied a tourniquet and rubbed potassium permanganate crystals into the wound. About a half an hour later he still felt pain, so a physician gave him a five or six cc shot of antivenin in the arm.[51]

Perhaps the most famous zoo herpetologist who was bitten was Grace Wiley, one of the few women snake experts in the 1920s and 1930s. Wiley was from Kansas and attended the University of Kansas, majoring in entomology. She had a passion for snakes, however, so she began collecting them. She amassed an enormous personal collection of 330 animals representing 115 subspecies. Her expertise and ownership of such a large

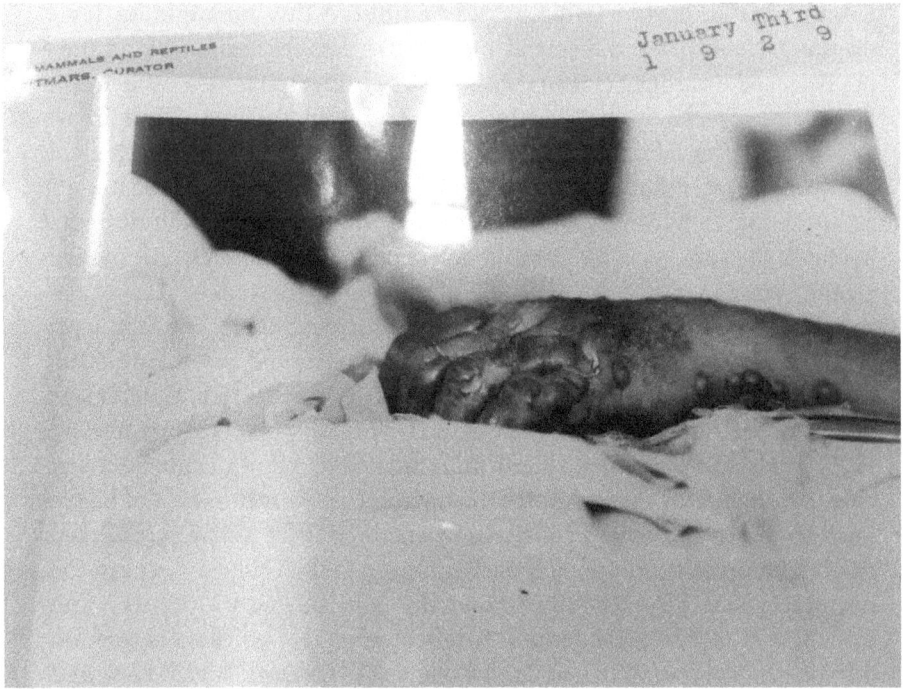

Roger Conant's hand after a bite from a rattlesnake (courtesy American Museum of Natural History).

number of the animals helped her get a job at the Minneapolis Natural History Museum. Unlike other herpetologists at the time, Wiley believed in gentle touch rather than force feeding. She believed that all snakes, including venomous ones, could be tamed. She spoke to them and stroked them until they became used to her and other human contact. After failing to heed the safety warnings of the Minneapolis Natural History Museum, Wiley took her large collection to the Brookfield Zoo (IL). While there, she let 19 venomous snakes escape because she failed to shut their cages. The director, Robert Bean, fired her and she took her snakes to Orange County, California, where she started a roadside zoo and starred in some movies with her snakes. Wiley was finally bitten fatally during an interview with a journalist on July 20, 1948. She was posing for a photograph for the piece with a cobra. She attempted to open its hood, and it bit her on the finger. Although she had a snakebite kit that by this time had antivenin in it, it was old and the serum had dried up. She lapsed into a coma and died about an hour later at Long Beach Municipal Hospital.[52]

Animal dealers who supplied snakes to zoos and later extracted venom for antivenin production were also bitten with some frequency. Rattlesnakes bit Ross Allen, the director of Ross Allen's Reptile Institute in Silver Springs, Florida. His institute marketed itself as the largest producer of snake venom in the United States. Ross was bitten several times, but one bite was particularly bad.[53] On this occasion, Allen was visiting rattlesnake hunters, who supplied his institute, in the western part of Florida, and he examined a box with a diamondback in it for possible purchase. He turned the box upside down and allowed the snake out so that he could catch it with his forked snake stick. His stick slipped, allowing the snake to turn its head sideways enough to bite his finger where it pierced a vein sending the venom directly into his bloodstream. He headed back to his car for the long drive to the hospital and within 30 minutes he was paralyzed, unable to work his hands or legs. His doctor, who was evidentially familiar with snake treatment in that region, made 50 incisions from his hand to his shoulder, applied suction, and injected 30 ccs of antivenin. He was also given a blood transfusion because he had lost so much blood from the cuts designed to get rid of the venom.[54] About 10 hours after the bite, he was in agonizing pain, paralyzed through much of his body, so weak that he could barely raise his eyelids, and unable to drink because his tongue was swollen. After 24 hours, the swelling moved across and down his back, down his chest and into his other arm. He remained this way for three full days until he recovered enough to have nervous tremors that shook his body. Doctors removed part of his thumb that had turned gangrenous, and he remained in the hospital for 10 days and at home recuperating for two weeks. It took him six weeks to return to work.

Soldiers

Another group repeatedly at risk were soldiers because they trained in camps spread around rural areas in the United States. The army kept records of all illness and fatalities and, not surprisingly, soldiers were bitten on frontier camps.[55] They took the bite problem seriously and noted medical officers serving with troops in the field were "particularly likely to be called upon to treat cases of this character."[56] Like everyone else, they had no real way of treating the bites.

John Chalmers Da Costa was professor of surgery and of clinical surgery at Jefferson Medical College in Philadelphia as well as surgeon to the Philadelphia Hospital and consulting surgeon to St. Joseph's Hospital, Philadelphia, but prior to that he served as a military doctor. In lectures

"The Scouts and the Rattlesnake" (Art and Picture Collection, New York Public Library Digital Collections).

to his medical residents, he liked to tell them that they had to treat bites "without proper appliances" and how he had seen one soldier "blow off his finger with a pistol the moment after it was bitten by a rattlesnake."[57] And this was a problem they had to cope with frequently. To take one case during the Civil War, Private Theodore E. Turner, from Troop D, 4th Cavalry, aged 29, was bitten by a rattlesnake at Fort Concho, Texas, on June 27, 1866. The snake bit him on the phalangeal joint on the left thumb and caused significant inflammation, so much so that it resulted in the destruction of the joint. He was admitted to the hospital in Austin, Texas, and the venom had completely eaten through the left lateral ligament. He was feverish, unable to sleep, and wanted to have his thumb amputated. After the doctors removed his thumb, he returned to duty.[58] Another private from the 13th Infantry near Camp Cooke, Montana Territory, in 1868, was bitten in the throat by a large rattlesnake. A fellow soldier immediately sucked the wound. The bite victim reported to the post hospital at Camp Cooke three hours after the bite. The doctors soaked a cloth in rancid olive oil, because that was all they had, and wrapped it around the man's throat. By that point the wound was hard and painful and bruised by the man who had tried to suck out the venom. This lucky soldier survived.[59] This, however, was not always the case. Private William Robinson (37 years old), from Troop B, 3rd Calvary, was stationed at Fort Cummings,

New Mexico. He was known for his good behavior and his snake charming abilities. He had evidently caught and held snakes many times in the past without incident. On the morning of July 13, 1869, he was on duty guarding sheep herders near the base and he caught a rattlesnake. He was immediately admitted to the post hospital complaining only of a little stinging sensation, as though he was bitten by a bee or wasp. The doctor cut open the wound, applied ammonia, and cauterized it, but Robinson was already physically weak. He began vomiting, his hand started to swell, and he took on a yellowish tint. He was given opium at night and woke the next morning complaining of numbness in his arm. Blood ran freely from his wound. He began complaining of neck pain and then complained of pain in the genital region. When doctors examined that area, it turned out that he had an iron ring, six-eighths of an inch in diameter, embedded in the soft tissue of his penis. The doctor asked why he was wearing the ring, and Robinson informed him that it was to preserve his chastity and it would be taken out once he was married. The swelling in his body from the venom, however, had reached his penis, which was now grotesquely swollen, and he could no longer urinate. The doctor and an assistant filed off the ring with "some difficulty." In the meantime, gangrene destroyed the finger that was bitten, and they amputated it. Over the next couple of days, Robinson started slipping away and despite trying to revive him, he died on July 16, 1869. The surgeon conducted a necropsy of his body shortly after his death and found that his tissue was softened on the side of his body that was bitten, and his blood was black and not coagulable.[60]

Rattlesnake venom was also allegedly used by Native Americans in the region to injure soldiers. At least one newspaper claimed that frontier soldiers were particularly vulnerable when local tribes collected rattlesnakes, had them bite the liver of a buffalo, and then used the blood and venom mixture of the buffalo as a poison coating for their arrows.[61] In other cases, soldiers were bitten trying to profit from rattlesnakes found around their camps. Sam Cherry, an army guide in the 1830s in Texas, killed large numbers around his camp. He claimed that rattlesnake oil would prevent rheumatism and filled large numbers of bottles with the oil that he sold to local stores.[62]

Much later in the 1940s, when soldiers were stationed in the west again to train for World War II, Laurence Klauber wanted to keep a record of the number of soldiers bitten by snakes. He had Martin Crimmins, a soldier, socialite's son, and amateur herpetologist stationed in Texas, send him data on bites from 3rd Army Surgeon, Colonel R.C. MacDonald, who treated soldiers for bites received during maneuvers. They were particularly interested in fatal bites. One of soldiers' fears training in the west during World War II was that they would be bitten while in the field. As a result, they passed along what we would call an urban legend in which a soldier was "advancing under machine gun fire which is held just above the bodies of the advancing troops in order to force them to keep down, who comes upon a rattler suddenly and raises up into the machine gun curtain with disastrous results."[63] There is no evidence that this actually ever happened, but they were occasionally bitten in their camps and this seemed like an even worse scenario. Army Surgeon MacDonald, for example, shared that there were about a dozen snakebites during his 3rd Army maneuvers. One of the soldiers was bitten in the summer during a night maneuver. When he threw himself on the ground, a snake bit him in the face.[64]

Domesticated Animals

Livestock was also struck by venomous snakes and treated similarly to the poorer humans who lived among them. To be sure, not all farm animals were victims. Pigs were sometimes voracious killers of venomous snakes, and thus they were good to have around. They were, of course, much more common as protection than other snakes were and useful because they were eventually eaten. Farm families could enlist them as allies, but not everyone felt so comforted by their work. Snake dealers who had pigs found that they cut into their business by killing rattlesnakes near their homes. One snake dealer in Pennsylvania had an "old sow named Jennie" who had a voracious appetite for rattlesnakes and used to kill several a day. The dealer knew when she had killed one because she ate everything except the head.[65]

But venomous snakes took a heavy toll on other livestock, including horses and cattle. In India, they put the death rate for cattle at about 2,100 a head yearly.[66] To combat the problem of snakes killing cattle (and people) in the late 1800s, the English government, under Sir Frederick Halliday, the lieutenant governor of Bengal, initially gave a small monetary reward for the dead body of every venomous snake brought to the magistrate in the district. In some districts, people brought in dead snakes "by the thousands." There were so many of them that the magistrate complained that he could not carry out his job because of the stench of putrid bodies.[67] As in India, one estimate is that in the United States in the mid 1920s, venomous snakes created over one million dollars in lost cattle in one year in Texas alone.[68] In the United States, rattlesnakes and cottonmouths bit cattle on the head, the feet, or the limbs. When farmers inspected their animals, they typically found bite marks where fangs pierced the skin. As with humans, sometimes these bites were not fatal and only required some minor wound attention that included, for example, driving the cattle into mud puddles and letting them sit there.[69] In some cases, however, extreme swelling around the area typically set in and the animal often became unconscious, its temperature dropped, its pulse was light, and finally it died. Other times they were bitten on the lips, which became thick and swollen, and if treatment was neglected, the swelling became hard and sometimes an abscess formed making it difficult for the animal to heal.[70] To put the problem in perspective in the United States, the Department of Agriculture described snakebite as the worst problem cattle faced in 1885. They were concerned about the loss of cattle from splenic fever or pleuro-pneumonia, but when they reached out to ranchers to help them reduce the death level in their herds, they noted that "snakebite seems more widely spread than any other malady."[71]

Given the widespread nature of the problem and the striking economic loss, one might expect that veterinarians in the United States would be as interested in a potential cure for animals as doctors on the front lines were for humans. However, as with humans, veterinarians focused primarily on snakebites elsewhere or dismissed the problem entirely in the United States. The *American Veterinary Review* was the earliest veterinary medical journal in the United States. When the *American Veterinary Review* discussed the issue at all, it was in their "exchange" section, in which scientists or veterinarians from other countries submitted small articles that might be of interest to Americans. The editors of the journal finally published a snakebite article in their 1922 edition, well after human doctors were discussing antivenin, and many years after scientists began doing animal experiments using antivenin. Pierre A. Fish, the author of the article, informed readers that death from snakebite was quite rare. Although we would assume that this referred to rare in the case of animals, it turns out that he was not at all concerned about them. His primary concern was about whether people were bitten, and if so, how they should kill the snake. Even the ideas about various rudimentary cures did not penetrate the veterinary profession by the early 1900s. People did not need to worry about the snakes, Fish shared with his readers, because "the most venomous of our native snakes live in lonely little settled districts on stoney or swampy land that can not be cultivated." Usually they disappear when people approach, and besides, even if people run into them, they can not propel themselves as far as folklore suggests. The only way to kill them, he shared, was "clubbing or shooting them." His only reference to any other animal was to dispel the notion that hogs are immune to snakebite. They were not, he insisted; they just had thick skin that was tough to bite through.[72]

As with other snake interactions, some of the earliest written sources about horse and snake contact came from other countries. Brazilians, for example, noted that horses and cows were vulnerable.[73] And the few early stories that appear in veterinary journals come from India. In one case, English military veterinarians were called to attend to their horses that had been bitten by cobras and kraits. Lieutenant E. Clive Webb, a veterinary officer at the Remount Depot in Mona, Punjab, India, was one such person. He reported attending to a one-year-old bay gelding bitten under the lip. When he arrived, the horse's face was swollen, with green mucus coming out of the nostrils and blood flowing out of the horse's anus. A variety of topical antiseptic treatments failed to stop the increasing fever, and then death, of the horse within a day. A two-year-old bay gelding was also bitten, and in this case the veterinarian identified the snake as a krait who had been sitting on the horse's hay. The horse reached down to eat and the krait bit it in the lip. By the time the veterinarian saw the horse, it was urinating blood and dripping blood mixed with mucus from its nostrils. It struggled to stand and had a high fever.[74] Although it was treated with some injections, it was dead within a couple of days. Cattle were also bitten, as we can see in the case of an English veterinarian who shared that a farmer's cow had been turned out one night and the next morning the farmer found her lying down and struggling to get up. The left hindquarter of her udder was "practically black." The family brought her back to the house and she did not rise for two days. Upon examination, they found a bite mark on her udder. She survived, but the bite site turned gangrenous and the skin sloughed away, leaving a large cavity.[75]

Like horses elsewhere, horses in the United States were bitten, and people struggled to save them. Small farmers who depended upon one or two horses for other kinds of agricultural work could be just as devasted as the large stock farmer losing a large number of animals. A rattlesnake bit Frank Corbett's horse in Jacksonville, Florida, on the nose. However, this lucky horse's head returned to its normal size after a few days.[76] On the Rio Grande in 1867, two horses were bitten by the same snake while grazing. Within a few hours, the glands around the head and necks of the animals were enlarged and mucus discharged from their nostrils and gums. Their eyes were glazed over and their pupils were dilated.[77] Depending upon the location of the bite, the horse often had to have dead skin removed if they recovered, but they frequently died within two to three days.[78]

Why was it that American veterinarians did not bother to address snakebite as a problem? Their explanation that it was rare was untrue from the perspective of stock animal owners in the west and southwest. Moreover, the excuse of the rarity of snakebite, which justified the lack of attention to the problem, also fit awkwardly with the many journal articles about other very rare conditions that happened with much less frequency. Veterinarians wrote in journals about rare deformities in animals that they surgically repaired, for example. These were case studies that were not going to help large numbers of animals or their humans. The answer again seems to lie more with the same problem that humans faced, and that was geographic bias. The veterinarians who edited and contributed to the *American Veterinary Review* were mainly from the East Coast. More narrowly they were from New York and Massachusetts. There were a couple of representatives from Kansas and Illinois, but they were the exceptions. The primary editor, Professor A. Laitard, was the correspondent for the Parisian Central Society of Medicine and, thus, he had even less incentive to discuss a problem that primarily affected rural Americans, particularly in the south and southwest.

In the meantime, American farmers circulated stories of bites and cures among themselves. In the "home and farm mazagine section" of the *Gazette-Times*, a farmer from Heppner, Oregon, recommended treating stock animals much the same way humans were treated. Once the farmer had determined that the horse or cow had been bitten by a snake, he recommended placing a ligature between the bite and the body. Clearly this was advice that would not include one of the most common bite places (the face), but instead assumed a bite on the legs. Once that was done, the farmer recommended making cuts on the bite spot and then cauterizing the cuts and bite site with a hot iron.[79]

Some farmers, although they were not stock farmers, did get some more professional help, but it came from an American zoo director and Brazilian scientists working on antivenin. One possibility, if the animals remained generally located at one farm, was to increase the number of harmless snakes there, as Klauber suggested to the lemon farmer in California. This was an idea that Vital Brazil, the Brazilian scientist who brought antivenin to his country and later began the process of bringing it to the United States, was experimenting with in the early 1900s. At the

Institute, called Butantan, in Brazil, where Brazil worked in 1913, the workers were collecting and breeding mussurana, who were the natural enemy of venomous snakes in Brazil. The mussurana is four or five feet long (or even longer), nearly black with a lighter underside and a mellow temperament. It survives by eating only other snakes and it is completely immune to the poison of the lachecis and rattlesnake groups. Its favorite prey is the jararaca.[80] Brazil urged Teddy Roosevelt, who came to visit Butantan in 1913, to encourage Americans to breed king snakes in the United States for the same reasons. King snakes feed on other snakes and can easily kill rattlesnakes because they are immune to rattlesnake venom. Raymond Ditmars had also experimented with this idea at the Bronx Zoo, and intentionally exhibited snakes and rodents together with the express purpose of showing how snakes could be good for agriculture.[81] A few faculty members at Tulane University's Medical School also urged farmers to buy or breed king snakes, gopher snakes, or other black snakes in an attempt to let one snake prey on another, and in that way rid the property of the dangerous animals. They brought venomous snakes into a Tulane laboratory and staged battles between them and the nonvenomous snakes to show farmers that they had an ally in their struggle. They encouraged the nonvenomous snakes because the "death toll by poisonous snakes" was "heavy" each year in the south.[82]

In addition to Tulane doctors encouraging farmers to either breed nonvenomous snakes or at least let the nonvenomous ones live, people who coped with snake problems also had a few, sporadic, attempts by state legislatures to help the problem.

Government Help?

Initially a few states tried to do something about ending the rattlesnake bite scourge. North Carolina, Pennsylvania and Iowa, for example, had legislators who pushed for programs or funding of various kinds to diminish the number of snakes or snakebites. Local people offered miracle cures that legislatures considered publicizing to help citizens. North Carolina's state legislature gave out a grant to find a cure for water moccasin bites in the late 1700s because of the large number of victims. According to one account, "a negro slave" claimed to successfully treat snakebites in the state and particularly recommended a plant cure. State legislators voted to grant his freedom and give him £200 for information about the cure.[83] Much later, in the 1900s, the Pennsylvania Department of Agriculture, Division of Zoology, had an exchange in which citizens of the state were asked to collect reptiles or amphibians and send them to the Division of Zoology by mail, complete with a record of where they found the animal, what its habitat was like, and what it ate. In return, the Division of Zoology would answer their questions about the animals and send them a "copy of the publication upon these creatures in our state." They regretted that they didn't have the funds to buy the specimens from the "patriotic" citizens who had sent them in. They requested, however that "snakes should be killed before shipping." People were sending the specimens in envelopes where they were crushed before reaching the department and thus unrecognizable.[84] Several states, including Iowa, New York, Minnesota, and Wisconsin, put bounties on rattlesnakes during the mid 1900s so that they could reduce their numbers. Hunters brought in dead snakes and were paid per snake. One county in Iowa, for example, had a 50-cent bounty on dead rattlesnakes. In Keokuk, Iowa, hunters had to bring in part of the rattlesnake's tail and rattles to the county auditor, located in the county court house, to receive their bounty.[85] South Dakota hired professional hunters to kill them. The practice spread to the southwestern states and eventually morphed into the rattlesnake roundups that have killed hundreds of thousands of rattlesnakes.[86]

The American federal agency that might have reduced snakebites was the Bureau of Biological Survey (hereafter referred to as the Bureau) housed under the Department of Agriculture. The Bureau exterminated many so-called pests to help farmers around the country. Their deadly war against birds, coyotes, and wolves is legendary.[87] They did not target snakes, however, as one of their noxious animals. As we have seen, part of the explanation for this lies with the fact that many snakes, including venomous ones, help farmers by eating animals that eat their crops, such as rodents. This is not the whole explanation, however, because as we can see from the case of stock animals, not all farmers benefited from venomous snakes. The bureau failed to focus on venomous snakes because one of their researchers dramatically miscalculated the number of fatal snakebites in the south and southwest. Dr. P. Willson collected the bureau's one and only study on venomous snakebite numbers in the 1920s. Unfortunately, however, he failed to actually determine the number of bites in the south and southwest.[88] He neglected to collect any bite data from entire states, including, for example, Mississippi. Part of the puzzle about why the United States government failed to see venomous snakes as either a serious public health threat or an economic drain on livestock farmers, then, is explained by this methodological error.

People Killing Snakes

The reality was that people were facing significant snake problems, whether the government wanted to help or not. So they often took matters into their own hands, waging a war against snakes. People killed far more rattlesnakes than rattlesnakes killed people. The amount of carnage was nothing short of astounding, and this is what Hornaday was nobly trying to prevent.

People killed rattlesnakes and other snakes around their homes and businesses for safety. Sometimes when snakes slithered into homes, they were met with shotgun blasts. Mrs. Daniel Bush, of Windgap, Pennsylvania, found a "huge rattlesnake" in her doorway and "blew its head off with a shotgun."[89] Sarah Sanford, who lived near Ellenville, New York, found a rattlesnake and a pilot snake in her hen house and cut off their heads with an ax.[90] A rattlesnake got into a pantry in a home in Georgia, ate some eggs, and in the process knocked the crockery off the shelves and woke the family who promptly killed it.[91] Mrs. Earl Williams, of Walla Walla, Washington, found a large rattlesnake curled up outside her kitchen door. One of her children alerted her to its presence so she got her gun and shot its head off. This was the second one she shot that season. The *Richmond Democrat*, a newspaper from Richmond County, Missouri, reported that a local optician's business was "infested with snakes for some time." Apparently the optician, Dr. Mitchell, spent a fair amount of time dispensing the animals from the premises to protect himself and his clients. The newspaper reported that one particular day had been "snake day" at the business because he killed a four foot-long rattlesnake.[92] Two men, A.B. Sampson and Chas Bent, rented a vacation house in a mountainous area of Arizona. Sampson awoke one night to the sound of a rattlesnake near the head of his bead. He woke up Bent, who was apparently also in the room and had a shotgun with him. Bent shot and killed the rattlesnake. He also put a hole in the floor in the process. When he examined the area around the snake, he discovered a large rat that the snake had followed into the house and bitten. It was evidentially after the rat when it woke up the man instead.[93]

Snakes, particularly venomous ones like rattlesnakes, were also the victims of economic greed. Snake hunters collected snakes that they killed and offered for sale either pickled or as skins. An Ethiopian immigrant, for example, lived in Connecticut on a hillside that afforded a large number and variety of snakes that he and his dog caught. He pickled and sold them to bars in New York, Philadelphia, and Boston.[94] Other times entire families of snakes were killed. Percival Heffner, in Fredericksville, Pennsylvania, claimed that his wife was attacked by two large black snakes, one of which chased her and the other tried to bite her on the face. Heffner rescued his wife from these two snakes and in the process learned that one of the black snakes had 68 young, all of which he killed as well.[95] Roger Conant, a famous herpetologist, curator of reptiles at the Toledo Zoo in 1929, and later director of the Philadelphia Zoo in 1967, had a collection of "several thousand specimens at home," all of which were dead snakes and other reptiles that he and others had killed for science.[96] Laurence Klauber added "500 specimens" to his personal collection one year to bring his personal number of living or dead snakes to 1,500. One hundred of these were rattlesnakes, both dead and alive.[97] Karl Kauffeld, the herpetologist at the Staten Island Zoo, captured and either held or killed 31 snakes in one day in a field study trip on Mt. Misery, in southern New Jersey.[98] Kauffeld took the trip with a property owner named Asa Pittman, whose family had lived on Mt. Misery for many years, and who was himself an amateur herpetologist. On one of the field trips, Kauffeld and Pittman caught "at least 200 rattlesnakes, most of them near the Mt. Misery den."[99] He found them sunning themselves on rocks near the den, beneath moss in a small spring. The scientists could capture them in such great numbers because they did the field studies that carefully documented their progress and habitat. The Pittman-Kauffeld study, for example, documented where the dens were on Mt. Misery, which streams the snakes traveled down to find food, when they left the den area in the spring, and when they returned in the fall.[100] Perhaps because they were killing snakes so much themselves, they recognized what the large-scale impact would be if many more citizens engaged in the practice. They warned others not do the same, particularly if people from the northeast joined those from the southwest in the practice of rattlesnake roundups that gratuitously killed so many of them for so little purpose. In 1906, Raymond Ditmars pointed out that the abundance of rattlesnakes in the east was "remarkable" and not understood by the urban dwellers of New York City. He reminded readers that although the southwest was "rattlesnake headquarters," the "abundance of poisonous snakes" in the eastern states was remarkable. Right across the Hudson River from New York City, the Palisades are "infested with copperhead snakes."[101] He warned his fellow urbanites that while they were sitting on rocks having picnics, they were blissfully ignorant about the snakes living underneath them and coming out to prowl at night.

Abandoning the sportsmen's bravado, he warned that "within two miles of a well known summering resort in Pennsylvania stands a pictur-esque mountain in full view of the numerous hotel verandas. Fortunately it is surrounded by veritable moats of river and swamp, deterring the sum-mer guests in making ascents" into the surrounding mountains. He pointed out that he had captured many rattlesnakes in that area. And in fact, the reptiles were so numerous that there was little novelty in catching them. Every year that he hunted for snakes in that region, he had found many of them. The "woodmen think little of slaughtering several hundred of the reptiles every autumn as the snakes congregate about the 'dens'—the hibernating quarters." And he only mentioned this mountain as an example of the many similar ones in the Berkshires (Massachusetts west-ern mountains) or those in Connecticut or New York.[102]

Sometimes the motive for killing a snake was simply pure hatred. One man from the Blue Ridge Mountains in the early 1900s waged what he described as a personal "war on snakes," particularly rattlesnakes. He made regular trips into the forest, partly to collect honey, but also to kill snakes. A newspaper columnist described his snake killing hobby as a public service.[103] A newspaper column shared a story about cowboys from Montana who fought a battle against rattlesnakes. They were hunting horses in a mountainous area when they came upon a snake den with a large male snake sitting on a rock in the sun. One of the cowboys who owned a gun began shooting at him and the snake allegedly struck back. The cowboy fired 26 more shots into the den just to kill the other "little warriors" before they left.[104]

Newspapers shared stories of snakes who were killed also to empha-size their size and potential deadliness. The animals were described as haunting or stalking an area for years until a farmer finally killed it. The *Crittendent County Press* (KY) reported that A.C. Maclanahan, a farmer who owned the Newcom Farm, killed a five-foot, seven-inch rattlesnake that weighed 21 pounds. To prevent anyone from disputing its size, he saved the skin to show to doubters.[105] Almost every one of the hundreds of rattlesnake stories in American newspapers in the 18th and 19th cen-turies stressed the number of rattles or buttons the snake had as a short-hand way of telling readers how long it had lived. This was designed to emphasize how scary it was that the animal had been living among the community for so many years.

Most often, however, people simply assumed that as humans they had the right to kill the snakes when they ran into them in their own habi-tats. Rather than let the snake simply go its own way peacefully, they pur-sued it and killed it. W.H. Randall, who worked on the New Mexico and

Arizona Railway Line, was on a trip to Santa Fe through the mountains. At a stop, he found a four foot long rattlesnake and killed it.[106] Edna Mckee of Oregon, Missouri, thought she was killing a small garden snake in her front yard, but realized later that she killed a rattlesnake.[107] A boy named Lake Eping, of South Carolina, killed a rattlesnake on his father's cotton farm. It was traveling along a cotton row when he saw it, threw a rock at it to disable it, and then stabbed it to death with a stick.[108] Robert Fletcher, a farmer who lived in Columbia, Kentucky, told a newspaper columnist that he had killed one rattlesnake every year that he lived on his farm.[109] Another farmer from Marble Hill, Missouri, reported that he cleared a meadow to plant and in the process killed 50 snakes.[110] Jimmy Spurlock, a farmer who worked on another man's corn farm in Gainesboro, Tennessee, killed seven rattlesnakes in one season.

Many years later in the 1940s and 1950s, Laurence Klauber compiled data on who was bitten, how, and where.

Laurence Klauber was one of the key herpetologists in the United States and was a central figure in helping bring antivenin to the United States (courtesy San Diego Natural History Museum).

Children were the most frequently bitten, but after that, the common denominator was that those bitten were men working outside in some way to provide for their families, usually through work of some kind, such as farming or gardening. Snakebites, in short, were largely a poor person's medical problem. Poor people, children, and working class men were by far the most likely to be bitten. Farmers and their livestock were at significantly greater risk than others. Urban, white-collar men in cities, in contrast, who took the occasional hunting or fishing trip, were at much less risk. But they had the greatest access to the print media and the most interest in furthering their hobbies of hunting and fishing in the woods. The result: a steady campaign of denial about the true cost of living with venomous snakes in the United States that hid the truth about the real dangers many Americans faced from these animals and that the animals faced from people. This was, in many ways, a kind of human-animal war consciously fought by people who lost loved ones and who wanted to live and work in generally safe surroundings. They knew that one accidental encounter could mean the end of their lives or their children's lives. It was better to rid the area of snakes rather than risk death. For their part, the snakes simply tried to defend themselves in their homes from large predator humans.

Luckily for poorer and rural Americans, some white-collar, urban professionals—namely doctors, herpetology curators, and herpetologists—worked with the snakes as well, and could give voice to the reality of how damaging snakebites really were and knew that they needed some kind of cure for their bites. In the meantime, people suffered through a range of ineffective and painful treatments, as we shall see next.

2

Cures

The Strange and Often Painful Treatment for Snakebite Before American Antivenin

In his advice to sportsmen, M.G. Ellzey assures worried hikers and hunters that most rattlesnake bites are survivable if readers take the simple steps he recommends, which include "clear[ing] the bowels by an enema of warm water and soap, to which may be added with advantage two [teaspoons] of spirits of turpentine."[1] This should quickly cure the problem, he assured, because rattlesnake venom was really not that dangerous. Similarly, another physician writing in the late 1800s assured readers of the *American Medico-surgical Bulletin* that there were actually no deadly snakebites. And in fact, "The bite of the cobra is not so deadly as is generally supposed." People exaggerated, he told his readers, but luckily for them he was there to give them the scientific truth.[2]

Writing about medicine in the United States in the 18th and 19th centuries, history of medicine scholar Elaine Breslaw paints a generally bleak picture. While European scientists and physicians were embracing specific causes for specific diseases, scientific discoveries of germs and viruses, and the need to test findings empirically, a large percentage of American physicians refused to make these adaptations. Breslaw writes mainly about American doctors' poor responses to infectious diseases like typhoid and cholera, where elite physicians refused to accept that bacteria and viruses caused illnesses and argued against inoculation even in the face of its obvious curative power. At stake was their power and prestige based upon arguing for different and ineffective cures like bleeding, purging, and placing heated cups on patients' skin to draw out some fantastical substance. If they acknowledged that they misunderstood the causes of the illness and offered ineffective or harmful treatments, then they risked losing the "real power in any healer's arsenal of cures" which was the "aura of authority and omniscience."[3] She notes that "as today a certain number of people recover from the most life-threatening conditions or go into remission without medical intervention, many health problems resolve themselves even if nothing is done. So too in the old days people survived despite [the lack of] appropriate therapies. That a few patients did recover was taken as proof of the healer to cure."[4] American physicians, she writes, were of a profession that was "more impressionistic than numerical."[5] Although they went through a period in which they were discredited, they climbed back up to the top of educated members of the elite class in the United States, and thus they were given significance deference.

We can see these themes clearly in the world of early snakebite treatments where American physicians, those who promoted their own treatments or wrote about treatments proposed by others, advocated dangerous and ineffective treatments.[6] Venomous snakes do not always deliver their venom for a variety of reasons, so people who are bitten by them are not always at risk of dying. Nevertheless, physicians wrote about their "cures" even when it was highly likely that the patient was not actually envenomated. In other cases, physicians used their instincts rather than any sense of science to promote a range of frightening and seriously dangerous treatments. And they frequently showed a kind of deference to the few people who were performing snakebite experiments on animals even when the results of the studies and methods were highly suspect if one thought about them logically. Non-scientific writers showed them extreme deference by promoting their cures through various kinds of literature, and in that way furthered the poor treatment for the scourge of bites.

Unlike infectious diseases, physicians and other healers in the United States who actually treated real victims did not dispute the cause of a patient's death or significant distress from a bite. They could tell that the snake had deposited some substance in the victim, and that it quickly spread throughout the person's body. So, the central question that physicians faced in this case was how to stop it from spreading. Was there a plant that they could place on the skin like the bark they used to slow down fevers? Should they place some kind of burning agent on the bite to stop the venom from spreading? What about simply cutting off the limb or the digit? What kinds of snakes were venomous? Was the snake venom a virus? When was it too late to stop the venom from spreading? What could they give patients to ingest that might stop it from killing them once it had clearly moved from the bite site to a significant section of the rest of the body? When we review their treatments, we find a wide array of approaches, some of which occur singly and others of which are grouped all together. One medical textbook writer in the late 1800s recommend snake stones, whiskey, and antivenin without making any distinction about which treatment worked the best. And worse, other writers, for economic, political, racist, or sexist reasons, denied that any treatment was needed at all. They claimed that people were either lying about their bites or the bite problem was simply not that bad. There were worse problems, the logic went, so we should focus on those, and by implication, let the bite victims die.

To understand what treatments physicians recommend, it is helpful to know how the major snake venoms in the United States hurt their victims. The two primary kinds of venomous snakes indigenous to the United States, who inflict most of the bites, are rattlesnakes and cottonmouths. The venom from rattlesnakes and cottonmouths in the United States have primarily hemotoxic properties, but some have neurotoxic ones as well. The hemotoxic elements of venom destroy blood cells and skin tissue, causing internal hemorrhaging. The venom disrupts the formation of clots so that blood cannot clot at all. As it spreads, it damages the inside walls of veins and arteries, all of which leads to massive uncontrolled bleeding in the tissues. This disrupts the delivery of oxygen to tissues by the blood. Without oxygen, the tissues in that area will start to die, which creates the massive tissue death that victims experience. The neurotoxic elements immobilize the nervous system and can affect the victim's breathing. Both coral snakes and some rattlesnakes have neurotoxic venom. Neurotoxic venom shuts off the body's cells' ability to communicate with nerves. They do so by inactivating acetylcholine, which is used to transmit nerve impulses from neurons to muscle cells. Without these impulses, the muscles stop working. This is fatal if it gets to one of our central muscles, the heart.[7] As we have seen, most of the fatal bites in the United States have come from rattlesnakes, so that meant that physicians were facing a guaranteed hemotoxic poisoning, and a possible neurotoxic poisoning. To try and stop the bites from killing victims, they turned to a variety of largely fanciful cures to help stop the spread of the venom. If patients were lucky in the 1800s, they received benign, but generally unhelpful treatments.

Benign and Generally Unhelpful Treatments

Physicians and scientific writers advocated a range of benign treatments that typically involved placing some substance or object on the bite site. In other cases, they advocated placing some human substance like saliva back on the animal itself. Some of these treatment suggestions came from looking to the practices of other cultures. In these cases, physicians or science writers typically advocated plant cures. At other times, however, religious and farming interests proposed a variety of magical cures, like placing animal parts on the bite site, using snake stones, or attacking the snake in a form of revenge in hopes that somehow that would cure the bite. For humans these were typically the most benign forms of treatment advocated and the least painful.

Placing dead animals on the bite site was one approach to snakebites. A rattlesnake bit five-year-old George Putnam, of Stony Fork, Pennsylvania, while he was driving the cows to pasture. His parents cut a live chicken in two parts and placed the meat on the wound. They also found, killed, cut open the snake, and placed its dead body on the swollen bite marks. Later a physician cauterized the bite, but doubted that it would do any good.[8] Like other sportsmen who wanted to encourage people to go into the wilderness, F.W. Hambleton, from Pueblo, Colorado, claimed that he had seen "many people bitten," but had never seen anyone die from a snakebite. He also claimed to know a young woman who was bitten, so "her mother applied the flesh of a freshly killed chicken to the wound. The young lady fully recovered with[in] a few days, and without any suffering."[9] There were a few other bite victims, but they simply had their limbs amputated, so Hambleton judged this a fairly minor problem.

Covering oneself with parts of the rattlesnake, giving children rattlesnake parts, or carrying parts of rattlesnakes was also recommended throughout the 1800s in the United States. One writer for the *Botanical Handbook*, published in Boston in the late 1800s, informed readers about beliefs in other states. People in Alabama allegedly believed, "If you put a string of rattlesnake bones around your neck, it will keep you safe from all harm." Those from Kansas believed, "If you carry a rattlesnake's rattle, it will cure or prevent rheumatism," or carrying a small piece of skin in one's pocket would bring good luck. Alternatively, a piece of rattlesnake skin worn around the waist next to the skin would prolong life. Americans from the southwest apparently believed that "headache may be cured by wearing the rattles of a rattlesnake in the lining of the hat." In western states, "Rattlesnakes' rattles [were] used to prevent children from having pain while teething." African Americans in New Orleans believed that rattlesnake necklaces hung around children's necks gave them immunity. Carrying a piece of the rattlesnake's skin in a pocket was supposed to bring good luck to the person who carried it as well.[10] Major Charles Lynch, of the Medical Corps of the United States Army, wrote the *First Aid Textbook for Police and Firemen,* published in 1914, in which he informed them that snakebites could be fatal, and that they should adopt the "Mexican plan" of "sleeping on the ground" surrounded by a "hair rope or lariat" because "snakes will not cross such a rope."[11]

Snake stones, which were sometimes actually rocks, and other times various other substances, were also championed as a potential treatment. They were small round pieces of stone or other hard substances, and sometimes they were small, perforated balls and rings of various kinds of ivory, strung together like beads. In Scotland, farmers gave them to cattle to chew if they were bitten by venomous snakes. Writers claimed that "some of them appear to be really efficacious." T.H. Peck, a writer for the *International Cyclopedia,* claimed that they were applied to the wound and absorbed blood from it, with the venom, before it entered the system. He insisted that this led to remarkable and speedy cures. The snake stone somehow magically adhered to the bite for a short time and then fell off, taking the venom with it. In the meantime, the physician or other caretaker rubbed the wounded limb in a downward direction to push the venom toward the stone and away from the heart. Peck relayed that two small snake stones, each the size of a large pea, brought from India, were known to have cured a man bitten by a cobra. In this case, these stones were actually composed of vegetable matter. Peck claimed that another snake stone made of bone was brought from Ceylon and that had cured a cobra bite as well.[12] So by extension, snake stones used in the United States to cure rattlesnake bites would surely work.

Plants, however, were the Holy Grail of cures. Their sheer numbers made for an enormous variety of potential cures. John King and Robert Newton, writing for the *Eclectic Dispensatory of the United States of America* in 1852, recommended American Aloe. They claimed that it was a used for flatulence, colic, obstinate diarrhea, and for snakebites.[13] They suggested that it worked as counter poison. P.L. Simonds, a British writer in the mid 1800s, believed that there must be a plant cure even though he acknowledged that physicians in this case were skeptical. He wrote for the *Journal of the Society of Arts,* a publication designed to connect scientific discoveries to practical applications.

Simonds reviewed all of the possible plant cures throughout much of the world and argued that there had to be some kind of "vegetable cure." He also thought venom was a virus, and refers to it as such throughout the publication. He wondered about the use of "powerful vegetables" such as "manchineel, hemlock, aconite, opium, nux-vomica, upas or antjas, tanghinia, henbane, datura, belladonna, and croton." He noted that in Ceylon, the "leaves and roots of the Croton tiglium are applied internally by natives in cases of snake bites."[14] If patients were given large doses of opium, that would make them very disconnected from reality, so he recommended jolting them with an electro-magnetic battery to wake them up.[15]

To test at least one of these plant cures, he shared with readers that a scientist by the name M. Mutis wanted to use criminals condemned to death in Santa Fe, New Mexico, as human subjects. He planned to see whether he could make them immune to snake venom by inoculating them with guaco. He and Mutis got the idea for trying guaco from "negros" who allegedly used the plant to make two incisions on the feet, two on the hands, and one on each side of the chest. They squeezed out the juice from the leaves and poured it on the bite spot. They also supposedly drank two spoonfuls of the juice per month for five or six months to build up an immunity to the bites, and then also carried the plant around so that it would have a "stupefying effect on the reptiles."[16] They had observed that an unnamed type of bird of prey who eats snakes would seek out the vine, pick the leaves, and plaster it all over their plumage and in that way repel any snakebite.[17] The Navy also recommended guaco because they had it on good authority that natives in Brazil used it. The consul of Brazil reported that guaco was "an important remedy for snake bites." It was also used for fever, rheumatism, gout, hydrophobia, syphilis, and cholera. They recommended one-half to one fluid dram of the plant as a cure.

Catherine C. Hopley, one of the few women who wrote about snakes, also shared native plant cures. She claimed that that healers used them "with more or less success." Indians in South America, she claimed, swallowed potent snakebite herbs in their region or inoculated themselves with "deadly vegetable juices." Like other proponents of plants, she insisted that one had to eat the plants regularly to get them to provide immunity. One possibility, she claimed, was that eating the plant might make the person smell repellent to the snake. Nevertheless, she acknowledged that scientists in the United States, like Weir Mitchel, had tested some 20 or 30 plants and found that all of them failed to cure snakebites. But, it was still possible, she believed, that standing near an ash tree might be a viable cure, because Oliver Wendell Holmes had apparently written about it in a story.[18]

Some American plants were recommended as well because they looked like some part of the rattlesnake or were named for the rattlesnake. C.E. Hobbes, in his *Botanical Handbook* from Boston, in the late 1800s, pointed out that cimicifuga has long pods that look like the rattles of the rattlesnake, and that is why people in the United States used it as a cure. Other plants, such as the yerba de la vibora, or rattlesnake weed (Dancus pusillus) of the Pacific Coast, were used as cures simply because they had name similarities. People believed that the cures must lie in the plants around where the snakes lived and a plant with that name must have been effective.[19]

Tobacco

Tobacco, however, was the American plant that was recommended or described as a cure the most frequently. Tobacco was recommended partly because it was easily available. Americans could not get plants from Ceylon easily, hunting for obscure American plants that might not actually grow in a particular region was futile, and partly, it seems, because on some level people seemed to recognize how foul it was when mixed with saliva in the case of chewing tobacco. If that was stuffed down any animal's throat, the story went, it would kill the animal. B.C. Coltrin, a miner working on the lower Rogue River in Oregon, was trying to catch his horse in a field when he was bitten by a large rattlesnake. He bled the bite and bound tobacco around it.[20] Farmers who were bitten shared their miraculous tobacco cures with others to spread the good word. In one case, an unnamed man wrote a story for the *Southern Cultivator*, a monthly magazine from Augusta, Georgia, that was dedicated to the "interests of southern agriculture." Its aim was "to elevate the character of the tillers of the soil, and to introduce a more enlightened system of agriculture, horticulture, stock breeding, and general farm economy."[21] The story, sent to the magazine in 1852, was on the efficacy of tobacco as a cure for snakebites. The writer's father had been bitten by a copperhead snake, whereupon he immediately applied "the juice of strong tobacco, mingled with saliva from the mouth, and so perfect was the cure that he did not lose a day from his business on account of it."[22]

Others were not so sure, however, that tobacco alone would kill the snake. For them it seemed that more revenge was needed. In this particular case, a Methodist preacher argued that two possible cures were presented, either saliva or tobacco. He refuted the argument by stating the following "facts." In the year 1800, while attending the General Conference of the Methodist Episcopal Church in Baltimore, he read Dr. Coke's Commentary on the Bible. Dr. Coke had argued that it is "undeniable that there is an actual enmity between the serpentine and the human race; and it is asserted, their juices are alike destructive to each other." He argued that the "prince of naturalists, the elder Pliny, who, as a heathen, must have been disinterested, asserts, that if the human spittle do but enter the serpent's mouth, it presently dies." He claimed to have tested the poison of human saliva on a snake while traveling with a companion to the Huntington Circuit Court in Pennsylvania. While riding to his appointment they saw a large rattlesnake coiled up in the road. Luckily they had a long, wooden cane with prongs, and they placed the fork over the neck of the snake.[23] He claimed:

> We then had a chance to spit into his mouth, which we did some three or four times. We then gently raised the fork to allow the snake to swallow the spittle, and after a while we removed it entirely. What was our surprise ... to see this snake exhibit every symptom of pain. He uncoiled himself—stretched himself at full length—ceased to make a noise with his rattles—and began to swell; and it was the opinion of us both, that in less than half an hour he had swelled to twice his former size. We regretted that we had not time to await the issue of the experiment, but as we had not, we killed the snake.[24]

This was a story that was shared by other American writers. Catherine Hopely, who wrote about snakes in the late 1880s, relayed an "old Virginian writer's opinion on man's ability to kill snakes with tobacco. 'Man carries more poison in his mouth than a snake,' said an old Virginian writer. 'He can poison a rattlesnake more quickly than it can him.'" Another writer claimed that a person could "kill a cobra by placing a drop or two of the oil from a dirty tobacco-pipe in a cobra's mouth." Supposedly two "woodsmen" in Virginia caught a snake and stuffed a quid of tobacco in the snake's mouth, whereupon it crawled a couple of yards and "convulsed, swelling and dying within a short time." Hopely claimed, "Leaves of tobacco as a plaister, or chopped tobacco as a poultice, are applied to a bite by the American backwoodsmen, after the custom of the Indians; or finally chopped tobacco, mixed with moist gunpowder and some pulverized sulphur formed into a plaister, and laid on the wound, and then set fire to." She also insisted that copperheads and rattlesnakes are never found in tobacco fields.[25]

Other plants were also described as useful for forcing down people's, snakes' or pets' throats. A reader of *The Plantation*, a southern farming magazine, for example, advocated using saltpeter and forcing it down the throat of the patient. One writer, for example, said, "In a recent number of *The Plantation*, he noticed [that] a gentleman from South Carolina, recommended placing saltpeter on the wound. He had never seen a person bitten by a Rattlesnake, but have seen dogs bitten and cured by forcing down their throats a large dose of saltpeter. He recommended giving salt-peter to humans as well, however, by giving them about thirty grains every half hour internally until the patient was cured. The physician allegedly assured him that he had never known this to fail as a cure."[26]

Painful Topical or Injected Substances

Nearly all other treatments recommended by physicians and writers were incredibly painful, violent, and also generally ineffective. Some of the treatments might annul the venom outside the body, but once it was inside, they only hurt the victim. Typically, the proposed treatment was accompanied by a testimonial to its effectiveness: A physician tried it and claimed that it worked on his patient, or a writer had heard of some story in which it worked.

Victims were treated with a variety of chemical substances, including nitrate of silver, caustic soda, and gold chloride. All of these agents could annul the toxic power of venom outside the human body. Unfortunately, however, they were much less successful when applied internally to bites, but that was how the venom killed people and animals.

The most common agents used to treat bites were permanganate of potash, iodine, ammonia, formaldehyde, and strychnine. Permanganate of potash was a salt-based substance that when mixed with water was effectively a disinfectant that protected against germs and infections. The potash part of the name came from producing wood ash and then collect-ing the results in large pots. Today it is used largely in fertilizer. A small amount placed on a bite site would have sterilized the area, but certainly would not have cured bites. Physicians typically recommended injecting it, however, into the wound, or a cut that they had made near the wound. It was also toxic to humans when injected at a rate that might have neu-tralized the snake venom.[27]

Iodine was another frequently recommended treatment. Like all top-ical disinfectants it was recommended partly because using water to clean out any wound was dangerous in the 1800s and early 1900s. Only boiled water could be used to clean out wounds and that might take longer than grabbing a bottle of disinfectant of some kind.[28] Dr. James Whitney, of

Woodford Col., Illinois, claimed that he had successfully treated rattlesnake bites by painting iodine on the bite. He painted the part that was
bitten as far as the swelling extended with four coats of the iodine, first.
Then he painted on four more coats before going to bed, and at four in
the morning. He believed that the iodine was absorbed into the body,
came into contact with the venom and then neutralized the toxicity. The
bite wound, however, was kept open the whole time for maximum access
for the iodine. This would have been tremendously painful and done nothing except keep germs away from the wound site as it spread.[29] A medical
school professor named Brainard, from Chicago, also recommended
iodine injections. He recommended injecting the tissues at the bite site
with "half a drachm to a drachm and [with] a half a solution, made of five
grains of iodine and fifteen of iodide of potassium in a fluid ounce of dis-
tilled water." After that, he recommended that physicians should apply a
cupping glass over the wound "as soon as possible." And then he directed
them to use a trocar—a medical device that is made up of a sharpened
metal tip to penetrate flesh, a hollow tube, and a seal. The purpose of a
trocar is to introduce other medical instruments into the body, so in this
manner, Brainard was instructing physicians to place the needle into the
trocar so that it could go under the cup and into the bite site to deliver
the iodine. He claimed to have done 40 successful experiments with this
technique on pigeons, kittens, and dogs.[30] Physicians also recommended
mercury to accompany the iodine. Brainard claimed mercury was "most
valuable" for curing snakebite, although it is deadly and he never clearly
explained how it was supposed to get into the patient's systems to coun-
teract the venom.[31]

Ammonia was a related cure that was frequently recommended and
sometimes debunked. One unnamed physician shared his ammonia cure,
and the story followed a familiar pattern: the physician was called out to
a house, tried a treatment, it worked, and now he recommended it to
everyone. "On August 1891, I was called in haste to see a boy four years
old, who was suffering from snake bite," he relayed to readers. The boy
had been bitten on the hand in two places by a rattlesnake. He gave the
messenger, who arrived by horse, ammonia water and told him to race
back three miles to the boy's home, soak a cloth in ammonia water, and
apply it to the hand and arm until the doctor could get there and take
over. He arrived at the house and found the little boy's hand "swollen
almost to bursting, as a tight ligature had been kept around the wrist since
it was bitten." He ordered the ligature taken off and then placed 25 drops
of aqua ammonia in half a glass of water and gave the boy a teaspoonful

every five minutes until the pain and swelling ceased. After 20 minutes, the child became easy and quiet. He continued this treatment all night every two hours. The next morning, he found the boy up and walking around the house. He did not recommend constantly giving people ammonia, but he did suggest it as an alternative to whiskey.[32] Part of the zeal for ammonia came from Australia. More of the Australian snakes had neurotoxic venom that caused lethargy as victims' breathing and hearts slowed. As a result, they were looking for some stimulation as a way to keep people alive. A Professor Hartford, from Australia, recommended using hypodermic syringes and injecting "ten or twenty minims of the strongest liquid ammonia directly into veins without killing the man on the spot." He claimed once again to have done successful experiments with ammonia in the late 1860s.[33]

Not everyone was so sure about ammonia. A small number of voices from outside the United States argued against its use. By 1877, the *Pacific Medical and Surgical Journal* informed its readers that ammonia was not an effective treatment. "A few years ago, our readers will remember [that] the injection of aqua ammoniae in the veins was vaunted as a preventative or cure of the poisonous effects of snake-bites," the anonymous author wrote. Australia had initially adopted it as a cure and "numerous cases were given which appeared to confirm" that ammonia treatment worked. However, experiments made in India by a commission of the medical authorities of Calcutta, proved the inefficiency of the treatment, at least for the bite of venomous serpents in India, the journal warned, and so at least Australians were less likely to get this treatment.[34] They were lucky because the results of the treatment were at best extremely painful, and at worst, caused death. Ammonia spread on the skin burned and killed the tissue. But enough ammonia injected into the body, as American physicians recommended so casually, could perforate the colon, causing bacterial products to leach into the peritoneum, which in turn caused acute toxicity and death.

Formaldehyde was a related disinfectant that was also recommended at times. It was called Formol, and it was a solution of 10 percent formaldehyde in water. It was also supposed to be an "infallible" cure for animal bites, rabies, lupus, and germs from dead bodies. In the case of snakebites, the cure was particularly painful, however. The puncture produced by the snakebite was supposed to be opened by a needle, pin, hairpin, or something of that nature. Once the bite had been further opened, Formol was dropped into the open would and spread around with the sharp instrument that reopened the snakebite. Or, alternatively the physicians could make an incision across the bite and drop the Formol inside. Once in the bite, they were supposed to knead and massage the wound to spread the Formol as much as possible.[35]

Strychnine was another dicey cure that some physicians recommended. Morris Rice claimed that it had been tried with significant success even though it was "a poison as terrible and deadly as the snake venom itself." He focused on the neurotoxic types of snake venom that stopped nerve centers throughout the body. It did not, he claimed, interfere with the fundamental structure of the nerve cells themselves. So, the good news was that strychnine had the opposite action of the venom and this, he proposed, was why patients should be given the doses in "exceedingly large quantities" while the patient was watched. One might guess that the patient should be watched for poisoning from the strychnine, but actually he felt that they needed watching for a "relapse" from the snake venom. He urged physicians that strychnine should be given "freely, and without regard to the quantity." There was "more danger of death ensuing from not giving enough, than from giving too much." But just in case they did not understand how much freely meant, he recommended one injection "within twenty minutes after the first injection." Very urgent cases sometimes required "as much as twenty minim of liquid strychnine in persons over fifteen years old." He claimed that this was safe, and that strychnine had no harmful side effects. "In India and Australia this treatment is considered the remedy par excellence," he assured his readers. And just for good measure, he reminded his fellow doctors that in all cases of snakebite it was good to keep the kidneys active and purge the stomach.[36]

Sometimes physicians and others who studied venom recommended poisons that killed the snake itself, believing that if that was ingested by the bite victim, then it would kill the venom inside the person as well. Carbolic acid and creosote were two such treatments. They both killed snakes when placed on them as one might expect, particularly in the case of creosote. When carbolic acid was placed on snakes it caused the snake to "double itself up in numerous folds, remaining as stiff as if cast in metal." People could also place carbolic acid or creosote around their homes to drive snakes away. They knew that a few drops of carbolic acid poured on the floor of their cages would also kill snakes in a very short time. Weir Mitchell recommended that every backwoodsman supply himself with a little of it because it was easily portable in small tubes. He also claimed to have experimented with it as a cure, which he applied to the wound, and claimed treated it successfully, but it had to be given "at once."[37] Although all of these treatments were painful and could kill the patients, they did not include actual physical mutilation. However, some physicians recommended that as well.

Cauterizing, Shooting and Ligature

Cauterization was one of the physically violent treatments writers recommended frequently. At their most ineffective, writers for medical journals sometimes recommended cauterizing near or next to the bite spot. George Shipman, who wrote for *The United States Medical and Surgical Journal*, recommended applying a hot iron next to the wound to arrest the poison. It was supposed to be as hot as the patient could stand.[38] H.K. Gilman, a first lieutenant for the USMC Bureau of Navigation in the Navy Department, wrote a field handbook for naval operations on shore. For insect bites and scorpion stings, he recommended extracting the stinger, but if it remained in the wound, he recommended rubbing "acetic acid, the nicotine from a pipe, or chewed tobacco, upon the wound." For snakebites, he recommended that one should "tie a string or handkerchief tightly above the wound and apply a caustic; if you have none, burn the wound deeply with an iron (or a ramrod) heated to a white head then use the utmost exertion to prevent the patient giving way to sleep, the usual accompaniment of snake-bites, and which often ends in death."[39] John Chalmers Da Costa was professor of surgery and clinical surgery at Jefferson Medical College in Philadelphia, surgeon to the Philadelphia Hospital, and consulting surgeon to St. Joseph's Hospital in Philadelphia as well. He acknowledged that most people do not have the proper implements to treat snakebites. However, he liked to tell students in his lectures that he had "seen an army officer blow off his finger with a pistol the moment after it was bitten by a rattlesnake," and thus escape envenomation. In general, he recommended making several cuts about the bite (a common recommendation as we shall see), cauterizing it with pure acid, then sucking the venom out or using a cup to somehow suck it out. Another possibility used by hunters, he claimed, was to cauterize it by pouring a little gunpowder on the excised area and apply a spark, or by laying a hot ember on the wound. If they happened to have a hot iron lying around then they should use that. Or, if a surgeon was around, then he should amputate the limb well above the bite. By the time Da Costa was dispensing medical instruction (1908), Albert Calmette's antivenin was available, but difficult for doctors in the United States to get.[40] Writers for *The Rural Efficiency Guide* recommended cauterizing the wound with a hot iron, or taking the approach that hunters did, which was to pour gunpowder on the wound and apply a spark or lay a live coal upon it.[41] Writers for the *National Druggist,* in 1908, described a letter from a pastor who claimed to have seen a method used by Bogan natives when bitten by venomous snakes. The person immediately went to a red ants' nest, stamped his foot to rouse the ants, then he or she placed the bitten part of their body in the ants' way. The ants swarmed the bite and then dropped off dead. This process of finding an ants' nest was supposedly repeated until there were no more dead ants, suggesting that there was no more poison coming out with the blood.[42] Dr. W.G. Stimpson, the assistant surgeon general of the United States Public Health Service, also recommended extreme measures when bitten. The wound "should be cauterized" by applying "carbolic acid or nitric acid on the end of a stick, such as a match stick or a toothpick," but noted that "most of these injuries happen in the wild, where such chemicals cannot be obtained. Cauterization may then be performed by heating a nail, a knife blade, or some other metallic object, such as a suspender buckle, in a fire and freely burning all parts of the wound. On hunting trips, a cartridge may be torn open and a little gunpowder poured on the wound and then ignited with a match."[43]

The American Medical Association also advocated extremely violent treatment methods when they finally got around to acknowledging the problem in 1908. They also immediately dismissed the only actual cure, antivenin, equating it with placing chicken parts or urine-soaked clothes on a bite. In contrast, they highly recommended cutting off arms, fingers, and toes. Removal of a toe, for example, was "justified if it could be done immediately following the injury, or later." Amputating fingers should "certainly be considered under similar circumstances." Besides, they said, bites on the finger were likely to be followed by joint problems and tendon problems, so the physician should not hesitate to remove the finger.[44]

Advocates of blasting off limbs also frequently recommended ligatures if one could not get to a gun or fire fast enough. Many people, they reasoned, would have some kind of string, rope, or handkerchief with them, so why not recommend that as the cure? The theory was that victims could stop the venom from spreading if the initial shock troops of topical burning agents failed to do their job. Perhaps they could just tie off the arm and the venom would never reach the rest of the body. And as a worst case scenario, they could have the limb amputated later. Writers admonished that "incredible force must be used to tighten the ligature, which even with a tourniquet or a stick to twist the cord to the utmost is scarcely sufficient to completely stop the circulation in the fleshy part of a limb."

Sometimes you had to make the ligature so tight that you cut into the flesh. In other cases, they acknowledged that even a grown man couldn't tie the ligature tightly enough. In this case, a scientist named Fayrer was experimenting with a dog who had been bitten by a snake in the hind leg. In another case, Fayrer also failed to stop the venom from killing a chicken who he allowed a cobra to bite in an experiment. He exerted the greatest amount of tension that a man could exert, but in spite of the ligature, the fowl showed signs of envenomation in 23 minutes, and in three-quarters of an hour was dead. Despite the lack of success from his experiments, he strongly advocated ligatures and informed others that they should not relax the ligament until the limb was "cold and livid."[45] Other times they recommended multiple ligatures. If one worked, then several must be better. John Warren emphasized that every second counted because "in many reported cases" victims' lives had been saved because of ligatures. It must be applied so tightly, however, that they might want to use a stick to turn the knot and really cut off all circulation. And, then they should make another ligature higher up because perhaps the first one did not work after all and the patient needed another ligature as a kind of second venom dam.[46] It is not at all surprising that when victims or their well-intentioned assistants succeeded in tying ligatures this tightly, victims often lost their limbs to gangrene.

Cutting and Sucking

In addition to ligatures, physicians and other writers recommended cutting the bitten limb or body part and sucking out the venom. In 1872, F.W. Hambleton was a member of the United States Surveying Corps. One of the members killed a large rattlesnake and swung the snake "in fun toward another of our party and the reptile struck its fangs in the man's hip." Unfortunately, they were a long way (around 200 miles) from a doctor, and had no way of treating their friend with any kind of chemicals, so they resorted to "the old frontier way of cutting out the wounded flesh." Two men held the bite victim while a third used "a dull pocket knife to cut a piece as large as a hen's egg from the flesh surrounding the bite." The patient screamed in pain during the procedure like "a calf under the branding iron." They then carried the poor fellow to camp and gave him enough "whiskey ... to have paralyzed 2 men." Simultaneously they also filled the wound with chewing tobacco, and bound it with cloths. Refreshingly, Hambleton acknowledged that their patient did not recover immediately, but rather "fell sick, either from the bite or the treatment," so they sent him by ox wagon for further treatment in Arkansas City. The victim later recovered, and Hambleton thought this made sense because he himself was once bitten by a water moccasin, but placed a freshly killed chicken on the site and was fine.[47]

As we can see from this story, the related treatment protocol promulgated into the early 1970s by physicians and science writers, and then firmly lodged in the American mythology about how to treat snakebite, was that people should cut the wound and then suck out the venom and spit it out. The cutting took a lot of different forms, suggesting no one had any idea what they were actually doing since if they really knew where the venom was, the cuts should all have been recommended for the same place. For example, no one was recommending that gall bladder surgery incisions be placed over the heart or on the leg. Once that surgery was developed, there was a clear consensus on the rough area to make the incision. Not so with snakebite. Should they scoop out the bite site? Should they make a slash across it? Should they poke it and open it up? Should they make several slashes up the bitten appendage? What about × marks? perhaps those would work better than slashes? There was no clear consensus, so patients were at the mercy of their particular physician's idea about where to cut, how to cut, and how often to cut open the wound. That is if they were treated by a physician. In other cases, they were slashed by friends and acquaintances who had even less surgical knowledge and technique. S.B. Higgens, of the *British Homeopathic Review*, recommended making incisions at the "lower point of attachment of the deltoid muscles, in the manner as for vaccination, and into these" introducing "small pellets of cotton (the size of a millet seed) saturated with an alcoholic tincture of the alconcito." He said that "care is taken to keep within doors and out of the wet and dew for from fifteen to twenty days, after which period the inoculation is concluded." He claimed that this process was successful because he tested it on dogs and none of them had died or even shown "any inconvenience" from a venomous snake.[48] The War Department's recommendation to the Hospital Corps in the early 1900s for snakebite was to cut open the wound, suck out the poison, and then cauterize it with "fire or caustic."[49] It is hard to understand why they thought this might work, but one writer's description of a bite helps us understand the limits of their understanding. P.L. Simonds argued that the bite of a venomous snake is like a cat's scratch. In contrast to the observations of all other people, he argues that it just scratches the surface. So, all one needs to do is cut out the area of the wound, which is roughly the "size of a six pence, or a four pence." The newly created hole should be cleaned and then the venom should be sucked out for up to two hours. If possible, the sucking should be done using "cupping glasses," but he understood that people are unlikely to have these with them. They do have their mouths, or someone's close to them that they can use, however, and that's what they should use unless they had a cup.[50]

Physicians and other public health writers continued to recommend these treatments even after antivenin became available in the United States. Two of the biggest advocates of the largely futile acts of cutting and sucking out the venom were physicians Dudley Jackson and Rhea Jackson, who had conducted about 700 live rattlesnake bite experiments on animals partly to debunk myths about the curative ability of home remedies, and partly to argue that cuts over the wounds and suctioning could remove venom and save lives. Jackson and Rhea did extensive, sad, animal subject studies on dogs who they injected with venom to trace the trajectory of the liquid through the body. Their advice was also championed by Colonel Martin Crimmins, who ran a military base near San Antonio, Texas, and played a central role in the distribution of antivenin. On the advice of Jackson and Rhea, Crimmins recommended placing cuts over the bites to withdraw the venom through a suction device. If that failed to work, he proposed making even more cuts further up on the body. For example, if one was unable to withdraw venom from a cut over a bite on the lower part of the arm, then they advocated making several cuts in a x shape on the upper portion of the arm near the shoulder and suctioning the venom.[51] In 1929, Jackson, for example, claimed that San Antonio hospitals had treated 17 cases of venomous snakebite by suction alone, with no deaths.[52] And finally, they advocated tying a ligature above the wound to slow the pace of the venom. When it didn't work, he blamed the bite victim as in this account: A woman from the San Antonio area was bitten by a snake in 1946 and died. Crimmins shared his version of the bite story to Laurence Klauber, a member of the San Diego Zoological Society, and amateur herpetologist. "We have had one death from rattlesnake bite this year. She was a very fat woman, about twice normal weight ... [the] tourniquets were useless and crosscuts [were ineffective] on account of the thick layer of fat" on her leg.[53] So, the problem was not the treatment protocol, it was the woman's fault.

There were serious problems, however, with all three parts of the protocol. They neglected to emphasize, for example, that suctioning venom only works if one can remove it within five minutes of a bite to have any effect.[54] Similarly, creating safe incisions of any kind requires a sterilized knife. Unfortunately, however, most Americans typically did not carry around sterilized surgical equipment (and still do not). To rectify this problem, Jackson created a snakebite kit, named the "Dudley," that included a sterilized blade and suction device. Most Americans did not have access to this product, and thus resorted to using whatever sharp object they could find only to kill themselves by tetanus infections brought on by a dirty knife.[55] And finally, ligature only makes sense if one understands how to use it, and if one can get to a hospital in a short period of time. Unfortunately, however, poor people living in remote rural regions of the country were tying ligatures around their arms and legs only to have gangrene set in because it took them so long to get to medical treatment.

Some of the problems created by the treatment advice advocated by Crimmins and Jackson are evident in the bite Ross Allen received. Allen was a professional snake collector and venom dealer from the Florida Reptile Institute. He was on a routine trip to visit his hunters who caught snakes in the wild. On his first stop, he lost his footing while trying to hold a five-foot diamondback rattlesnake. The snake succeeded in biting him on the thumb. After he caught the animal, he applied this recommended first aid by placing a tourniquet on his arm and by cutting his hand open in three places. Luckily for Allen, passengers had accompanied him to get the snakes and thus drove him toward help. They sped through the woods to avoid the deep sand they had gotten stuck in while traveling to the snake hunters and then caught the road for the remaining 27 miles to Ocala, Florida. The tourniquet, however, failed to stop the venom that rapidly spread through his arm and into his body. In 30 minutes he was paralyzed and unable to use his hands or legs. In the car, he made three more cuts, applied suction and injected 30 cc of antivenin. When he reached the hospital he was "totally helpless and only able to talk, in spite of the first aid" he received.[56] At the hospital, the doctors made 50 incisions from his hand to his shoulder, but his arm continued to swell and the pain remained intense. A special nurse "kept up suction" for nearly "24 hours."[57] He had lost "considerable blood" from the first aid so he needed transfusions.[58] Although he received morphine, it failed to entirely dull the pain. Within 24 hours the swelling spread from his arm to both shoulders, his back, chest, and head. Muscles in his legs, face, and stomach shook for around six days. By the fourth day, doctors had to remove part of his thumb because gangrene had set in. Ultimately, Allen survived because he received antivenin.

Raymond Ditmars, the herpetology curator at the Bronx Zoo and strong advocate of antivenin once it became available, advocated using ligature and razors because he recognized that antivenin was still out of reach for most people. In a newspaper article designed to help Americans recognize venomous snakes and treat their bites, Ditmars told readers that they should "apply a ligature above the bitten part, open the fang punctures with the blade, massage and suck the wound, and then shake up a few crystals of permanganate in the bottle of water, washing the wound with a few drops at a time of this amethyst-colored solution. After twenty minutes of this treatment, the ligature must be removed."[59]

Even by the 1950s, people were still trying to use the tourniquet and razor method as the following account reveals. On August 22, 1953, Robert Hellman, a snake hunter, tried to capture a rattlesnake on Highway 40 in Moffat County, Colorado. The snake had been partly run over by a car, but Hellman and his travelling companion, Edward Mockford, a biology graduate student at the University of Florida, decided to take it anyway. While putting his hand around the snake's head, it bit him on two separate fingers. Mockford hailed a passing car so that he could administer first aid while they were taken to the hospital. He tied two tourniquets on Hellman's lower arm instead of his fingers. He used a razor blade sterilized in alcohol to make a single cut across each puncture would, but Hellman conceded that they were "probably not deep enough to do much good." Then they used an old-fashioned rubber bulb and metal cup as suction devices, which he again noted were "relatively ineffective on the small, rounded surfaces of a finger and very painful ... because of its hard edges which tend to dig into the already bruised tissue." Later a "completely ineffective secondary cut was made on the side of the left forefinger about one half inch above the bite [which] succeeded, ultimately only in confusing the doctor as to the site of the bite on that finger."[60]

Cutting limbs and bitten body parts and then trying to suck out the venom lasted well beyond the 1800s as physicians and other scientific writers promoted it as a heroic, but generally futile cure. Most commonly, however, patients were given alcohol.

Alcohol

The most recommended treatment for venomous snakebites was alcohol. The type depended upon what the patient and doctor could access, although the higher the alcohol content the better. For the rarer, upper-class patient who was bitten, doctors recommended wine and even more rarely brandy. Because most people who were bitten were poor and in rural areas, however, the drink most recommended was whiskey. Doctors and writers who promoted this treatment did so for a couple of understandable reasons, and others that were muddled and misguided. On the positive side, at a minimum, alcohol numbed the terrible pain and made the snakebite bearable. If venom was spreading throughout the body, moreover, the need for a painkiller of some kind was acute. Further, if the treatments previously described were attempted as well, the patient would desperately need a painkiller. Limb or digit removal, deep cuts, or burning substances injected in an already extremely painful, bruised, bleeding bite site might actually happen if a patient was completely knocked out with the most likely narcotic available. Doctors and science writers felt safe in advocating alcohol, then, because there was no way that they could implement their other treatments unless their patients were effectively heavily anesthetized. And they realized that the truth was the bite was agonizingly painful, and they could provide some help in at least minimizing the pain to the extent possible.

When it came to arguments about using alcohol as an actual cure for the bite itself, the reasoning was very murky and further illustrates Breslaw's argument that physicians, and we would add, science writers, had no qualms about completely fabricating potential cures. The other clearer source for the reputed cure was a kind of mythology of western frontiersmen. They claimed to know their lore and used that as their reason for recommending it. It is also clear that part of the claim for alcohol likely originated in India because of the neurotoxicity of cobras. The stimulant part of the drink might have kept cobra (and water moccasin) bite victims alive longer, or appeared to do so because it would have helped keep the heart beating at the same time that the snake venom was stopping the patient's heart from beating. There is no doubt that an actual bite from a cobra with venom in it would have killed a person regardless of gallons of whiskey, but at least the patient might have appeared to last a bit longer.

The problem with the Indian approach in the United States, however, is that alcohol is a pain numbing stimulant that also breaks down platelets. Hemotoxic venom from rattlesnakes, for example, works by breaking down red blood cells and forcing the patient to bleed out. Giving them whiskey in that case would have only made that situation worse by further killing the body's ability to create platelets to stop the bleeding. So, other than pain numbing and temporarily making the patient appear more alert because they were getting a stimulant, alcohol was in no way a cure.

It was recommended for everyone until three forces challenged it as a cure, two of which we will focus on in this chapter. First, Temperance movement advocates argued against its unfettered use, and second, the first wave women's movements, and the increasing focus on recreational experiences for all Americans, including young women, placed advocating enough whiskey to float a battleship in conflict with ideas about what proper young women should do.

In India, the British recommended wine for cobra bites. Writing for the *Monthly Homeopathic Review*, S.B. Higgins recommended "pure spirits of wine, or 95 percent alcohol or the best high wines that can be procured." The physician or lay person healer was supposed to "put five drops (no more) of the preparation into half a tumblerful of pure water; pour the water from one tumbler into another backwards and forwards several times, that the preparation may be thoroughly mixed with the water, and administer a large tablespoonful of the mixture every three or five minutes" until it was finished.[61] Clearly, this was a recommendation designed overwhelmingly for the wealthy in India, and most likely for whites.

In the United States, in contrast, whiskey was the recommended drink even in the southwest where tequila was available as well. The Navy's recommendation for sailors bitten by snakes while on shore was that "no time should be lost administering spirits." Further, there was no need to worry about causing intoxication because doctors could supposedly give a "very large quantity" without causing intoxication.[62] Doctors who were also researchers, like Weir Mitchell, claimed that people could drink bottles of whiskey or brandy and not notice the effects. William Gore, a 22-year-old stone cutter from Fort Lee, New Jersey, was bitten by a rattlesnake when he kicked at its head. Instead of retreating, the rattlesnake defended itself and eventually bit Gore on the finger. House Surgeon Dunning, at Manhattan Hospital, gave him "an ounce and a half of whiskey an hour" so that he was "drunk all the time."[63]

Age was initially not a barrier to alcohol treatment as long as it was given by physicians or other healers in the home. Catherine Hopely claimed, "A girl of 14, who when bitten by an Australian snake, drank three bottles without being intoxicated!" And that "Dr. Weir Mitchell found that delicate women and young children under the influence of snake poison could take 'quarts of brandy without injury, and almost without effect.'" She also claimed that a "Mr. Walter Nightingale reported in the Field, January 14th 1882 that 'a little girl two years old, bitten in the hand by a "horned viper" ... had administered to her brandy and milk in occasional doses without any visible effects, until a whole bottle of brandy had been thus swallowed! The child recovered; and the force of the argument seemed to rest on the astounding quantity of strong spirit that could be taken to overcome the venom without producing intoxication.'"[64]

The whiskey cure was endorsed by Dr. Charles Allen's experiments on snakes in New York City. Allen collected venomous snakes from Florida, including the diamondback rattlesnake and the water moccasin, and brought them back to his home that also served as a laboratory. Unable to keep all of his snakes at home, he kept part of his collection in Central Park. He recommended whiskey for bites, although he was somewhat unique among writers in the 19th and early 20th centuries in noting that most people would kill themselves with it if they drank a whole bottle (let alone as much as they wanted as some advocates suggested). In contrast, he proposed whiskey in moderation to "prevent heart failure."[65]

Other science writers were more blunt about the real benefits of alcohol. Catherine Hopely had stayed in Iowa when streets were uncleared, and unlike the East Coast, city-dwelling writers who liked to deny the problem of snakebite, Hopely pointed out that people were frequently bitten by rattlesnakes. Because there was no medicine, people turned to whiskey and they got drunk instead. In contrast to other writers who asserted that one could ingest large amounts of whiskey and not feel any effects, Hopely contended that there was a "violent combat" between the whiskey and the snake venom. George Terhune, a teamster from Nevada, stopped his horses to get a drink from a spring and was bitten on the hand. Although he wanted to kill the snake, he withdrew the bung from the whiskey, drank it, and took some "tobacco from his pocket, saturated that with whiskey and applied the poultice to his hand." He kept drinking whiskey as he drove his horses to his destination that he reached the next day. He removed the poultice and found that the wound had "turned green," but he survived. Hopely pointed out that backwoodsmen resorted to this cure rather than other "local torture" because it deadened the bite victim's sensibilities, stopped his suffering, and sent him into a happy state where he was oblivious of danger. She admitted that it was somewhat low class to be "dead drunk," and instead just for appearance's sake of the "loyalty to science" and the profession of medicine, physicians should use some other cure as well.[66]

Hopely recommended alcohol as a treatment based on her experiences in the midwest, but even the best hospitals in the United States used whiskey. Writing for the *Medical and Surgical Reporter* in 1888, Charles Dulles noted that the treatment was deep intoxication until the patient recovered. They "saturated" the victim with whiskey or some other alcohol.[67]

Not everyone deserved the cure, however, according to science writers in particular. Some people were fakers, and these were the poor, rural men. Hopley claimed that African Americans pretended to get bitten just to drink whiskey. Indeed, "a planter himself" had told her "that Sambo would sometimes prick his hand or foot with a thorn, and crying out 'Rattlesnake!' fall into well assumed agonies, in his preference for a spirituous somniferousness to get out of cotton-picking." When the planters realized the fraud, they offered some of the rest of the horrific cures, so she claimed that the false claims became less frequent. Science writers claimed that southern planation owners assured them that during cotton-picking season, "Sambo" would allow himself to get bitten to drink alcohol and rest. The overseers were given alcohol to give to slaves in case of snakebites. There was no sympathy for the pain of these workers. In contrast to the kind words about numbing pain, and few other alternatives, African Americans were described as getting "helplessly drunk." To punish them, the plantation owners then withheld the painkiller and just used injected ammonia, which they claimed stopped the claimed frequency of the bites.[68]

Prohibition advocates also disagreed that alcohol should be used for anyone at all. They dismissed the pain and the lack of other readily available real cures by downplaying the bite problem and arguing that snakebites in America (and India) were less of a problem than the "serpent of alcohol," or they denied that bites killed people. One unnamed prohibitionist columnist claimed to cite an also unnamed scientist who informed readers that rattlesnake venom was "seldom strong enough to kill an adult." People who drank whiskey were described as alcoholics who faked their bites to drink more.[69] They were people who scratched themselves on "brambles" so that they could drink to excess.[70] Prohibitionists gleefully noted that unnamed scientists had found that alcohol did not cure bites. They also noted that intoxication killed more people and created far more negative costs in many ways. They pointed to how expensive it was to run a court that cost "$100 a day" for a trial that resulted from the purchase of fifty cents' worth of alcohol and ran for two days. This daily "spectacle" of working with alcoholics happened every day in their communities when they had to pay $200 for "one man's privilege of taking two or three drinks of whisky." They argued that far more people had been killed by intemperance, which they claimed was about 60,000 per year, compared to the roughly 48,000 deaths per year caused by cobra bites. A person bitten by a cobra died quickly, the argument went, but alcoholism caused prolonged suffering and agony. A snakebite only affected one person, they claimed (clearly incorrectly), but alcoholism ruined families. People were not wasting time and money when they were bitten by snakes, but they were when they were in saloons. Venomous snakes did not cause "crime, prostitution, pauperism, mental and physical ruin, and the hereditary disease which accompany the American saloons." So the real serpents people needed to kill were the saloons.[71] A related argument was that rattlesnakes were more noble because they gave people warning that they were about to strike, but alcohol killed people "in a sly, lying way." Some of the more moderate prohibitionists acknowledged that drinking some alcohol made sense to dull the pain of a rattlesnake bite, but they resented that the rattlesnake bites were used by proponents of alcohol to keep it available to everyone.[72]

They particularly disliked the idea of giving alcohol to children, and warned that there was never any justification for that. They made the elitist claim that there were not that many snakebites in the United States so there was no need to worry about needed pain killers or cures.[73] Prohibitionists sometimes referred to a saloon as a "snakery." One unnamed newspaper columnist for the *Belmont Chronicle*, in St. Clairsville, Ohio, asked readers to imagine allowing a person to move into town and set up a snakery in which (presumably he) would come into town and set up a business. The business would have cabinets with drawers and cases with glass tops. He would keep the snakes, including rattlesnakes and copperheads in the drawers and "sell bites." A rattlesnake bite would "cost 6¼ cents," for example. When the snakes got cold, the businessman would lie them out on the sidewalk to warm them up. While they were warming, schoolchildren would come by and stop and look at them. In this way he could get the children hooked on the snakebite (metaphorically the alcohol). In this case, the writer argued, parents would quickly drive the businessman out. But poison from the "rum cup," the writer proposed, was worse than the "deadly fang" of the snake. Why? Because in the case of the snake, no one was at fault, but in the case of alcohol, people were morally guilty of drinking and giving alcohol to children. The answer was better to work and pray for a law that banned alcohol.[74]

People in local areas, however, fought back against the attempts by prohibitionists to take away alcohol as a cure. In Minot, South Dakota, for example, a local German doctor recommended against using alcohol. In this case he was not doing so because he was a prohibitionist, but rather because he correctly pointed out that it was not an effective cure. Fearing the spread of prohibition and the loss of their potential numbing agent in the case of a bite, the local newspaper fought back. One of their unnamed writers noted that a "whole lot of miners" in the region could attest to its effectiveness and hypothesized that the doctor must have gotten some of the "North Dakota Prohibition whiskey palmed off on him," and this was why he failed to see its excellent numbing and curative effects.[75] As we have seen, farmers also used alcohol to treat ranch animals, which meant that they needed access to the drink. The *Chicago Herald* reported that whiskey in New Mexico was used to treat snakebites in sheep. The story gleefully noted that Prohibition had failed to stop alcohol for either people or sheep, and that when the sheep ingested it, they staggered around "the prairie" with a "jag on that would make an old bummer wild with envy."[76]

When children started attending organized activities outside of the home, science writers modified their advice about snakebite treatment in general and got rid of the recommendation that children should drink altogether. The rise of the Boy Scouts and their time spent in the wildness posed real potential problems for bites, particularly because Boy Scouts went into the wilderness and gathered their own natural history collections (they called them museums) from the plants and animals that they found. In contrast to the post–environmentalist movement ethic of leaving nature alone (take only photographs, leave only footprints), the early Boy Scout approach was to capture and bring home nature. This meant capturing snakes, including rattlesnakes. Ray Ditmars, the herpetological curator at the Bronx Zoo, warned Boy Scouts against collecting these animals because, although it was true that sometimes the boys could safely catch one, other times they were bitten. At a minimum they faced agonizing pain, and in the worst case scenario, they faced death. So, what should medical writers tell boys in the woods who might get bitten? Did they want them getting out their tobacco and putting it on the wound? Shooting off the bitten limb? Slashing themselves with knives? Shooting strychnine into themselves? How about ingesting as much whiskey as possible? The answer was no to all of the above. By the early 1900s, *The Boy Scout's Manual* advocated sucking out the venom without making any cuts and tying a ligature that they loosened every so often to let "a little poison escape into the body." If the bite seemed bad, they recommended keeping the ligature tight and losing the limb. They omitted telling the boys to cut themselves or drink hard alcohol. The boys could use ammonia, but only as a disinfectant on top of the skin, or ingested when combined with water.[77] The occasional news story reinforced the wisdom of this approach even if it was never clear that the snake had actually included any venom it its bite. The *New York Times* had a column that updated readers about the Boy Scouts' activities around the country. In one case, we learn that Leon Bindrup from Logan, Utah, was on a hiking trip with his troop when he was bitten. He was climbing a hillside and reached up to grab a ledge when a rattlesnake bit him on the hand. He shook the snake off and started to run back to get help. Suddenly he stopped and remembered his training about bites. So he pulled out his pen knife, cut the bite area, "sucked out what poison he could from it," and then had a tourniquet applied by a companion. The unnamed columnist reported that no ill effects resulted from the bite, but it is highly likely that there was no venom in the bite to begin with.[78]

Conversely, girls in the outdoors got no information at all. Girls were simply instructed to avoid venomous snakebite. And ignoring all of the little girls who had been bitten and died in the past, they informed these girls that bites were not really a problem. Lina Beard and Adelia Beard's *On the Trail: An Outdoor Book for Girls* omitted recommending any immediate help whatsoever. If a bite happened, it was the girl's fault because people could "almost always avoid" snakes, they insisted. Citing Hornaday's fictitious statistics on bites, they assured girls that "out of seventy-five million people not more than two die each year of snake bites." Because the book was directed at the comparatively rare, urban young woman venturing into the wild for recreation purposes, they could make the same fictional statements that they made to the same race and class of men earlier. The solution, they said, was that somehow someone needed to just kill the snake and show the girl that it was undoubtedly just a harmless snake. The authors said that the real problem was the hysteria of the girls who were actually worried about being bitten by a venomous snake.[79] Once the snake was taken to someone (it is vague to whom the snake should be taken) to be identified as a harmless snake, then everything would be fine.

Rationality Layered on to Irrationality

There were science writers and physicians by around 1910 and later who began making much more accurate statements about snakebites and the need for treatment. They were clearly influenced by Albert Calmette's invention of antivenin for use against cobra venom. At times, these writers urged Americans to get some of it if they were going to spend time in tropical areas with venomous snakes, although they do not say this explicitly. The creation of a cure, even a very limited one, suddenly created the environment in which at least some science writers could say that the problem was real. Once again, the writers most likely to acknowledge the problem and the potential treatment were often those who were most in contact with snakes. But in spite of their rationality about antivenin, they had a kind of stratified approach to treating bites, in which they layered on cures from the past and culminated with the recommendation that victims get treated with antivenin. Generally, moreover, they were extremely vague about where one got Calmette's antivenin.

The accurate statements about the definite need for treatment came from people directly responsible for the lives of others who worked in areas with significant venomous snake problems in the United States. Miners were very clear that workers bitten by snakes needed immediate treatment. In their first aid instruction, they said that "snake bites are usually very dangerous."[80] Lieutenant W. Culbert Lyon, writing for *The Military Surgeon Journal* in 1910, argued that American troops in the field were particularly likely to be called upon to treat snakebites. He further pointed out that where a snakebite happened on the human body made a difference, e.g., a strike to a bone was less dangerous than one to a vein, and that whiskey was "most dangerous" as a cure from his observation. Similarly, potassium permanganate was "over-estimated and of very little value." He recommended Calmette's antivenin, but noted that it was "not easily obtained in the United States on account of the small demand for it."[81] E. H. Winston, writing for the United States Navy Department of Medicine in 1921, also began to get more accurate, although he layered on previously bad treatments. He recommended that field medics make a tight bandage around a bite, slash the wound with a sharp knife two or more ways and at least as deep as the puncture, squeeze it, wash it with permanganate of potash dissolved in water, work, massage, suck, and wash to get all of the venom out. He then recommended medics stick small bits of gauze into the wounds to keep them open. He pointed out that whiskey and brandy were not good cures, and instead they should call a doctor immediately who should arrive equipped with antivenin and strychnine tablets.[82]

Highway engineers get the prize for the most accurate and detailed recommendations to their workers. They knew that snakebites happened, took them very seriously, and gave their members the most detailed information available about where to actually get antivenin. They explicitly told their workers, "Do not give alcohol or ammonia." And, in contrast to the bravado of the sportsmen, these more practical men, who actually ran into venomous snakes more often, noted that "poisonous snake bites must receive instant treatment." They recommended a ligature first, followed by cutting the wound so that it bleeds freely, sucking the wound, spitting out the contents, and washing the mouth afterward. Then they recommended that a "concentrated solution of potassium permanganate should then be poured into the wound or better injected with a hypodermic syringe." In contrast to other official publications, they suggested loosening the ligature in ten minutes to allow the blood to circulate freely at intervals of ten to 15 minutes. When engineers were working with "more dangerous tropical snakes," they recommended they use a "hypodermic injection of Antivenene serum," which would be injected into the "cellular tissue of the right or left side of the abdomen." If there is time, the skin should be cleansed before the shot. Unlike other organizations or physicians, they actually told readers where to get the French antivenin. The serum could be obtained from "Les Establissements Poulene Freres, 92 Roue Vieille-du Temple, Paris." They also provided the actual dose of 10 cc (contents of one flask) for smaller venomous snakes and 20 cc, or two full doses at once, for cobra bites. They also pointed out that it would last in dried form.[83]

Once French antivenin became available, even remotely and with great difficulty, then at least some science writers began to take all snakebite seriously, even the nonvenomous ones. Writing for general practitioners, William Parks told physicians in 1912 that he could not understand why any snakebite was dismissed. Because "bites of animals may in some cases be followed by blood poisoning, to which the patient subsequently succumbs, and yet the animal be an innocuous one." How would a doctor feel who had passed up a black snake bite as unimportant if the patient subsequently died from the bacteria from the bite? He warned that the doctors who failed to treat all bites risked losing patients who would believe that they were not taken seriously. He pointed out that relying on people to bring in the snake to determine whether it was venomous and then treat it was fanciful. Sometimes, he noted, "even the patient only gets a glimpse and it is gone." Should they just trust luck, he asked, or should they treat it seriously and apply all of the possible treatments? He for one treated all snakebites "in as thorough a manner" as he knew how.[84]

The 19th and early 20th century cures for snakebite in the United States and elsewhere reflected the culture and prejudices of the people administering the cures and writing about them. However, there were accurate voices in the conversation about cures. In 1892, Arthur Brown, the superintendent of the Reptile House at the Philadelphia Zoo, told a reporter for the *American Notes and Queries* periodical that "whisky was not an antidote for snake poison" but rather a "popular fancy" and pointed out that it could actually "carry the effects beyond the stimulating and exciting stage."[85] More commonly, however, physicians and other science writers recommended futile, painful, and fictitious cures. It took until 1919 for the U.S. Public Health Service to recommend against whiskey. And even then, they were still suggesting that ammonia was a cure.[86] The truth was that physicians and science writers had no idea how to cure a snakebite, yet had lots of prejudice against many of the people unfortunate enough to get bitten. Because snakebite was not as common as it was in India, there was really no reason to spend much time looking for a real cure in the United States, the logic went. Writing for *The Archives of Internal Medicine* in 1908, the physician Prentiss Wilson dismissed the problem. "It is doubtful," he said, "if the morbidity and mortality from snake bite in the United States will ever demand the preparation of an effective antivenomous serum." In contrast, people in India really needed antivenin because more people died there, he informed readers. Besides, there was really no need to worry about this problem because the venomous snakes in the United States are only found in certain parts of the country. They were "only in the group of states roughly indicated as extending from mid Texas to the Carolinas," and, surreally, he said no one should feel that there was a real problem because 99 percent of Americans were not bitten by rattlesnakes. Without any proof (in fact it seems that he must have completely fabricated the statistics), he insisted that the mortality of snakebites from all cases was 10 percent, but with coral snakes it was "25 to 50 percent, water moccasins, 17 percent; large species of rattlesnakes, 11 or 12 percent." The tragic nature of these made-up facts was that they were printed by someone who was regarded as an authority in one of the most prestigious medical journals in the United States.[87] As we shall see, however, luckily for citizens in the United States, there were people who did not dismiss the pain and death, were willing to help everyone, and knew that an actual cure was needed.

3

Antivenin

Bringing the Real Cure
to the United States

Victims of snakebite in the United States desperately needed help from people who actually knew what they were talking about, were honest about their findings, could make the medicine, and effectively get it to the people and animals who needed it. The process of bringing antivenin to the United States relied on the previous work of antivenin creators, the specific help of Brazilian scientists, the United Fruit Company, zoo snake house curators, and American railroads to finally get the treatment to people. Creating the antivenin and distributing it, however, was no easy task, partly because the people involved sometimes had alternative agendas that had nothing to do with curing snakebites, as we shall see in the case of Afranio do Amaral. But there were also a range of scientific questions that needed answering first. Could cobra antivenin, made by the Pasteur Institute, be a cure-all for venomous snakebites in the United States? If not, could one type of rattlesnake venom cure all rattlesnake bites in the United States? If that was not true, which kinds of rattlesnakes would need to be collected to create an antivenin effective for most rattlesnake bites? Where could they find these different rattlesnakes? Did rattlesnakes in zoos already produce enough venom or did they need to constantly capture them in the wild? Who was going to continuously capture them? And who would get the antivenin once it was available? These were the difficult questions that antivenin proponents in the United States had to answer as they struggled to get the treatment out to people that would finally end many of the ineffective, harmful, and sometimes barbaric methods of treating bites in the past.

Albert Calmette and Vital Brazil

Initially, proponents of antivenin in the United States hoped that French scientist Albert Calmette's cobra antivenin would cure venomous snakebites in America. Calmette was a student of Pasteur who created his initial serotherapy laboratory in French Indo-China after a nearby bombing war between France and China drove large numbers of cobras into the village of Bac-Lieu near Saigon. Forty villagers were bitten and several of them died within a few hours.[1] The tragedy prompted him to search for a cure for snakebites that he found by slowly injecting cobra venom of into a horse to allow it to build up immunity to the venom. Although Calmette initially hoped that cobra antivenin would cure all venomous snakebites, scientists in Australia, the United States, and Brazil tested the antivenin on snakebites from venomous snakes in their countries and found that unfortunately this was not the case.[2]

Vital Brazil, a Brazilian scientist, read about Calmette's work and was motivated by his own experience with snakebite victims to replicate the work. He was born in 1865 and his family moved from Minas Gerais to São Paulo. His parents had severe financial difficulties, so Brazil worked his way through high school and medical school. He graduated from the Faculty of Medicine at Rio de Janeiro in 1891, at the age of 26, and then returned to São Paulo to become an inspector for the State Sanitary Department. During that period he fought outbreaks of yellow fever and cholera. In 1895, he left the Sanitary Service and set up practice in Botucato, a small town on a railway line that abutted farm property that included coffee and cattle ranches. It was here that he encountered problems with snakebites. The two kinds that he initially focused on were the jararaca and the South American rattlesnake. When the jararaca bit people there was "an intense local reaction with rapid and progressive enlargement of the affected part due to hemorrhagic oedema. Where survival occurred, loss of a part of a whole limb due to dry gangrene was common. In [rattlesnake poisoning], the local reaction was mild with haemorrhagic oedema limited to areas around the bite; nevertheless signs of neurotoxicity such as ptosis and asphyxia later ensued." He set up a small laboratory to study the venoms of the two snakes and test current remedies, including plants. In 1896, he read the work of Albert Calmette on anti-toxic serum that could neutralize the effects of cobra venom. He was so inspired that he closed his practice and got a job as assistant director of the Institute of Bacteriology under Dr. Adolpho Lutz. While at the Institute, he began his own experiments on animals to see if he could immunize them against snake envenomation. In 1899 he was called to investigate an outbreak of bubonic plague, and later the director of the Sanitary Service placed him in charge of that research (he, himself, began to come down with the symptoms of the plague, but was nursed back to health). The Sanitary Service purchased a farm in Butantã, nine kilometers from the center of São Paulo, so that Brazil and other state-employed scientists could develop an anti-plague serum. In 1900, in a converted barn, he began to work on a snakebite cure. Brazil estimated that 5,000 people died in Brazil every year from snakebite, not counting the "nameless hundreds of Indians," and he estimated that snakebites cost his country $8,000,000 annually.[3] In 1901, the institute in Butantã opened under the name of Institute of Serumtherapy with Brazil as the director. While he was producing anti-plague serum for distribution, he was experimenting with creating antivenin in horses and mules. "In December 1901, Brazil demonstrated to an audience at the School of Pharmacy, São Paulo, that a fresh sample of Calmett[e]'s serum offered no protection against neurotoxic rattlesnake venom and exerted only a very weak neutralizing action on haeumorrhagic jararaca venom." He produced an "anti-bothropic serum prepared in Butantan and announced that he was producing an anti-ophidic serum, a polyvalent antiserum consisting of a mixture of anti-crotalic and anti-bothropic serum, which he realized was the answer to the uncertainty concerning the venomous species involved in most natural accidents."[4] He had created the first antivenin for venomous snakes in his area.

Brazil set up a venom supply distribution system in which railways allowed the free shipping of snakes in exchange for serum and syringes: One vial of serum in exchange for one venomous snake; six venomous snakes got one a syringe and needle in return. The institute sent interested people (often farmers) equipment to capture the snakes, and boxes for their transport. Brazil included a questionnaire with each ampoule in order to document the snakebite accident, clinical signs, and the effect of the treatment. He undertook an aggressive public health campaign that included educating farmers and other laypeople in rural areas (including teachers and authorities in the interior), participating in conferences, demonstrating the use of antivenin, and writing publications that highlighted the health problem of snakebites. His campaign was very successful. He placed around 5,000 vials of serum in the hands of people and sent the antivenin to other Brazilian states as well as Argentina, Uruguay, Venezuela, and Cuba.[5]

He also brought vials of antivenin with him when he visited other countries, including the United States, to give talks on the subject. He saved a zoo keeper's life at the Bronx Zoo during a visit in 1916. On the morning of January 27, a man named Toomey was bitten by a newly arrived Texas diamondback rattlesnake. He was using a device to clean the cage, and the large snake darted out and bit him on the hand, leaving one deep wound and two deep scratches. The Bronx Zoo had antivenin on hand from Pasteur's Lille Institute in France, but it was made for cobra bites and was shipped as small yellow granules sealed in glass tubes, because granualization meant the serum kept longer. Unfortunately, however, this required adding liquid to the crystals to make them injectable, but that took a long time and the patient suffered a great burning pain in his hand. The doctor associated with the zoo, Dr. Van der Smissen, was called, and he administered the serum (ligatures had been used, but it was decided against cutting the wound, although someone did try to suck the venom out). The doctor took Toomey to the hospital where his symptoms got worse, presumably because they had the wrong antivenin. By this time, Toomey was very weak, with severe chills, and began to go into a coma-like state. His arm swelled to an enormous size, as did his glands. The swelling spread over half his breast and down toward his abdomen, accompanied by "marked discoloration" of the swollen area. They gave him strychnine to revive him, whereupon he started to vomit profusely. Luckily, another doctor at the hospital, Dr. Gustav Langmann, had done a lot of research with snake venom. He happened to know that Vital Brazil was in New York for the Pan American Congress. They located Brazil, who had fortunately brought rattlesnake serum with him to demonstrate at lectures. He gave Toomey's physicians the fluid serum which they injected without delay. "The effects following the injection of Dr. Brazil's serum were astonishing. Within a few hours there was a complete cessation of vomiting and chills. Within twelve hours the great swelling that had involved the arm and a considerable portion of the body, had decreased one-third by actual circumfrence measurement of the arm and rapidly receded from the breast. The areas of intense discoloration also faded. He was discharged from the hospital in three weeks. The Instituto promised to make the serum in liquid form for quicker application, and the Bronx Zoo purchased and stocked its cabinets with anti-lachesis (for moccasins, copperheads, and old-world type tree vipers) and anti-crotalus serums."[6]

Butantan and Afranio do Amaral

One of Brazil's students, a man who played an even larger part of bringing antivenin to the United States than Brazil himself, was Afranio do Amaral. Born in Belém do Pará in 1894, he studied medicine at the Federal University of Bahia and was later hired to work at Butantan. He was handsome, bright, wealthy, ambitious, and vain. By 1919 he was directing the institute, which by that point was 5,220,000 square feet of countryside and housed 4,053 venomous snakes representing 59 subspecies. Frank Carpenter, a journalist who visited Butantan, described it as "a city surrounded by thick walls of concrete and fences of iron, and about which inside the walls runs a deep moat of fresh flowing spring water, in which the citizens swim back and forth at their pleasure."[7] Each snake had its own small dome-shaped house. There were large white buildings with pitched roofs, plenty of trees, but also large sections of well-maintained cut grass. The snakes were held outdoors in the open air in a zoo-like enclosure that looked to be about three-quarters of a football field long, surrounded by a manicured walk of dirt. The enclosure itself had a low cement wall and on top of the wall was a black metal fence, supported at intervals with a cement half-column. Inside the wall was a water moat that surrounded the enclosure. In addition there were a few longer tubular structures placed along the side of the enclosure that also functioned as snake dwellings. Each snake house had its own little yard in front of it. The place looked like a snake subdivision, with paths of dirt laid out between igloo homes complete with their own front, side, or back yards, depending upon where they were placed. There was a solitary tree within the community and a large gate with a Greek-style impediment top that marked the entrance. Workers were protected from the snakes by wearing mandatory gaiters, following instructions for not stepping on or aggravating the snakes, and using forked sticks to render them helpless. Assistants at Butantan, like the directors, dressed elegantly, as though they might be going to work at an office, appearing in dress shoes, dress pants, a white-collared shirt, a trench coat, and a fedora.

At a barn on the property, horses were injected with venom on a regular basis, with small amounts at first and then progressively larger amounts. They received additional doses every day until the blood of the animal contained enough of the venom for the serum. Do Amaral told journalists that the horses "thrived" on the venom. He claimed that they gained weight during the injections, but once stopped they began to pine away and lose weight. He claimed that by the end of the year, a horse who went through the process had enough venom in his blood to kill 2,000 horses who had not been treated at all. One treated horse could supply serum for a year or more. If they continued to receive occasional doses, they could serve as a serum source for a long time.[8] Eventually do Amaral developed two techniques for producing antivenin: a fast technique, and a slow technique. In the slow technique, he extracted the venom and dissolved it in equal parts of a normal saline solution and glycerin. Next he gave horses subcutaneous injections of small doses of venom every few days for six months. By the end of that time, a typical horse could resist a dose about 10,000 times larger than the initial dose of .05 milligrams.[9] In the faster process, he injected venom neutralized by the pre-collected antivenin from the slower process. Because the venom was already neutralized, it allowed him to inject larger quantities sooner to accelerate the serum-producing process.

By 1915, the institute had sent out more than 46,000 tubes of the serum for snakes.[10] Working under his mentor Brazil, do Amaral similarly engaged in a public health campaign to advertise his medicine and to cut back on the number of people who needed it. He spent his time admonishing farmers to wear shoes, for example, because he believed that most of them did not. At demonstrations, he illustrated the protectiveness of rawhide against a snakebite. He further dramatized the problem by sharing the story of a farmer who was bitten on the foot by a venomous snake. By the end of the week, the skin on the foot had sloughed off, and then the whole foot fell off. The farmer brought the foot in his jacket pocket to show do Amaral.[11]

Before do Amaral assumed the directorship of Butantan, it had 100 horses used for antivenin and riding. But do Amaral was a complicated person. On the one hand he was dedicated to saving lives, but on the other hand he was vain and sexist. He began his day at 7:00 a.m., patrolling the institute's entire property by horseback, partly because some of it was impassable by car, but also because he liked to ride. Before do Amaral, the institute had mixed breed horses, but with his arrival things changed. He claimed that he bought what he called purebred English horses because they produced better antitoxins. Later, when the state brought charges against him for poor management of the institute, his defense was to claim that nearly 75 percent of the mixed breed horses were bad producers when he was first hired at Butantan. It was a matter of efficiency, he claimed, to get rid of the majority of the institute's original herd and reinvest in thoroughbred horses. If Brazil had to pay for the animals, then they should not have to keep animals that failed at their jobs. As a result, he purchased three thoroughbred mares that he named Tessalia, Madreperola, and Heloisa. All of them had the kind of genetic stock that he claimed (without evidence) would make better antivenin. He kept another called Acacia, a mixed-breed horse. The real purpose of getting purebred horses, however, was entirely personal. Do Amaral loved beautiful horses and showed Acacia in competitions. He bought her for the institute, and then from the institute, showing her twice and winning both shows. He later sold her in a private sale after she proved her value in the ring. The other horses, he later acknowledged, had various physical defects that made them poor show horses. Tessalia, for example, had a scar on her right leg, and Heloisa had scars on her knees from a fall. Do Amaral then maintained purebred horses for sport and commercial ends at the institute's cost and they were cared for by institute employees. These were shown in events in São Paulo in his name (rather than the institute's), and he received various prizes from the competitions.

In addition to using public money on show horses, he also used it to dramatically improve the house on the property where his family lived. He went on a building spree for his house, making it into a lavish affair, spending over $100,000, an extremely large amount for Brazil during the early 1900s, all at state expense. He was later accused of locking an intruder in a garbage holding area as he patrolled the grounds and of sexism in dealing with his employees. He disciplined a woman for wearing a riding habit to work. She complained to her union, and this charge was later used against him by the state in the investigation of his extravagant spending at the institute. In his defense, he claimed that it was his "responsibility to guard the moral standing of the Institute, especially among the women, married and single, who worked there and to reduce the alarming situation created by the ingress of females into the work force in the hot lands of Brazil."[12]

By 1910, Butantan had produced crucial antivenin for South American rattlesnakes, lancehead snakes, coral snakes, and a polyvalent serum designed for cases where the bite victim and doctor were unable to determine the exact type of snake.[13] The world was watching, and Brazil was far ahead of the Americans, who really needed help. As a result, they called on do Amaral to help them bring antivenin to the United States, although he would become involved with Americans first through their corporate proxy, the United Fruit Company.

The Antivenin Institute

Although Vital Brazil pioneered a great deal of the antivenin work in Brazil, the United Fruit Company continued to lose workers to death from snakebite. In addition, do Amaral believed that the number of snakebites and fatalities were increasing as more people were pushing further into the wilderness for a variety of work and recreational reasons. The problem was particularly acute in the tropics where he claimed that countries struggled to attract immigrants to cultivate the land because of their legitimate fear of venomous reptiles. What was at stake, as far as do Amaral was concerned, was the very "conquest of the tropics."[14] As a result, the United Fruit Company's Medical Department asked do Amaral to study the magnitude of the snakebite problem in Central America. With better scientific information, the company hoped to standardize their method of coping with venomous snakebites. The United Fruit Company was also connected with Harvard Medical School and therefore with Thomas Barbour, a herpetologist and director of the Museum of Comparative Zoology at Harvard.[15] Barbour knew do Amaral and Brazil through his connections with herpetologists around the world, his work with zoo directors, and his personal collecting trips.

Do Amaral and Barbour had to decide whether to set up an antivenin lab in Boston or Philadelphia. Harvard, and they, were in Boston, so that was appealing for proximity reasons, but Mulford Labs in Philadelphia was already established and they would not have to start from scratch.[16] But how could they catch the snakes? There were certainly plenty of rattlesnakes in Pennsylvania and in other locations in the northeast, but Mulford Labs did not have the employees to dedicate to hunting them. Simply hiring these employees would have been difficult because of the system of capitalism in the United States. The Brazilian system of handing out antivenin for free only worked in a state-sponsored and -funded public health system, in which the Butantan Institute got paid by the state to make the antivenin. Somehow the American lab had to make a profit. So they asked professional and amateur herpetologists around the country including, for example, Klauber in San Diego (whom they both knew from their herpetological professional association), to work for them for free while the pharmaceutical company and do Amaral would get paid for their work. Unlike the Brazilian haphazard system in which farmers randomly turned in snakes and received vials of antivenin in exchange, Klauber and other professional and amateur snake handlers, as we shall see, would capture the snakes for free, extract the antivenin and purify it for free, and only be reimbursed for the expense of shipping the snakes and venom back to Mulford Labs.

Why did these herpetologists work for free? Their motivations were complex. Part of the answer lies in the stories we have already seen about the horrific nature of snakebites and their proximity to them. They were already hunting and capturing live snakes that they held at home or in their zoos, and as a result, they were in danger of bites themselves. It was in their personal medical interest to have an effective cure on hand. They were also the experts who Americans around the country were turning to when they were bitten, so to have a cure on hand would have helped them play that role. They loved to get out into the countryside and hunt snakes. Klauber kept a diary of the number of snakes he collected on his evening excursions around southern California, and it is clear that he relished being out on the road in the evening looking at the beautiful sunsets and enjoying the outdoors. And finally, they enjoyed one another's company and had enormous respect for the Brazilian and French scientific discoveries. These were scientists, and they were eager to learn about how to stop these terrible side effects from a bite. If they had to donate their labor for free for a while, so be it.

Even though the herpetologists collecting for Mulford Labs were prolific, they could not catch all of the snakes around the country themselves. So, Klauber set up a deal with railways in the United States that was similar to the Brazilian one. The Santa Fe Railroad Company station attendants caught and sent rattlesnakes to him in San Diego. He also had a similar deal with the San Diego & Arizona Railway Company that brought him a few "C. cerastes from the Colorado Desert."[17] He gave do Amaral the names and addresses of other animal dealers and amateur herpetologists from whom he might get snakes and venom, including K.C. Beck and Company of Hutchinson, Kansas, a wild animal seller; Colonel Martin Crimmins of Fort Bliss, Texas; Charles Evans from Phoenix, Arizona, an animal dealer who regularly sold snakes in his district; the Snake King of Brownsville, Texas; and Hiram Yoder of Normanna, Texas, another snake hunter.[18] It is likely that do Amaral knew some of these men before. Barbour, for example, worked with Crimmins as well as other herpetology curators at zoos, such as Ditmars (Bronx Zoo) and Conant (Toledo and later Philadelphia Zoo), so do Amaral had a large network of potential donors around the country.

The additional problem that do Amaral faced was that he did not really know the United States, and he had been given the flawed and dismissive Bureau of Biological Survey that claimed that there were only a negligible amount of snakebites around the country. How could a pharmaceutical company justify producing antivenin if the federal government effectively claimed that there was no significant public health problem? To better study the problem and dramatize it, Barbour sent do Amaral on a research and driving trip around the country. In the American southwest in 1925, do Amaral concluded that there were "more than 1,000 cases of snake-bite by poisonous species" per year, rather than under 200 as the Biological Survey had mistakenly calculated.[19] He found that the highest mortality rate from the bites occurred in the southwest, where 35 percent of the victims died.[20]

During that trip, he also met Martin Crimmins, among others, who would help him set up his supply chain for his lab. To advertise the work he was doing, do Amaral distributed a two-page description of this planned antivenin laboratory at Mulford Labs to the amateur and professional herpetologists who would serve as free labor in his supply chain.

In conversations with do Amaral and through the literature he handed out, they learned that Mulford Labs, under do Amaral's direction, planned to purify and concentrate two versions of serum for distribution: one version for humans and another for cattle. The laboratory would be called the Antivenin Institute of America. The Mulford Company had gotten its start by successfully creating a serum treatment for diphtheria that it marketed as hygienic and reliable. The process for creating the diphtheria antitoxin is similar to that for antivenin in that horses were used to create the serum. At their facility in Glenolden, Pennsylvania, the company had laboratories and stables where they drew blood from horses and then slowly created the antitoxin by reintroducing small amounts of the diphtheria, mixed with horse blood, back into the animal until it reached complete immunity to disease. The process typically took around a year, after which the serum was made with the horses' antibodies. The Mulford Company, then, had already engaged in the same scientific work that likeminded scientists around the world were experimenting with to create antivenin, and that helped convince do Amaral's supply chain that their labor would result in an actual cure produced in the United States.[21]

The antivenin lab was divided into two sections: a neararctic section that focused on snakes in the United States and surrounding areas, and a neotropical section that worked on antivenin for snakebites from Central America and northwest South America, at the request of the United Fruit Company. Do Amaral would serve as the director of the Antivenin Institute as a whole, and Raymond Ditmars, the curator of the Herpetology Division of the Bronx Zoo, would serve as the neararctic director. The supply distribution system in the United States was subdivided into the New York, Philadelphia, New Orleans, San Antonio, and San Diego substations. Almost all of the substations were chosen because each of these cities had a zoo. The zoo meant that they had a herpetologist nearby who could serve as a source of venom by milking the venomous snakes in their collection, and identifying snakes who bit people. When people were bitten and went to the hospital, the first logical question they were asked by the attending physician was "what kind of snake bit you?" If it was a non-venomous snake, the treatment could be very different. Sometimes people brought (and still bring) with them the snake who bit them, if they killed it afterwards, but more frequently doctors have to rely on the victim's description. The problem that doctors faced in helping patients was that they did not necessarily have any biological training in types of snakes, so zoo snake-house curators were called into emergency rooms by doctors to identify snakes. Zoo herpetologists were some of the few qualified people in a city who could accurately identify a snake, so they played a crucial role in the distribution and public health campaign to prevent deaths from snakebite once antivenin was available. Do Amaral placed William Scheppergrell in charge of the New Orleans station, because of the Audubon Zoo, and Laurence Klauber was in charge of San Diego, because of his work in the San Diego reptile house.

Do Amaral asked retired Colonel Martin Crimmins to create the antivenin stations around the southwest (particularly in Texas). Crimmins was concerned about the snakebite problem because he commanded Camp Bullis, Texas, and found that he had one rattlesnake bite for every thousand soldiers. While in Texas, he became interested in "publishing information about snake-bite and its proper treatment, and issued bulletins to soldiers and lectured in these schools, so that non-scientific people could distinguish poisonous and harmless species."[22] Like other herpetology curators, he too had been bitten by a rattlesnake and knew how painful it was.[23] Crimmins already kept statistics about venomous bites and also kept statistics on civilians, discovering that in 1928, 130 Texans were bitten by venomous snakes. While he could keep detailed statistics on Texas, he found that other states were less willing to share their bite tolls, a fact that he attributed to real-estate agent pressures to suppress negative information about their areas.[24] Do Amaral later reported that his antivenin substations in the southwest had collected venom from over "4,000 rattlesnakes, as well as many from copperheads and moccasins."[25]

Thomas Barbour, curator of reptiles at Harvard's Museum of Comparative Zoology, was in charge of the whole neotropical section that was subdivided into two substations: one in Telas, Honduras, directed by Douglas March, and the other in Ancon C.Z., Panama. The neotropical section was connected with the Medical Department of the United Fruit Company and Harvard University's Department of Tropical Biology. The

United Fruit Company initially funded do Amaral in the United States, so he was beholden to its board, which consisted of a further mixture of university researchers, army brass, and doctors employed by the United Fruit Company. Each of the antivenin stations in those countries either caught and sent the snakes to the Glenolden lab, or they held on to the snakes at the antivenin station, milked the snakes, and sent the venom along to Glenolden. Just as in Brazil, do Amaral furnished the antivenin stations with snake boxes that the workers at the substations packed and sent back to Glenolden.

Zoo directors and herpetologists used the snakes at their institutions at the reptile house to collect large amounts of venom. Ditmars recalled handling "as many as a hundred during a couple of hours."[26] He used the same snakes repeatedly, however, because their glands would refill within a matter of days so that the same snakes had venom to extract again within a week's time. Each snake, however, only produced a few drops of venom so he had to use many animals to reach an inch of venom in a drinking glass. The color of the liquid varied from white, clear yellow, amber, to greenish depending upon the type of snake. But all of the liquid was dried and stored for laboratory purposes at the zoo. It was easily reconstituted by dissolving the dried flakes in water and kept most of its original strength. When the venom was dried, it was poured into flat dishes and the plates were placed under a bell to avoid contamination. When the venom dried it crystallized and flaked off somewhat. Working with the dried product was dangerous because even small particles, once inhaled, could produce some of the same symptoms as an actual bite.

Problems

While zoo directors like Ditmars had some knowledge about creating antivenin, the group had a lot left to learn and thus encountered difficult questions and problems as they worked through the process of creating their product. Initially they planned to make two serums: a polyvalent for "all of the most important American poisonous snakes" and one monovalent serum for the "dreadful Central American 'Fer-de-Lance snake' which causes a great many deaths every year and has become dangerous to the United Fruit Company's plantations."[27] Just as in Calmette's case, however, they were unable to make a polyvalent that cured the bites of all venomous snakes in the United States. They realized this as they began testing rattlesnake venom alone and found that it differed significantly by type, size, and habitat in the country. Rattlesnakes from the Cape Region, California, had venom that differed in toxicity from those found in Arizona, for example. They did not know this until Klauber collected a subspecies of rattlesnake he named *Crotalus confluentus nuntius*. Klauber then milked the snake and studied the venom yield where he learned that it had a lower level of venom than other rattlesnakes. Once they figured this out, they shipped venom by subspecies to make sure that Mulford Laboratories knew how toxic a particular kind of venom was likely to be. This would, in turn, determine how much of the venom they injected into the horses for the purpose of creating antivenin. Determining the toxicity of various rattlesnakes required time-consuming mail exchanges between Klauber and do Amaral. To take one example, Klauber sent do Amaral rattlesnakes and wanted to know their different toxicity levels. Do Amaral informed Klauber that he had determined that "the venom of C. atrox shows the same closeness to that of oreganus, and it is also close to that of C. confluentus." One "cc. of a monovalent antivenin I have prepared for Crotalus atrox ... neutralizes 3.8 mgm. of this venom" and also "neutralizes 3.2 mg of C. oreganus venom and only 2.7 mgm of C. exsul venom."[28]

They wondered whether they should concentrate on collecting large snakes or small snakes for their venom, and they questioned whether certain rattlesnakes who looked alike were all the same subspecies. Through their studies, they concluded that smaller rattlesnakes yielded smaller amounts of venom, but that the venom that they did have was more toxic.[29] They realized that Crotalis terrificus consisted of three different subspecies: terrificus, durissus, and basiliscus. Although these three different subspecies were superficially a great deal alike, they might have had different venom levels. Their range included part of Northern Mexico, but their subspecies morphed there into slightly different colors making them harder to identify. They wondered whether combining these varieties of venom under one heading called "Terrificus" might give the laboratory a false impression of the average venom level in each batch.

Another problem they had was that it was difficult to run the centrifuge. They tested the toxicity of the venom by squeezing the venom glands from several individuals of the same subspecies and collected them together in a conical glass. Then they used a centrifuge to remove cells, saliva, and colloid before they dried the venom. If this was not done correctly, the batch was useless. Do Amaral initially had a difficult time getting his assistants in the field (like Klauber) to run the centrifuge properly. The secret of the purification was to let the centrifuge run as long as necessary to make the yellowish color of the venom absolutely clear. A large batch could take three to four hours to be completely centrifuged. Once they had the dried venom, they mixed it together with similar samples to obtain a composite sample, representative of that type of snake. They had to do that to make sure that they did not get venom from one snake from a subspecies who happened to have venom with low toxicity at that point. This process gave them a "definite quantity of venom in each cubic centimeter."[30]

By 1927, do Amaral's operation had 38 horses receiving venom and developing antibodies for the serum. He hoped to improve his technique so that his antivenin could neutralize eight to ten mgm. per cc rather than only a little over five mgm. He claimed that his antivenin would be "nearly three times as strong as the best serum we had prepared before in Brazil and about five times as active as any prepared in France or England for India."[31]

The method of extracting the venom depended upon the size of the snake and the placement of their fangs. If they had a large rattlesnake, an assistant caught the snake immediately behind the head with a noose-stick and then placed the snake so that its head was resting on the edge of the table, unable to bite anything. Then another person used a metal hook to catch the snake's upper jaw under the rostral and tip the head back. Then they placed the rim of a porcelain cup with a handle or some other container under the fang points and in the process drawing the fangs downward and outward into the erect position. They slid the cup underneath the fangs to catch the venom. Klauber did not recommend using a piece of rubber stretched across the cup, as others did, in an attempt to give the snake the feel of biting into something and thereby (in theory) increasing the venom yield. Instead, he preferred to push on the glands of the rattlesnake to stimulate the venom production, and he pointed out that the diaphragm interfered with their ability to accurately measure the venom yield because some of it inevitably spilled on the rubber. For large snakes, this was a two-person operation with the assistant holding the tail of the snake so that it did not thrash around and disrupt the extraction process. Smaller rattlesnakes were caught and handled by a single person who could hold on to the head fairly easily with one hand. In San Diego, Klauber also used a different method of extracting the venom from small snakes because their fangs did not protrude as far. He milked the snake directly into the tube that led to the centrifuge.[32]

If the venom from snakes differed by type, then it became crucial that the handler know the type of rattlesnake that they had in their hands. This was easier if the snake came from a zoo, because they had time to study the animal and know its type, or they bought snakes from a dealer who captured them in a particular region. The problem, they discovered, was that zoo snakes were less prolific venom producers than wild snakes. According to Klauber, "my experience to date would indicate that our snakes secrete very little venom under the conditions in which they are kept at our zoos. In general I get good quantities from fresh snakes, but I secure so little from old specimens that I am beginning to believe it is useless to take the time to re-handle them every two weeks."[33] This meant that they had to go frequently on snake-hunting trips to capture fresh snakes for the Antivenin Institute. Crimmins alone claimed to have extracted venom from over "a thousand specimens" that he forwarded on to do Amaral.[34] They had about 40 copperheads and water moccasins in the laboratory, but hoped to have over 200 by 1927.[35] Do Amaral primarily wanted live snakes and venom sent his way, but he was also interested in dead ones because he claimed that they furthered scientific knowledge.

Because they could not rely entirely on snakes in zoos, snakes had to be captured in the wild. This meant identifying the snake accurately, which was a big problem because everyone involved, including the top experts at that time, sometimes lacked the basic ability to identify snakes correctly. This extended all the way to the highest experts in the field because they were still trying to identify and map the habitat range of snakes in the 1920s. So herpetologists working on antivenin spent a great deal of time trying to nail down the exact geographic distribution of particular sub-species of venomous snakes, partly because this interested the scientists themselves, but also because in theory it could help doctors who were visited by bite victims to know that no coral snake, for example, had ever been sighted west of the Rocky Mountains in the wild.[36] Even the elite researchers in the country, including Klauber and do Amaral, often disagreed over which snakes were which—a fairly important problem. For example, Klauber once thought that he was sending do Amaral a Crotalus tigris, when he was really sending a C. oreganus.[37]

A constant source of worry and discussion among the antivenin creators was what they would do if they couldn't find the snakes in the wild, even if they knew which ones they were looking for, and even with the help of paid and volunteer collectors. Klauber worried about not finding the snakes necessary to get venom to send back east. He prowled the back roads of San Diego country many nights during the spring through the fall looking for rattlesnakes on the roads. He took countless hiking trips, either alone or with colleagues, into the mountains looking for rattlesnakes to capture. But many times he came up short. Sometimes the snakes just were not there. "I have been able to forward you little in the way of local specimen of C. oreganus and C. exsul, having only three junveile specimens available," he wrote do Amaral. Thus far, he noted, "our season has been extremely disappointing. Whether this is due to heavy rainfall or lack of interest on the part of our customers, I cannot say. To date only one adult rattlesnake has been brought in, where as last year at this time we had some thirty large specimens."[38] He had been all the way out to Mountain Springs on two trips and only captured "one small Hypsiglena."[39]

Even when they could get the snakes, they struggled to get a consistent supply of venom from the animals. The conditions of snakes in the field varied. Some were healthy and some were sickly. An ill snake yielded very little venom, but was easier to catch. Whether the snake had recently eaten determined their venom yield. If the snake had just eaten, it would be some time before they could get any venom. If the snake had tried to defend itself by striking at its captor or striking at the box in the train or car, the venom was spent as well. Seasonal conditions also affected gland activity. A snake's venom supply varied around hibernation time. When they reached the serpentarium, the snakes were placed in a box in the dark for two weeks in hopes of restoring their venom. Klauber advised giving the snakes space because if they were crowded and afraid, they would bite each other and thereby cut back on the amount of venom. Carelessness in the laboratory often led to fang breakage, which further diminished venom collecting.[40]

Another problem they had was communicating with one another in a scientific manner. In addition to working for free, the members of this antivenin network also wrote their findings about their work for one another. They shared it in a journal they produced, the *Bulletin of the Antivenin Institute of America*, to bring as much of the herpetology world together as possible, and to help them focus on the problems they faced. Its editor, do Amaral, used the journal to publish original scientific research on snakes alongside semi-popular articles on a range of topics, including taxonomy, biology, geographical distribution, economic and public health efforts, physiological effects, and the production of antivenin. He hoped to reach a wide audience that included museum workers, biology departments in universities, public health officials, doctors, and researchers interested in antivenins. And he hoped to reach out to everyday people as well. He thought its readers would include nature lovers, campers, tourists, and a range of workers whose jobs brought them into contact with venomous snakes. The *Bulletin's* mission was to share scientific information and educate the public about the dangers of venomous snakes. In the era before easy access to journals, either through significant libraries nearby or much later through Internet access, the medical world had to rely on one another to share their studies. As a result, they had to take the time to mail one another requests for reprints of studies. The truth was, however, that mainly scientists and connected and well-read amateur herpetologists had access to the journal, and even they sometimes struggled to keep copies. Thomas Githens, who worked as a doctor and antivenin researcher at Mulford Laboratories, had to request Klauber's recent study on the levels of venom in a particular rattlesnake because even though Klauber had sent it to him, a colleague "walked off with it," leaving the laboratory with a crucial lack of information.[41]

The Railroads Balk

Scientists may have hoped that everyone interested in snakes would enjoy reading their publications and contributing their labor to ending the scourge of snakebite, but this was not the case. By the late 1920s, it looked as though Mulford Labs was going to have problems with their railway collection system. Railways had initially gotten into the business of transporting snakes to herpetologists like Klauber for complicated reasons. Part of the explanation was that the United Fruit Company had financial interests in some of the railways, so they directed the company men to undertake the project. And part of the explanation was railroad workers and passengers were bitten by snakes, so they had a vested interest in finding the cure themselves. So, as we have seen, they too were initially part of the free labor that served as the distribution system to herpetologists and then on to Mulford Labs.

There were problems with this system early on. Railroad workers typically did not know the exact subspecies of venomous snakes, and it was not always clear to Klauber and do Amaral exactly where the snakes came from. The best they could say was that the snakes came from somewhere in the vicinity of the railway stations. Stationmasters at the various stops along the line sometimes captured the snakes themselves and other times they seemed to have come from other people in the surrounding areas who brought them to the railroad to send along. They used a slip noose at the end of a stick and dropped the snakes into muslin salt, flour, or sugar sacks. They were also instructed to label the sacks by placing the locality on a slip of paper that they attached to the top of the bag. Once the snakes were at the stations, railway workers packed them up in boxes given to them by do Amaral for that purpose. Railroad conductors, however, were uncomfortable having the snakes on the trains.

They had to be continually convinced to maintain the system by visits and correspondence by do Amaral and Klauber to remain in the business of capturing and transporting the snakes. If they had their druthers, they would have gotten out of the business very quickly. And in fact, part of the railroad threatened to stop collecting the snakes. In 1927, they protested that capturing the snakes was a waste of employees' time. They complained that the snakes were too dangerous to transport, and they threatened to raise the cost of transporting them to $600 per year.[42] What had seemed like a good idea initially, to collect snakes at stations throughout the west to help their own workers and passengers, no longer seemed worthwhile to them. In May of 1927, W.K. Etter, the general manager in Los Angeles, sent a letter to the division passenger agent in San Diego, who in turn forwarded it to Klauber, in which he said that his railroad should no longer have to transport rattlesnakes because antivenin had been successfully created. They were unclear on why they needed to continually supply so many snakes and serve as unpaid labor for Mulford Labs. Klauber replied that they continued to need the more exotic snakes for "experimental work," and they would need a continuous supply for antivenin.[43]

The problem for the antivenin lab, however, was that the railway was crucial for getting subspecies that were too far out of range for most of the zoo directors collecting snakes around their work or homes. Laurence Klauber wrote to do Amaral in March of 1927 and confessed that he was not certain about whether he could get the laboratory any more Mohave Desert rattlesnakes. The "superintendent of the desert division protested that his men were putting in too much time collecting specimens and as a result put a stop to the shipments."[44] He suggested that do Amaral get the United Fruit Company officials to talk to the leaders of the Santa Fe Railway Company, located in Chicago, and persuade them to continue participating. After all, the United Fruit Company needed the whole antivenin enterprise to succeed. Do Amaral took Klauber's advice and complained to the United Fruit Company and Harvard.[45]

The Antivenin Institute needed to keep the Santa Fe line involved because they had stops all throughout the Mohave Desert as well as a route up through mountainous parts of Arizona. Without this regular supply of snakes, they would have to send an expedition into the mountains for the sole purpose of collecting, or they would have to pay individual hunters to find the animals. Do Amaral was particularly worried about the loss of rattlesnakes from the San Bernardino area because it was "the most interesting snake region in the United States."[46] The railway was also the "major source of C. cerastes" for the lab and the "entire source of C. tigris and the larger snakes from the Mohave Desert."[47] They had to determine the "nature of the venom" in these subspecies because "should any or all of these venoms prove to be similar to that of C. atrox atrox, C. exsul, C. oreganus, or any of the other common species," Klauber wrote, then he presumed that do Amaral would "no longer require venom from the rarer species; but on the other hand should any of these venoms prove to be materially different from those of the other species, then you will require a continuous supply for your immunizing work in order to make your product completely polyvalent."[48] The Mulford Company also finally broke down and gave free syringes of antivenin to the Santa Fe Railway Company as a way to pacify their growing frustration with collecting large numbers of snakes for free to make money for another company. The Santa Fe Railway Company had a Medical Department and they sent the antivenin there.[49]

Luckily for Mulford Labs and the antivenin effort, they were able to keep the railroad participating. In a letter to Klauber, in April of 1927, do Amaral shared that he has "gotten the Santa Fe Railway System again interested in snake capture," and he had just received a letter from their vice president reaffirming this fact. Do Amaral was asking Klauber to let the Santa Fe Railroad know how many snakes he needed and which kinds.[50]

Distribution Problems

Another challenge they faced was getting the medicine to people who needed it, even when the Mulford Lab was producing the product. Initially, as we have seen, Vital Brazil and do Amaral exchanged free vials of antivenin for venom when they visited the United States. They made these exchanges primarily with members of their antivenin network (zoo directors) who then did the best they could to get the drug to people who needed it. To take one example, a rattlesnake bit a man in Ithaca, New York, and Ditmars was called upon to send antivenin north. His daughter sped the vials to Grand Central Station where the director of the New York Central Nightflier picked it up and shaved precious minutes off his trip up north to deliver the serum. From there it was picked up by a driver who charred the car's floorboards speeding to the hospital. Unfortunately, however, Ditmars himself was running out of antivenin because he had given much of his stash to bite victims in the southwest. He felt guilty about asking the Brazilians to donate more antivenin, so that was not an option, and they could not sell it to him because the Public Health Department required that medicine was tested on humans before distribution in the United States. This was the central reason that Mulford Labs could not distribute their antivenin quickly—it had not yet been tested on humans. Although it was clear many people had been saved by the antivenin before it was legally approved, the product "was barred from the United States if he attempted to sell it."[51] He could donate the Brazilian antivenin to Americans, and they could in turn distribute it, but no one could make a profit on the exchange. Do Amaral gave Crimmins over $2,000 worth of donated antivenin for the southwestern antivenin stations.[52]

Crimmins faced significant distance barriers in the southwest, so he created a system of military airplane transportation to hospitals. In California, Navy planes took bite victims to hospitals, and in Texas, Army aircraft "covered 2,600 miles" bringing antivenin to bite victims.[53] He picked up bite victims and flew them to the nearest hospitals or the closest airstrip to an antivenin station. On the whole, their emergency flight system worked, although there were times when rescue victims could not be rescued because they were too remote. A venomous snake bit an aspiring priest while he was vacationing at a summer camp at Port La Vaca, Texas. Although Crimmins tried to send the antivenin by airplane, he found that there was no landing field nearby and the roads were so poor that it would have taken eight hours to travel 150 miles by car. In this case, the young man died.

In 1927, Crimmins began running out of antivenin because of a rash of snakebites. In desperation, he immunized himself with venom by injecting himself with repeated small doses and became "*in person* a stock for emergency cases."[54] He immunized himself so often that he looked pale and spent when he came to donate blood to the hospital. Laboratory experiments on animals confirmed that his blood could cure venomous snakebites on animals. Doctors in San Antonio, Texas, used his blood on humans twice, both times on children. The first child died within 72 hours of receiving his blood, but the second one lived. One the same day that the second child survived, the United States Public Health Service authorized the production of antivenin on the grounds that it had now been tested on a human.[55]

By May 4, 1927, do Amaral boasted that he had produced the strongest antivenin ever created. He told his colleagues in the antivenin network that it had "been approved by the Public Health Department in Washington and a license [was] granted for its distribution through the agents of the Mulford Laboratories."[56] Once Mulford received approval from the United States Public Health Service to distribute antivenin, the company relied heavily on zoo herpetologists to get the drug to people who needed it. People were contacting Klauber frequently about how to get a supply of the antivenin.[57] After the laboratory started making money, they began sending Klauber a fairly small amount of money, about $100, to purchase the supplies that he needed. One year, for example, he decided to use the money to buy sidewinders because he was unable to catch them on a regular basis.[58] "From all I hear the demand for the product [from Mulford] has been very gratifying in both San Francisco and Los Angeles," do Amaral told Klauber. And "I have no doubt that there have been large sales elsewhere, particularly in the Southern states."[59] To thank Laurence Klauber for his work in milking the snakes and sending the venom on, Mulford gave the San Diego Zoo "as many free syringes of [their] Antivenin as necessary." Their pharmaceutical representative for Mulford, then called an agent, was based in Los Angeles and sold extra vials, at a 25 percent discount, to the San Diego Zoo, which the zoo could then sell to hospitals to make a profit.[60]

As late as 1945, zoos in the United States were still milking snakes publicly to send to the company, now called Sharp & Dolme, that produced the antivenin. Roger Conant used milking snakes as a way to both increase his revenue and add to the venom stock. He admitted that his "chief interest" was the "selfish" goal of conducting their extractions in public, where visitors could watch the proceedings. The zoo sold tickets for this show based upon the idea that a pharmaceutical company, then producing the antivenin in 1945, needed the zoo to extract it because their efforts were focused on aiding the fight during World War II. The justification for the show was that World War II had made it impossible for Sharp & Dolme to tap into their customary suppliers, and so zoos would do their patriotic part by filling this gap. Not coincidentally, the zoo also made a profit charging extra for the admission to the show and charging the pharmaceutical company up to $25 for each gram of venom, depending upon the type of snake.[61] Similarly, Ross Allen, the director of the Reptile Institute, in Florida, claimed that he had to milk about "10,000 snakes" for "war needs."[62]

Sensing a business opportunity in venom, soldiers returning from World War II inquired about the idea of becoming rattlesnake farmers. Laurence Klauber received "a number of inquiries" from them and responded by discouraging the idea because "the demand for venom is sporadic," and it was "much easier to catch fresh snakes in the wild."[63] This was not entirely true. When corresponding between themselves, Klauber and Conant were candid that rattlesnakes were one of the easier "specimens" to keep in captivity, and thus the returning veterans could either hunt the animals or farm them for antivenin without serious risk of loss. Conant, for example, informed Klauber that although rattlesnakes rarely feed in captivity, they "seem to have a good life without" food.[64] Their motivations were no doubt noble in the sense that that they were primarily concerned with the danger inherent in working with the rattlesnakes, and they hoped to warn a potentially large crop of new farmers away from getting into the business of venom extraction. But it also did not hurt to dampen the competition from thousands of potential competitors in the venom-producing market.

In an interview in 1926, a Butantan employee named Joaquim summarized the institute's work on antivenin. He said, "You have often read of many methods supposed to cure snake bite. Making a ligature, sucking out the venom, taking brandy and cathartics, and keeping the puncture open with a packing of sterile [bandanges] all are recommended." But from all of their research at Butantan, they were "convinced that all the familiar recipes are quite futile. The snake venom fixes itself on the nerves, in the tissues and blood, with devastating rapidity. Once you are bitten, it is too late for any cure except serum." Indeed their daily work with snakes had upset "a whole raft of superstitions."[65] Although unfortunately many groups continued to advocate placing a tourniquet on the limb, cutting the wound, and sucking out the venom, all to the patient's detriment, they now also began recommending antivenin. By 1921, the United States Navy's *Hospital Corp Quarterly* insisted that whiskey and brandy were not cures. Instead bite victims should seek a "doctor immediately who should arrive equipped with antivenomous serum."[66] To be sure, there were continuing problems with antivenin. Some people had allergic reactions to horse and sheep blood (another animal later used to create the serum), and for years doctors continued recommending that bite victims use ligatures and razors to slice open the wound and somehow suck out the venom, as they had recommended before the cure of antivenin.[67] In 1970, for example, doctors Newton C. McCollough, from Orlando, Florida, and Joseph F. Gennaro, a professor at New York University, pointed to studies on dogs in which they had survived with the cure of incision, suction, and tourniquet. In one case, half of the dogs survived if treated this way within three minutes of a subcutaneous injection with venom. Other studies claimed that the longer the suction occurred the lower the survival rate. And their own studies showed that "multiple incisions" following the direction of the venom "did not produce fruitful amounts of ... venom by suction." Still, they noted that physicians or lay people in the field could make cross marks "singly, vertically, horizontally, or in a cruciate manner," but they should not "penetrate the subcutaneous or deep fascia." They recommended making a "superficial incision" by "tenting the skin," to make suction more efficient. And, without taking a stand on the treatment, they noted that "excision" and "amputation immediately after the bite have long been advocated."[68] Drug stores sold antivenin kits that came complete with tourniquets, razor blades, and suction bulbs into the 1970s. Doctors also continued to raise questions about the kinds of people who got bitten at that time. One doctor and scientific researcher team, for example, noted that "envenomation in the United States may be accidental, suicidal, or homicidal. Now, humans in contact with snakes were actually not just children playing or a variety of people in professions that might bring them into contact with snakes, they were possibly murderers."[69]

It was not until around the 1980s that medical associations like the World Health Organization began recommending that people simply get to a hospital as fast as they could, once they were bitten by a venomous snake, to get antivenin.[70] Hospitals now get antivenin directly from pharmaceutical companies primarily, and only turn to zoos in emergency situations. But as late as 1980, zoos were still overwhelmingly the place where antivenin was held. Thirty-one out of 37 antivenin holding sites were in zoos. It is not surprising the experts on snakebites by the 1980s recommended that doctors contact zoos for antivenin.[71]

Today, consumers can buy antivenin themselves without a prescription thanks to the work of the Red Cross, which produces and sells it directly online for venomous snakes found outside of the United States. For 139 Euros, anyone can buy Neuro polyvalent antivenin for cobra, king cobra, banded kraits, and malayan kraits, for example. The vials are good for five years if they remain unopened. The company that produces the antivenin is called S.A. Snake-Antivenin.com and is located in Brussels, Belgium. They say that they mainly work with professionals, but will not fill orders over 1,000 Euros.[72] Doctors Without Borders reports that as many as 100,000 people a year are killed by venomous snakes, so access to antivenin is crucial.[73]

In the United States, however, people are not allowed to get antivenin directly. Doctors still maintain complete control over people's lives in this situation and the antivenin produced is a direct legacy of the history of antivenin in the United States and Brazil. For many years, Wyeth Pharmaceutical Company, a subsidiary of Pfizer Pharmaceutical Company, made an antivenin called Antivenin (Crotalidea) Polyvalent, Wyeth, which neutralizes the venom of rattlesnakes, copperheads, cottonmouths, Fer-de-lance, other subspecies of Bothrops, the tropical rattler, and the bushmaster, among other snakes in these regions of the world.[74] They stopped making that and today only make a product called Snake Equine Antivenin that treats the bite of coral snakes. Rattlesnake antivenin today is made by BTG International Pharmaceutical Company and is called CroFab. It treats water moccasin bites as well, and it is made with the help of sheep rather than horses.

Medical authorities today are very clear on the danger of snakebite, the need to treat it with antivenin, and to let people know that the additional methods of treating snakebites are not benign. Today, the Texas Poison Control Center takes calls about bites and informs people to go straight to the hospital. But before they get there, they tell callers, "Do not cut the wound and try and extract the venom by mouth," "do not use ice or a tourniquet," and "do not drink alcohol."[75] BTG also gives very different advice to doctors, emergency technicians, nurses, and bite victims than they received in the past, and their suggestions capture a revolution in thinking about who gets bitten and how they should be treated. In a video presentation on their website, they dramatize how two people get bitten by a snake. In one case, a teenage boy is riding his mountain bike, he stops to take a break, gets off his bike, sits in the grass, leans back on his hands in some tall grass, and a rattlesnake bites him on the hand. Another boy, this time elementary school age, is playing outside in nature, lifts up a rock to look underneath it, and is bitten by the rattlesnake. Both of these examples illustrate the company's correct understanding that more rattlesnake bite victims are men than women and they are more likely to get bitten on the extremities. The use of sympathetic innocent young men is also illustrative of their desire to help people get treatment. These were not people who "deserved" their snakebite because they were intentionally playing around with a venomous snake, they were accidental victims. One was doing the healthy activity of exercising on his mountain bike, and the other was simply a small child playing. No snake charmers here. The advice to the public from the company is to immediately loosen clothing by cutting it if necessary, rather than tying off the limb with a ligature, then calling 911 so that emergency medical technicians can get to bite victims quickly. Time is tissue, they note, and even a small amount of venom scraped across the skin can cause harm. Once in the hospital, they draw lines around the advancing envenomation (rather than using any device to try and suck it out) to evaluate its progress and treatment. The Crofab is mixed with saline and given to the patient intravenously. Several vials are used over a 6–8 hour period. A doctor is there to make sure that the patient does not develop an allergic reaction and to monitor and treat the extent of possible side effects of the snakebite, including vomiting or neurological problems.

The problem now with the drug is its enormous expense. And the expense is reinforcing the class divide that always skewed the bite problem. The poor who do not have health insurance are particularly vulnerable in snakebite cases. One Missouri man who lacked insurance and was bitten refused treatment because he could not afford it.[76]

Thanks to antivenin, under ten people a year typically die from the bites today. BTG has fought to keep competitors off the market, even though they made the equivalent of $98 million selling close to 8,000 vials of antivenin in 2014. The antivenin costs around $2,300, and patients can receive anywhere from four to over 100 vials, depending upon the severity of the bite. Unfortunately, however, hospitals in the United States mark up the price far beyond the manufacturer's cost. Todd Hassler, from San Diego, was one of the 7,000–8,000 people bitten by rattlesnakes every year. His hospital bill totaled $153,000; $83,000 of that was for the Crofab that the hospital administered, even though he did not receive the large number of antivenin vials that severe bites require. Instead, the hospital marked up the cost of the antivenin tremendously in an effort, they claim, to get more money from insurance.[77] The same Crofab antivenin sells for just $100 per vial in Mexico. Leslie Boyer, the founding director of the University of Arizona's VIPER Institute, realized that she did not know why antivenin cost so much and did a study of what it actually costs to make the drug. She did a cost data study of every part of the manufacturing process and developed a pricing model. She found that "fees and costs for licensing, regulation, and hospital profits amount to 27.7 percent of the overall cost, and clinical trials made up just 2.1 percent. The cost of making the anitvenin, including research and development, animal care, and plasma harvesting was just 0.1 percent." The remaining 70.1 percent was due to hospital markups used in negotiations with insurance companies.[78]

We can also get a sense of the other costs involved today by reading Justin's story, posted online. He was 13 years old, taking part in a camp near Yosemite in July 2012. He and his fellow campers were resting about 4.5 miles from the trailhead when he was bitten on the palm of his hand while sitting on a boulder. The snake did not warn him at all, it simply bit him. The camp director called the hospital and a helicopter waited for him at the trailhead. The helicopter flew 30 minutes to a hospital in Modesto, California, but his bite was too severe to treat there so they flew him to the UC Davis Medical Center in Sacramento. While there, he was given 30 vials of antivenin. The doctors performed a fasciotomy in which they cut open his arm from the palm to the middle of his bicep to relieve the extreme pressure from the bite swelling. He spent 35 days at the UC Davis hospital where he had eight surgeries in which doctors cleaned out dead tissue from his arm. They then created a skin graft from his leg to close the open wound on his arm, for a total of ten surgeries. He had four months of occupational therapy after that, and then flew to Duke Medical Center in North Carolina for a follow-up surgery in which doctors performed a vascular flap procedure that entailed taking a section of skin and muscle from his back and attaching its blood vessels to the ones in his arm. In the process, he had two more emergency surgeries because of blood loss. After six months more of occupational therapy, he could move the fingers in the hand that was bitten only two to three millimeters. Justin does not tell his readers how much the hospital bills for all of this cost, just that it was "paid by my insurance of course." He does tell readers, however, that he had "$700,000 worth of helicopter flights."[79]

Antivenin, then, has become a cure for people who can afford it, and it is now accompanied by elaborate surgeries and physical therapy for the unlucky victims. The push for a cure started off as a way to help poor people who were disproportionately bitten, but has become part of the same expensive medical system in the United States that plagues Americans in so many ways. As we shall see, however, rattlesnakes have also made money for other Americans through their use in entertainment.

4

On Stage

Traveling Acts, Circuses and Zoos

Americans made money from snakes through entertainment that ultimately hurt the snakes and created snakebite victims. Snakes were captured, sometimes mutilated, held in environments that were unnatural to them, and eroticized, all for profit. Most of the champions of snakes were themselves questionable and on the margins of American society. So anything they might say about the snakes' virtues were highly suspect. And some Americans believed that any injury that the performers sustained while working with them was deserved. Rattlesnakes and black rat snakes were the most common performers. The rattlesnake's venom gave it a universal appeal, and the black rat snake's size (up to eight feet), made it a common performer as well. The rat snake lent itself to performances because it was non-venomous and preferred to flee rather than confront danger. However, it would rear and strike if it felt threatened, so its great size and ability to stage a show when provoked made it a favorite local performer. Once animal traders began importing exotic animals, however, they were soon cast aside for the more beautiful boas from around the world that became the staple of circus acts. Simultaneously the American rattlesnake, usually the timber rattler, made its way into both circus freak shows and zoological snake demonstrations. As educational institutions, one of the ways that zoos taught Americans about snakes was through feeding demonstrations that were as much entertainment as they were education. Large boas were often force fed animals while several zoo keepers lifted the snakes. Later zoos also used venomous snakes as entertainment through snake milking demonstrations, in which they removed the venom from snakes to help create the antivenin that protected snakebite victims. Although they were educational, these shows clearly had sexual overtones by virtue of the act of milking an animal that looked like a phallic symbol. As a result, when the entertainers were bitten, there was a clearly biblical sense that the snakes were temptation and the people bitten received their just rewards.

Early Snake Stories and Performances

Snake stories in local newspapers were one of the earliest forms of entertainment. Writers contributed clearly imaginary tales designed to shock or amuse readers. The black rat snake, hereafter called the black snake, was a common character in these stories, although rattlesnakes appeared as well. They sometimes started with the disclaimer that the writer understood that the story was not true. They just wanted to check and make sure that nothing like this had really ever happened and then relayed the stories. Sometimes the stories involved fantastic and improbable battles between animals. A writer to the *Boston Morning Post*, in 1833, claimed he saw a black snake cut into three pieces and then reconstituted.[1] Other papers had a section called "Snake Yarns" that regularly featured both black snakes and rattlesnakes. The daughter of the Reverend Squires, of Centerville, Massachusetts, supposedly awoke one day to find a giant black snake under her pillow. Plenty of stories concerning black snakes involved battles of some kind either between two subspecies of snakes, or between snakes and humans. Walter Adams of Bedford Station, New York, for example, supposedly killed a black snake measuring 12 feet in length.[2] Snakes were breathlessly described as cannibals, and editors regularly printed stories that might have had a grain of truth, but quickly moved to the realm of fantasy. A man from North Carolina, for example, claimed to see a black snake eat a garter snake. However, a few days later, he found the black snake with the garter snake poking its head out of its belly. The consumed snake had supposedly eaten a hole in the black snake, and the fearless man rescued the more endearing garter snake by killing the black snake.[3] In another story, a man claimed to hear of someone else who discovered a snake in his cellar suspended between two spider webs. The spider had lassoed the snake's head to immobilize it and was drinking its bodily fluids.[4]

Snake stories were also used to show how tough Americans were. There was no messing with our reptiles because they could be as dangerous as anyone else's snakes, particularly our old enemy the English. In one story, a medical student traveling north for a conference brings a rattlesnake aboard a steamship. It initially attracts a great deal of attention as his fellow travelers ask him to make the snake perform by rattling for them. After awhile this gets tiresome, and he stows the snake in a box in a smoking room. While the student is smoking with other passengers, he listens to a member of the British military, who was visiting the United States, boasting about how dangerous cobras are and how tame American rattlesnakes are by comparison. Another passenger recounts a story of a rattlesnake that got loose on board and bit someone. The fellow travelers then supposedly gave the owner hundreds of whip lashes and tarred and feathered him. Suddenly the medical student's rattlesnake appears under the chair of the English soldier's chair and bedlam ensues. The medical student catches the snake and throws it off the side of the boat before anyone can identify it as his. In the process, however, the English soldier embarrasses himself by trying to flee, so we are reassured that our snakes are indeed scary.[5]

Sometimes the stories preceded traveling family acts that then recreated the story for people in towns. One fictional story was about a large black snake who supposedly charmed a blue-eyed girl from New Hampshire. The story, biblically resonant, sexual, and loaded with racial prejudice, is about a young girl who repeatedly visits a large black snake who lives at the boundary of the family's property. The snake charms the girl and gets her to bring it her supper in the evenings. She falls in love with the snake, begins regularly to bring it her dinner, and starts wasting away. The father grows alarmed, confronts the snake, and kills it. This fictional newspaper story circulated throughout a few New England papers and evidently inspired one family to cash in on its popularity. The Hill family created a traveling act that toured through New Hampshire and Massachusetts in the mid 1850s trying to re-enact the loving relationship between the girl and a large snake. In the Hill family's version, at her mother's urging the blue-eyed young daughter would open a box with a black snake in it. Then she would carefully reach in and grab the snake behind the back of the head and pull it out of the box. She let it settle on her lap and draped it around her shoulders to entertain the crowd. Mr. Hill was eventually arrested in Massachusetts after one of his performances in Cochituate. The police attended the show and then detained the father on charges of cruel and unnatural exposure and endangering the health and life of a child. Apparently the child had snakebite marks from previous shows.[6] These were crude traveling shows that preceded the more professional circuses of the early 1900s in America that cashed in on audiences' desires to see large, preferably dangerous snakes.

Circuses

When we imagine late nineteenth- and early twentieth-century American circuses, a number of images come easily to mind: colorful posters, elephants on parade through town centers, the big top tent, lion tamers, pageantry, acrobats and daredevil stunts, clowns, top hats and ringmasters, and—in the margins—the sideshows. Although not a headline act for most circuses, snake charmers and snake pits nonetheless attracted their fair share of fascinated and horrified circus and carnival patrons, and on occasion provided reporters with sensational stories of escapes and attacks. Prior to the 1930s, the lack of antivenin for snakebites, as well as a deep-seated cultural loathing of snakes, assured that for the circus, bad snake news was good publicity.

Circuses are of course closely associated with elephants, lions, ponies, and other mammals that are easily trained. Snakes, however, cannot be trained to any great degree, and thus did not make good candidates for true animal shows. There could be no snake equivalent of Jumbo, even if one carnival did advertise "Jumbo the great snake."[7] Yet, circuses travelled with snakes, sometimes with lots of snakes, and occasionally, circuses prominently advertised their snakes. In a large circus such as the Ringling-Barnum, the snakes might even make it into the opening parade, appearing en masse with their handler in a windowed wagon—a kind of "Venom in Vegas" on wheels.[8] More often, it seems that snakes were a regular feature in the sideshow area, called "geek shows," where they had added an appropriately exotic, dangerous, and freakish air to the circus since the 19th century. Barnum & Bailey circus spokesman Tody Hamilton promised New York reporters in the spring of the 1906 that it had "the most marvelous collection of snakes ever congregated."[9] In 1926, the *New York Times*, in its long-running annual story about the Ringling Brothers–Barnum & Bailey Circus's return to Madison Square Garden, declared the circus "better than ever," thanks in part to a big increase in "freaks," including "the snake charmer."[10] Among the geeks and freaks, the circus snake made its company.

The snake *was* a circus freak. Its exotic origins, mysterious habits, and horrifying appearance evoked the same feelings of fascination and revulsion as those produced by the Siamese twins, bearded ladies, sword swallowers, and other human inhabitants of the sideshow. Although most circus histories give only passing mention to snake handlers and charmers, their presence—and their appeal—occasionally erupted to grab headlines. In those moments of mayhem when snakes escaped or attacked, they fully lived up to their promise.

Types of Snakes and Acts

But what kinds of snakes would be right for a circus? Should performers use American snakes or more exotic ones? If snakes could not be
trained to perform like other animals, how were they used in acts? To
evoke horror, revulsion, or curiosity, a circus could pursue several strate-
gies, sometimes simultaneously.

Ada Moore, snake enchantress, handling a python (undated photograph by H.A.
Well; courtesy Circus World Museum, Barbaroo, Wisconsin).

As with giants, strong men, and fat ladies, size mattered. As a reporter wrote in 1924, "It is the big snake that draws the crowd when the barker begins his patter before the tent."[11] Depending on the region of the country, a snake charmer was among the more popular freak acts, sure to "gather a crowd."[12] Many Americans, especially rural ones, would have seen snakes in the wild, and they were used to larger black snakes and rattlesnakes. Imported boa constrictors and pythons, by contrast, were exotic, fat, and long. Most boa species grow to around six feet, with some reaching as much as 13 feet long. Several python species, including the reticulated python, can reach immense lengths. So too can the anaconda, which is occasionally mentioned as a circus snake. A 1935 photo of a female snake charmer for the Cole Brothers Circus illustrated the clear value of a large snake: the charmer holds the snake, thicker than her arms, in a Statue of Liberty pose; the python's head thrusts aggressively toward the charmer's smiling face; its tail end coils on the ground. The snake is at least nine feet long, and although not venomous, it looks mighty dangerous. Even smaller snakes, if paired with smaller performers, evoked some kind of reaction. In one photograph, young Wisconsin performer, George W. Hall, Jr., stands by a table, a partly coiled snake held in his right hand, appearing ready to strike his face, while a second and much longer snake is draped around his neck.[13] Female snake charmers, or "snake enchantresses," who generally performed in somewhat revealing costumes with snakes draped and wound suggestively around their bodies, likely preferred working with larger, nonvenomous snakes. When boas or pythons were unavailable, the native eastern indigo snake, a large (up to seven feet) blue-black species, proved a good choice because of its impressive size and docile nature.[14] For real effect though, a python in the 20-foot range was a showstopper.[15] Circuses then offered the same erotic entertainment as the traveling black snake show, but they professionalized it by hiring adult women who could give their relationship with the snake more believability.

Venomous snakes, of course, heightened the sense of danger. Rattlesnakes and cobras were good bets here. The rattlesnake was native and easily acquired, and it looked and sounded threatening when coiled in a defensive posture. Similarly cobras, with their elevated heads and distinctive hoods, left no doubt as to their intentions. Best of all, venomous snakes actually *could* be dangerous, so their handlers gained some instant credibility. In reality, though, rattlesnakes and cobras could be defanged; sometimes their mouths were even sewn shut. Mrs. Beverly W. Haight, an "amateur" snake handler who set up in a Columbus, Ohio, park during the summer, claimed that she could tame a rattlesnake in two days, but a common saying among herpetologists is that the question is not *if* one will be bitten, but *when*.[16] A "hot" (i.e., not defanged) venomous snake was always potentially dangerous.

Finally, as anyone who has seen an Indiana Jones movie knows, there is nothing worse than being trapped in a small space with a huge, writhing mass of serpents. Thus, the "snake pit" was popular. It consisted of an enclosed space filled with snakes in which a performer would stand, sit, or lie down, handling numerous snakes at once, offering them to the audience, and sometimes getting bitten. Snake charmers would often perform with a box full of writhing snakes from which they would select first one and then another, in escalation of size and danger. The snakes themselves were generally harmless, either defanged rattlesnakes or domestic gopher snakes and the like, but the sight of so many in one place was horrifying to many. Ringling Brothers–Barnum & Bailey traveled with "dens of snakes" at least into the late 1920s.[17] Relatively inexpensive (rattlesnake suppliers paid eight cents a pound in 1922), snake pits were no doubt attractive to smaller circuses and carnival shows.[18]

One performer recalled how his carnival's snake pit worked to both frighten and fleece viewers. Outside the 20- by 30-foot tent, a banner advertised "Rose, Wild Cannibal Girl from Bohemia, eats them alive!" Inside, paying patrons discovered an eight- by 16-foot square pit filled with defanged rattlesnakes and nonvenomous "king snakes, blue bulls, whip snakes, yellow bulls, [and] water snakes." In the center sat the "geek," who was a man "acting like a wild gal playing with the snakes, putting their heads in his mouth" while a "whip boy" fired a blank gun, cracked his whip, and tried to keep the geek under control. When the geek, brandishing handfuls of snakes, lunged out of the pit and into the crowd, pickpockets relieved panicked and fleeing patrons of their wallets.[19]

Barkers and sensational banners convinced other patrons to shell out hard cash for serpent oddities that did not quite live up to their promise. The "hoop snake" myth—the claim that a snake can form a hoop and roll around like a wheel—was widely believed, but of course turned out to be an empty promise. Two-headed garter snakes and albino pythons were real, although not so large and monstrous as advertised.[20]

If the snake pit and other sideshows could be more scam than show, some acts promised and seemingly delivered true horror. Most notable, no doubt, was the live snake eating act. As late as 1938, a carnival featured an "African" who ate live snakes, apparently following the path blazed by Will "Steamboat" Davis, who performed as "Bosco, the Snake Eater" for the Barnum & Bailey and Ringling Brothers' circuses until 1906, when he began a life sentence in an Iowa prison (where he died in 1927). Harry Houdini described Davis's snake eating act as "disgusting," and claimed that it led to the barker's cry "he eats them alive."[21] However distasteful, Davis's act made an impression. In the first decade of the twentieth century, his show was a popular attraction at venues such as the Jackson Homecomers Festival (Missouri), and Virginia Tech students gave the nickname "Bosco" to a brilliant professor who "made mincemeat of sophomores."[22]

On the other hand, snake shows were not all humbug. P.T. Barnum hired Arlan F. "Doc" Randle to run an "educational snake exhibition." Costumed as "Princess Marjah," Mrs. Randle assisted, discussing the finer points of snake science as she held up the snakes Doc handed to her. In fact, the Randles actually had studied the available snake literature closely, and their act featured fact, not just sensation. Over the years, the Randles purchased nearly a thousand snakes from the "Snake King" (W.A. King) of Brownsville, Texas, and they made as much as $100 a week. Their "star" was Otessa, a 16-foot python.[23]

Snake Suppliers

One measure of the ubiquity of snakes in circuses can be found in the frequent stories about snake dealers. These stories consistently describe numerous animal dealers selling large quantities of snakes to circuses. In the snake trade, there were two distinct markets. One was for imported species, the other for domestic. The imported snakes were more exotic, larger, and more expensive, but it seems that many circuses had a supply of each kind on hand.

Circuses and other traveling acts in the mid to late 1800s often used local snakes that they caught for performances. Sometimes acts would move to areas that had a plentiful supply for their shows because of the high snake death rates. So the physical geography of the snakes' native habitat determined the routes that the acts took. By the turn of the century, however, circuses could get snakes from snake farms, freeing them to perform in any profitable town or city.

For domestic snakes, especially rattlesnakes, circuses turned to dealers. "Snake Men," as they were called, sold indigenous snakes throughout the country. Some of them, for example, sold their goods to steamboats traveling up the Chattahoochee and Flint rivers. Nationally, circuses purchased many of their rattlesnakes in the 1890s from Charles Bishoff, better known as "Montana Charley" or the "Rattlesnake King of the Rockies," for his frequent trips to the west for collecting purposes. He had outfitted a boat that he used for living quarters, transportation, and storage space. A small section in the middle of the vessel was used for his family's living quarters, which was surrounded by rattlesnakes in cages. He sailed the snakes down the Missouri River with the eventual destination of New York.[24]

Sometimes dealers were also showmen as well. One unnamed dealer who chronicled his experience for a newspaper column in the *McCook Tribune* (Nebraska) explained that that he spent his summers in Pike County, Pennsylvania, where there were hundreds of rattlesnakes. The area attracted "city people," who were primarily from New York and spent their summers in the mountainous region, and wanted rattlesnake hides and buttons. The tourists stayed in a boarding house, and the snake dealer supplied the owner with skins and rattles. He earned $2.50 for a large skin and had a contract to sell over 100 of them the next summer. Some buyers had the skins stuffed and mounted, and others had them made into cigar cases, belts, pocketbooks, card cases, and slippers. Another local snake dealer, named Elijah Pelton, held over 200 rattlesnakes at his place in the woods and handled them for a fee. His house became a tourist attraction, and the experience was enhanced when he informed his customers that he had collected the snakes from the immediate vicinity of his home.[25]

Perhaps the biggest rattlesnake dealer was William Abraham Lieberman, also known for his trademarked name the SNAKE KING. W.A. "Snake" King, who opened his "Snakeville" business in Brownsville, Texas, in 1908 after 20 years of selling out of San Antonio, was a primary supplier for snake charmers, circuses, and carnivals. In addition to rattlesnakes (he had 8,000 ready to ship), he dealt in imported snakes, birds, and mammals that were of interest to circuses and zoos.[26] He claimed to have sold four tons of rattlesnakes (all defanged) to museums and "circus performers" in 1908.[27]

When enough of their domestic snakes died, snake charmers initially sent letters, and later telegrams, to Lieberman asking him to send a particular kind of snake or later a "mixed fixed" box to the next performance town.[28] Lieberman set up his "Snakeville" farm in Brownsville, Texas, because of its plentiful supply of snakes. Initially he collected the snakes on his own by setting up collecting camps with his wife and painstakingly gathering them from the wild. He quickly realized, however, that paying people, primarily ranchers, farmers, and hunters, to bring in snakes was more efficient. On Saturdays, people from the surrounding areas drove their horse-drawn wagons to the farm filled with a variety of animals, as well as snakes. He kept rolls of one-dollar bills on hand and made a show of slowly counting out single dollars so that the farmers felt the heft of the money for the trade. The surrounding area, however, soon ran out of snakes, and Lieberman was forced to look across the Mexican border. Realizing that they were losing a potentially profitable investment, Mexican customs officials imposed a head tax on rattlesnakes. Lieberman forced the customs officials to count the snakes themselves and out of fear they opted for a fixed tax per box, rather than on individual snakes. To keep his prices low to sell to circus performers, Lieberman decided against importing the snakes, but local ranchers and hunters complained enough to officials that they abandoned the tax. Lieberman's low regard for snake life in general, moreover, caused the depletion of snakes in the region. He could have raised baby rattlesnakes or other snakes at his farm, but elected to kill them all off every time a female snake produced offspring, using the absurd argument that the infant snakes were too dangerous.[29] Later hunters also used the arguments that young rattlesnakes in general were so dangerous that they demanded a bonus price as compensation for the risk of catching them.

Circus performers also got exotic snakes from well-known animal dealers in New York who imported them from around the world. One estimate is that circuses (along with zoos and natural history museums) bought somewhere from 700 to 1,000 snakes from India, South America, and Africa per year during the late 19th century.[30] They had to consistently replenish the snakes because they died so quickly. Pythons were the particular favorite of circus performers because they were large, exotic, and generally safer than local venomous snakes, although pythons do have very sharp teeth, and an untreated bite could become seriously infected. Probably because keeping a large snake alive was not always easy, it seems that there was always some demand for pythons. Pythons eat infrequently, but even trained herpetologists could not always get them to eat in captivity and so had to resort to force-feeding. Travelling in a variety of climates and conditions was not conducive to good health either, and many reportedly died after getting overheated in their glass cases during street parades.[31] Others, such as a 28-foot python, succumbed in winter by getting badly burned by heating stoves.[32] Many died because they were handled so often at night that they did not get enough rest.

Luckily for snake handlers, in the absence of today's legal restrictions, the supply of imported snakes was seemingly limitless, at least until World War I interrupted international trade. During that unhappy period, one snake enchantress, Mademoiselle Maxine, longed to trade in her "gallery" of snake pictures for a "couple of good live constrictors."[33] Animal shipments to New York resumed in 1922, and the *New York Times* ran numerous stories about the demand for pythons and their price ($20 for a seven-foot snake; $700 for 25-footers). The Ringling Brothers circus got the first big python to arrive—a 28-footer.[34]

In the early and mid 19th-century circus, when pythons were relatively rare in the states, a showman could apparently make good money, if their later recollections are to be trusted. John Nathans claimed to have not only earned a healthy income with his 14-foot boa "Old Rube," but also to have sold Rube for a $7,500 profit. In his act, he simply bent his body over like a bridge and allowed the snake to crawl over him. Or he fed Rube a nine-pound live turkey or a pair of live chickens by holding the fowl by the head while the snake ate them. At the feedings, he charged 50 cents a person, and apparently the crowds were quite large. George F. Bailey also saw the economic value of snakes in his circus. His circus had exhibited "a great many of them," and although he himself had never handled them directly, they had greatly enriched his coffers. He believed that their danger was minimal, but he certainly benefited from the belief that snakes could kill their handlers by crushing or biting them. By the 1880s, the price had come down significantly, with smaller boas costing about $5 per foot.[35] Still, when "Princess," a 103-year-old, 920-pound, 28-foot-long boa constrictor died in 1906 (of "indigestion brought on by overeating"), it was described as one of the circus's "most valuable assets."[36]

Even a snake that did not make it to the circus could make for a good story. In 1895, Captain MacDuff, who piloted the steamship *MacDuff*, brought a shipment of pythons, as well as other reptiles, to New York from Singapore. The ship had encountered bad weather outside of New York and only six of the initial 13 survived the trip. One gigantic 23-foot python had perished during the storm after wrapping itself around a hot stove. As the ship neared the Statue of Liberty, the python was thrown overboard. The large snake floated up through Hell Gate into the Long Island Sound where it was spotted by people who believed that it was a sea monster. The sea monster rumors proved great sport for citizens from Long Island who were experiencing a less than exciting summer, and the water was soon full of boats searching for the dead serpent.[37]

When reporters turned to circuses, the chances were good that any named person featured in a story about snakes was a "freak" of some kind. The *New York Times* thoroughly approved when in 1913, the Barnum & Bailey Circus brought back the freaks, including the snake charmers, after a five-year hiatus. "Who wants elegance in a circus? the management asked, and the answer was 'Nobody!'"[38] A lengthy *New York Times* story from 1916 announced, "Giant the Best Man at Midget Wedding." Performed in the center ring of the Barnum & Bailey Circus's opening-night Madison Square Garden show, the ceremony featured a "procession of freaks" who lent their support to the happy couple: Miss Elsie Reineking, a three-foot-tall snake charmer, and her betrothed, the somewhat shorter Francis Short, a clown. The flower girl, Mlle. Maxine, was a snake enchantress. Although there were no snakes in the ceremony, a giant boa brought Elsie and Francis together a year earlier when Francis rescued Elsie from a near-swallowing (or so the story went).[39] When the circus was in the city two years earlier, the *Times* ran a long story about "Zip" and the other Barnum freaks' dinner at Healy's restaurant, where the cloakroom attendant refused to check Maxine's live, nine-foot boa.[40]

Since snake charmers were mostly women, their newspaper profiles tended to play up the gendered implications of handling snakes, emphasizing how unusual it was for a *woman* to not fear snakes. An out-of-work circus snake charmer, Mrs. Donald Moore, was turned away by the Volunteers of America Relief home because she wanted to bring "her two pythons under its shelter."[41] In the provocatively titled "Snakes in Bed," a reporter examined how snakes were undermining Walter B. Hedler's marriage. In 1895, Hedler, a wealthy New Jersey harness maker, married Evelyn Stansfield, a "snake hypnotist" for a circus. Although other hypnotists "fondled" defanged "serpents," Stansfield "made reptiles that retained their fangs submissive by the weird defiance of her eye." Hedler hoped that "his pretty wife" would give up her passion, but three years later their household was still filled with snakes. Finally, on the night of December 3, 1898, he could stand it no longer. On that evening his wife came into bed at 11 p.m., bringing "three of her snakes, great, slimy, venomous things.... She brought them into the bed with her, and all my protests could not stop her. I was terrified, but finally lay absolutely still in the hope that the horrible creatures would ignore my presence. They did so for a time, crawling over and about me, but my quivering flesh probably gave me away, and one of them finally put me to the test by stinging me viciously. It was too much." Too much indeed as Hedler later filed for divorce.[42] When it came to snake enchantresses, apparently they were better appreciated from a distance, at the circus.

A 1925 New York City radio broadcast of a "live" circus underlined the erotic implications of a woman charming snakes. Lew Graham, Ringling's long-time announcer, conducted this virtual circus with panache.

His introduction to the snake charmer must be quoted in full to be fully appreciated:

> And next, ladies and gentlemen, next is Mlle. Cleo, of whom no doubt you've all heard. Positively the world's greatest trainer of ferocious, poisonous vipers. Ab-so-lutely without fear, a marvel of all times. Step close now, but carefully, carefully, and note the steel-bound den. It literally teems with writhing, angry, fearsome, poisonous vipers. And this little lady, this frail little girl, Mlle. Cleo tames them all. I will now request Mlle. Cleo to command Big Dick, the giant python, to stand on his tail and hiss. Stand by and Richard the python, 32 feet in length, will hiss for you.[43]

In Chicago, reporter Paul Gilbert joined Mlle. Cleo on stage to experience what handling snakes was like. Cleo's act was advertised with a large banner portraying her as "a sort of modern Eve, a huge green serpent coiled around her neck whispering his wicked secrets into her ear." When Gilbert met Cleo, he noted that "her hand lingered in mine for some time," and he described her "fairy" like appearance and "scanty" dress.[44] These two reports are especially useful because they offer detailed, contemporaneous descriptions of how a snake show was "sold" to circus patrons. The announcer's pitch and the visual details, faithfully reproduced in these newspaper stories, surely enticed many readers to go and experience Mlle. Cleo's show for themselves.

Sometimes it is not news until something goes wrong. The sideshow snake pit always featured a geek who pretended to eat snakes, but in 1937, a Walter L. Main Circus roustabout "went berserk and entered the sideshow tent while the show was in progress and suddenly leaped into the snake pit and bit one of the snakes in two."[45] This may have been one of the few times that even pickpocketed customers felt they had gotten their money's worth. In a more tragic incident, two young boys playing on the Sun Brothers Circus lot discovered a bottle with a picture of a snake on it. Thinking it was lemonade, the boys drank what was later "believed to be a mixture of something used to stupefy circus snakes." One of the boys "died in convulsions that evening."[46]

The escaped snake, hiding anywhere and eluding capture, was a stock figure of horror. When Charles Reiche & Brothers, a major New York animal dealer, lost a 30-foot African python while passing City Hall square, panic ensued, as the "monster seemed a creature of the imagination" capable of snatching a "newsboy or other delicate morsel among the bystanders for a meal."[47] That python was recovered, but a black snake that supposedly escaped from Sautelle's circus in 1906 became a local Virginia legend, making "a noise like a horse" as it glided through the brush. The 11-foot "monster" was so terrifying that squirrel hunters "were afraid to shoot it."[48] Another 11-foot snake, found alive in a Pennsylvania dump, was declared a circus escapee, since the circus grounds were not far away.[49] During the summer of 1932, residents of a west-end St. Louis neighborhood were "terrorized" by a "giant python" and its companion who got loose from a circus snake charmer.[50] Citizen encounters with escaped snakes provided a real element of human interest. When a boa escaped from its cage on a train, it was finally discovered "curled snugly around a fat man, who sat apparently asleep." After the snake was removed, the man awoke and "declared that he had never slept better in all his life although he had been a trifle warm."[51] A defanged rattlesnake that escaped from the John Robinson Circus while it was visiting Portsmouth, Ohio, was dispatched with a hoe by alert citizen Robert H. Huffman.[52] A Chicago policeman emptied his revolver into a six-foot boa constrictor that a circus left behind when it pulled up stakes.[53]

Although venomous rattlesnakes were sometimes defanged, "hot" ones always posed a risk, even if one snake pit performer claimed that "the rattler is really one of the easiest snakes to handle."[54] A young employee of the Dan Rice Circus, Tony Cuellar (22), disproved this when he "dropped a pocket comb into the rattler's cage" and was struck trying to retrieve it. Rushed to a hospital, he was "feared dying."[55] James Reilly, better known as "Slippery Reilly," spent a decade or two as a circus snake charmer until in the summer of 1884 the "unfortunate showman" met a rattlesnake that he could not charm. Drinking a huge amount of whiskey did not save his life. On stage even in death, he was subjected to a semi-public autopsy that revealed the massive tissue damage suffered in his left arm, left lung, and heart. The students and doctors left the autopsy with their curiosity satisfied and with souvenirs: small vials of Reilly's blood.[56]

Handling snakes offstage could be hazardous, as several incidents illustrate. The Forpaugh Circus, which was performing in Detroit, Michigan, in June 1891, exhibited a boa constrictor, named "Old Nick" for its "wicked disposition," in a sideshow. Henry Prince, a snake charmer, took the snake back to his cage for the evening and was nearly strangled to death by Nick. A teamster heard a groan in the tent and "found Prince black in the face and nearly strangled with five coils around him." The story becomes somewhat less believable when "cowboys were summoned from the big tent, who lassoed the boa" and then "slashed [it] several times" before it released its grip and Prince regained consciousness.[57] Another story, with details that seem embellished by either the reporter or the sources, concerned a Welsh Brothers Circus performance in August

1903. The circus included a snake sideshow in which a woman charmer, named Van, performed with an 18-foot python. As she was trying to get the snake out of its cage for a performance, she lost her grip, allowing the python to wriggle free and fall to the ground. At this point, the python supposedly slithered over to a nearby Indian Brahma bull and coiled around its hump. The bull tried to get it off with its horns and Van tried to pry it off as well. Van was bitten by the snake, whereupon she "dropped to the ground and fainted." The bull successfully skewered the snake with its horns, causing its death. Van's bite was cauterized by Dr. E.S. Parker of Rockway, and she survived.[58]

The most sensational attacks were by pythons, whose bites usually came in connection with an act going horribly wrong. Although snake experts frequently described pythons as gentle, harmless snakes, they have numerous, very sharp teeth that curve backwards and sink deeply into flesh. Bert Uber, of South Sharon, Pennsylvania, learned about the danger of standing too close to the snake charmer. As the charmer wrapped his 12-foot snake (probably a python) around his neck, the head came close to Uber. In a flash, the snake struck, lacerating Uber's nose with its sharp teeth. In standard medical practice of the day, the doctor cauterized the wound, leaving Uber with an unfortunate souvenir from the circus.[59] In New York City, "a sawdust ring battle with an enraged python sent two circus performers to a hospital ... and gave spectators at the show the creeps." The snake in question belonged to the Castrenelli aerial acrobatic troupe, used at the beginning of their Ringling Brothers' show for "local color for the Bamboyo rope act." On this day in 1932, while being carried to the ring, the 25-foot-long, "hungry" snake bit acrobat Octavio Castrenelli and aerialist Alfredo Cardona before it could be "subdued." Despite a "large" wound to Castrenelli, the band kept playing and the show went on. Still, Bamboyo later said that he felt "a circus ... should be able to get along without a python."[60] Elsewhere, Labero, a professional hypnotist, failed to hypnotize a "huge python," and circus goers were treated to the spectacle of the snake biting Labero's hand so viciously that one tooth broke off; calmly, the hypnotist went on with the show, turning his attention to guinea pigs, rabbits, and other less dangerous creatures.[61] Ralph Smith, a snake charmer with the Ingalls Carnival Circus, was bitten three times by a python that had to be pried off him with "clubs and pitchforks." His cauterized wounds were described as "grave."[62] Snake charmers with venomous snakes typically prevented the venom sacks from releasing their liquid by sewing them up, for example. It was impossible, however, to completely remove the danger from a boa constrictor, so it is probably for this reason, as well as their size, that these snakes were the stars of the snake shows.

Some newspaper stories stretched credulity but were designed to publicize the circus. In a wild 1897 story, the *New York Times* reported that the Smithsonian's Walter Ralston had supposedly captured a 33-foot python that had been "terrorizing" residents of a Florida island after its supposed escape from the sinking of a ship carrying a circus.[63] Described as having a "bucket" sized head and "long, cruel looking fangs," this monster was not the end of the story. Ralston claimed that he had seen signs of a larger python, perhaps 75 feet long![64] When circus performers shared stories of historical snake incidents with reporters, the line between fact and fiction seemed to blur considerably. In 1902, a group of circus performers shared a story with an Iowa reporter about an incident that that happened "long ago in Texas." In this case, a 19-foot anaconda escaped from its cage during a show and crawled over to where a giraffe was lying in the sun enjoying a nap. The snake moved onto the giraffe and coiled around its head, tightening its grip. Meanwhile a clown was entertaining visitors in a tent. The giraffe jumped up with the snake around its neck and ran into the tent, twisting its neck around in an attempt to shake the animal off. The giraffe pranced "round and round the ring, slashing the air and whipping the canvas roof" or "slamming the snake down on the ground and jumping around like a crazy June bug." The circus hands felt at a loss for what to do in this situation and waited to see how the battle would turn out. The spectators initially believed that they were watching a part of the show in which a fake rubber snake was coiled around the giraffe. After about five minutes of watching the struggle more carefully, however, they realized that they were watching a real struggle between the snake and giraffe. At which point they "wanted to go home in short order" and "slipped out from under flaps of the tent, scrambled over the backs of seats," and generally got out of the tent in any way possible. The panic, meanwhile, caused more distress for the giraffe, who began to run faster and faster. The giraffe eventually smacked the bottom half of the snake off of its neck onto a pole in the center of the ring, allowing 14 men to rush out and grab that section of the animal. Another circus performer seized an axe and killed the snake by cutting it in half. At the end, they were "all glad it had to be the anaconda to bite the dust."[65] In 1907, a boa constrictor reportedly got out of its sideshow cage, made its way to the main tent, and encountered an elephant. In what sounds like journalistic license, the snake "coil[ed] itself around the elephant's body," leading to "shrill trumpeting" and a "rush for the exits" by frightened patrons.[66] These stories sounded a bit too much like the sensational sideshow banners that advertised the snake acts, but their dramatic appeal was undeniable.

A Kind of Scientific Circus

Zoos were the other major institution that placed snakes on stage. Zoos around the world, and in the United States, were created as scientific educational institutions. The idea of the public garden designed for recreation, education, and scientific study came after Louis XVI's collection was opened to the public in Paris, and the London Zoo opened in 1828. Germany also housed similar institutions in cities like Berlin and Frankfurt, and wealthy Americans traveled to these zoos and brought the idea back to the United States. American city zoos started for a variety of reasons, but some of the largest ones, like the Philadelphia and New York zoos, emulated European zoos to the extent that they could. Their express purposes were public education and recreation. The education would come from collecting and displaying different kinds of animals so that the American public could tour the grounds and see what the animals looked like in reality, rather than in the fictional accounts of writers and artists of the past who sometimes made up the appearance and behavior of animals, as we have seen in the case of snakes. They were also designed as institutions to preserve rather than kill animals. Records of zoological gardens date to ancient times and they parallel the very long history of killing animals for sport, food, or the visual method of taxidermy as a method of displaying them. So, in the context of their early times, zoos were the better option for an animal compared to death for food or killing for the purpose of stuffing and displaying in a museum.

The idea behind zoos is clearly illustrated through the founding of the National Zoo. The Smithsonian was one of the American museums with a large collection of stuffed animals that hunters had given for the purpose of justifying and paying for their hunts. Giving the animals to a charitable institution was a tax write off for wealthy Americans who went on hunting excursions and brought back animals. William Temple Hornaday was one such hunter and later an expert taxidermist who worked for the Smithsonian. Through his own experience of hunting, he realized that he and his fellow hunters were exterminating animals in the American west. He subsequently became an advocate for preserving American species, including, for example, the American bison, and as we have seen, American rattlesnakes. His ideas and taxidermy work caught the attention of the director of the Smithsonian, Samuel Pierpont Langely, in 1887, who subsequently appointed Hornaday to create a National Zoo dedicated to recreation, science, and the protection of American animals. Under Hornaday, the Smithsonian campaigned for a new zoo that would serve as a "refuge for the vanishing races of the continent."[67] The additional goal, however, was the advancement of science. Just as the Smithsonian's stuffed animals educated Americans, so would these animals, with the added benefits that their movements, smells, and behaviors could be observed.

To be sure, there are varieties of individual mammals that guests could learn about, so zoos exhibited them, but they could not compete with the huge number and varieties of reptiles. Elephants come in a few different types from different continents, and large cats are the same, for example. But the numbers are relatively limited and therefore require less time and scientific investigation to determine which ones are in the wild. In contrast, there are thousands of snakes and other reptiles, and this gave scientists interested in animals and the outdoors a perfect area of study that could continue for years. Zoo directors like William Mann, who eventually ran the National Zoo from the 1920s through the early 1950s, and Roger Conant, who directed the Philadelphia Zoo, got their start as young people collecting snakes and other reptiles and corresponding with herpetologists in zoos. As we have seen in the case of antivenin, the number and possible questions about them were endless. Where did they live? Were there subspecies? What size were they? What color? How did they reproduce? Were they venomous and if so, to whom?

Zoos capitalized on the scientific possibilities of the vast collecting necessary for scientific study by going on extensive collecting trips around the world. We can see the scope of this work through William and Lucille Mann's collecting for the National Zoo. In 1925, William Mann was appointed director of the National Zoological Park. In 1926, he led the Smithsonian Institution–Chrysler Expedition to Africa, an expedition to Central America in 1930, British Guiana in 1931, the National Geographic Society–Smithsonian Institution Expedition to the East Indies in 1937, Argentina in 1939, and the Firestone–Smithsonian Institution Expedition to Liberia in 1940.[68] Lucille Mann traveled with him on these expeditions as an unpaid laborer who helped collect, feed, and transport the animals back to the United States. Prior to that point, Lucille Mann, like so many people, was afraid of snakes and had very little experience with them. Partly to get his wife acclimated to them, he once brought home a small snake, hid it in his pocket, and then introduced it to Lucille and other friends at a card game. In another instance, he insisted that they babysit for a friend's corn snake, named Elaine Cleopatra McGuiness. Mann also started a group he called the Vivarium Society, which was a more open version of the Washington Biologist's Field Club, that met on Plummer's Island. The Vivarium Society was an amateur herpetological group dedicated to young people who liked to keep cold-blooded pets. They met in the zoo office and mostly boys brought whatever their current pet was, and it was "nearly always a snake."[69] At one of her first meetings, a young man brought two black snakes coiled around one another that the group passed around. The point of the society was both social and educational, like the zoo itself.

The capturing and exhibiting of animals, however, was the real purpose of the zoo and at that time they took elaborate trips to bring animals back from the wild. These were the days before breeding programs and before significant animal welfare legislation, so when zoos wanted to expand the animals they housed, they typically either traded with one another, or if they had the funds like the National Zoo, they could get them from their native country. At one point, for example, Mann wanted reptiles from Central America, rhinoceros from India, and giraffe from Africa, so they designed their collecting trips around these goals. They chartered ships or took freighters because they could transport a lot of animals in that way, because the ship owners could get tax write offs, and because they did not have the tranquilizing agents that they did later so when they put a large cat in a cage, for example, it was wide awake and likely unhappy most of the time. Airline transport of animals only became more reasonable when the numbers were lower and they could tranquilize the animals for enough time to safely get them into the plane. The reaction of other passengers on the freighters varied when they arrived with "several hundred snakes."[70] They typically tried to hide the snakes and did not discuss them with the other passengers. They generally kept other passengers out of the freight areas with the animals to make sure that no one got hurt. The captains and crews of the ships knew, however, and had to enter the freight areas at times because of their jobs. As a result, like the train crews in the United States who collected and transported venomous snakes for antivenin, they were not always particularly happy about the snakes. To make the job seem more appealing, the Manns would strategically introduce the captain to more gentle animals they were transporting, like giraffes. In one instance, they won the friendship of a particularly resentful and hostile captain by bringing him down to the holding area and letting him pet some giraffes they were transporting.

They "collected everything that came along," and they came home from one trip, for example, with "several hundred kinds of turtles" because the local people, or natives, as she called them, just kept bringing them.[71] They did some excursions into the wild to capture the animals as we shall see, but much of their collecting was done by staying on the ship, putting the word out that they were in town, and meeting with local people who brought the animals to their ship or freighter to sell. In other cases, the animals were on sale in markets in the cities, and they simply bought them by going to the shop or walking through the open market to see what was for sale for food or as pets. William Mann's theory was that it was better to accept any animal that local people brought because if word got out that they were not taking any new animals, then they might miss out on the really unique animal that they had not yet acquired. So they brought back lots more animals than they initially wanted or needed. To be sure, they were limited by some local permitting laws on very rare animals. The Dutch, for example, required permits for some animals. But on the whole, the lack of animal welfare protection anywhere in the world facilitated their collecting. To collect the animals, they hired local people because they knew where to go in the wild, which markets had them, and which people already had them as pets and might be willing to sell them. On the Mulford Exploration of the Amazon Basin, they brought back "forty cages of monkeys and parrots and all kinds of things."[72] William Mann brought back 1,700 animals from his Chrysler expedition, many of which were snakes.[73] Their help on trips was enormous at times as well. On their trip to Liberia, they had "sixty or eighty boys" who helped them with their hunting. The Manns had four men each who carried their hammocks.[74]

In 1930, they went on a collecting trip to Central America, specifically to collect reptiles. They took trips to Havana, Panama, Barro Colorado Island, and Honduras. Sometimes the United States had facilities, companies, or connected scientists who served as their hosts. The Barro Colorado Island center was connected with the American Museum of Natural History, for example. And the biological study area in the Canal Zone was financed in part by Thomas Barbour. The Barro Colorado Island station was a small place consisting of a laboratory with a few bedrooms, a bathroom, a common area, and a kitchen. Only the elite stayed in these places though, not the poorer people who were involved in the circuses. Alice Lee Roosevelt Longworth beat Lucille Mann as the first woman to get to stay on the island, for example. Lucille Mann's job on the island was to collect snakes, which was evidently not very successful on that particular trip. In Honduras they went to a little town called San Pedro Sula, where there was a man who collected snakes to milk them for antivenin. They stayed for a few days and bought the entire collection of venomous snakes, which they placed in canvas bags and took with them on the train back to the coast to their ship. They also collected reptiles at the United Fruit Company station at Tela, which was a plantation right on the coast. The company also ran a quasi-research station where a few young college students lived and did research.

On their trip to Monrovia, Liberia, the Manns were inducted into the Snake Society. They were staying in Belleyella, in a military garrison, and one of the soldiers stationed there offered to introduce them to members of the local Snake Society. They decided to do it because they thought that some of the men involved might know where the best snake collecting places were and help them capture them. They made a monetary gift to get into the society, so the people involved were using them as well for economic gain.[75]

When it came to snakes, the purpose of all of this collecting was to stock the recently constructed reptile house that Mann built with funds from the New Deal. In addition to the snakes he had collected, captured, or bought on his trips, he had snakes coming in from around the United States. A "friend" in Texas had "nineteen cages of rattlesnakes ready to send," for example.[76] As we have seen from the zoo network that produced antivenin, his friend was likely either Martin Crimmins, or possibly the Snake King. Mann had wanted his reptile house to serve three related goals. First, he wanted it to be a fun and educational experience that combined the enjoyment of the circus with learning. To that end, he wanted a representative collection of snakes from the United States and around the world. Unlike tigers, snakes came in an enormous variety, and he wanted people to understand nature's complexity. Second, he wanted guests to get to learn a little about the animals' natural habitat, so the reptile house was on the cutting edge of its time in enlightening people about the plants and landscape that the animals lived in, even if these were often just painted background scenes. And the final purpose of the reptile house was to get Americans to respect the reptiles by learning about their power, which in the case of rattlesnakes and cobras, included the ability to kill people. He hoped that people would become fond of them if they saw them in the context in which they could not get hurt or at least not have contempt for them.[77] Although his snake and other reptile collection was for American citizens, it was also aimed at his fellow elite herpetologists and ichthyologists. This was a state-of-the-art institution, a kind of geek show for people who knew about the global representation of snakes, minus the scantily clad women. The American Society of Ichthyologists and Herpetologists called the building "an outstanding development in public education in America" and formally thanked Congress for funding the project. Mann's building influenced other zoos in Toledo, Chicago, Detroit, and San Diego, among other zoos.[78]

Although they did not offer any scantily clad women as part of their snake show, they did have snake theater that took a variety of forms. Some zoos, like circuses, had snake pits. The differences were that that they were permanent and more attractive. The Toledo Zoo's reptile house was designed in the Spanish architectural style, and inside the house, in the center of the room, was a snake pit sunk into the floor surrounded by a wooden fence and some potted plants. The Detroit Zoo also had a snake pit in the 1920s that was permanent, outdoors, and spacious. There was also actual theater involving snakes that consisted of a poor version of the circus acts. The Detroit Zoo had theater performances that lasted from the 1930s until the early 1980s. The main attraction, initially, was Jo Mendi, the cigar-smoking and whiskey-drinking chimpanzee who performed 12 to 14 shows daily at the zoo theater. One of Mendi's fellow performers, later in the 1960s, was Maureen, a 14-foot python who was brought on stage and held by a male zoo keeper to demonstrate her size. The Detroit Zoo also let Leonard Nimoy (who played Spock on the original *Star Trek* series) hold a python in 1976 when he visited the zoo as a way to get photographs of a celebrity that were in turn used to advertise the zoo.[79] Sometimes snakes were also taken out of their enclosures to educate guests in a kind of impromptu educational display. Karl Kauffeld, the curator of reptiles at the Staten Island Zoo, took snakes out to display to small groups of young guests in the mid 1930s. And Dr. Patricia O'Connor, a staff veterinarian at the Staten Island Zoo from 1947 to 1970, regularly offered educational shows in which she took an indigo snake to hospitals, nature clubs, and hobby groups. At a time when disabled children were kept out of school, O'Connor did special lectures in which she invited them to the zoo to learn about and touch the snakes. The St. Louis Zoo had regularly scheduled python snake feeding shows in the 1930s that were held in a grassy outdoor area. Large crowds of people formed a semi-circle and watched the show. The zoo placed a large python on a long tarp and several zoo keepers held its body while another zoo keeper force fed the python a meal. The final, perennial theater favorite was milking snakes for their venom, which the zoos in turn gave initially to do Amaral and later to the Mulford Pharmaceutical Company. Like the feedings, these were staged affairs that zoos sometimes charged admission for as well. The number of actors involved depended upon the size of the snake. Cobras took more men to hold them still than rattlesnakes, for example. Sometimes the audience members were also given their own nonvenomous snakes to pass around during the show so that they could feel something akin to what they were watching. In the 1940s, the Barrett Park Zoo on Staten Island had two educational shows at 3:00 and 4:00 p.m. on Sundays in the reptile wing. They forced a rattlesnake to strike at something, milked venomous snakes, and handed around nonvenomous ones.

The purposes of these theatrical and educational performances were complex. Herpetology curators, as we have seen, knew first hand the devastating consequences of bites, so they wanted to let other people know just how difficult it was to hold large snakes, how quickly venomous snakes could strike, and how much venom they could produce. Starting with the arrival of the automobile, they also believed that increasing numbers of people were heading into the wilderness where they might very well get bitten. As a result, the educational lectures served as one of the few rational sources of public health information about how to prevent death

Park employees holding a snake, 1906 (Art and Picture Collection, New York Public Library Digital Collections).

from venomous snakebite. Raymond Ditmars, the reptile curator at the Bronx Zoo, urged hikers to wear long pants and leather leggings when they hiked. He also suggested that they not reach above their heads to rock ledges that they could not see. But another central reason that zoos had to have educational shows was a legal one. In a particularly important court case, Blanche v. Guzzi, the judge concluded that zoos could house and exhibit dangerous animals because they were educational institutions. That idea was later placed into the major piece of animal welfare legislation in the United States regulating zoos, the Animal Welfare Act, which protects a zoo's right to exist as long as it is exhibiting animals for the purpose of educating the public. As the animal welfare movement emerged, interest groups like the Humane Society of the United States and sympathetic zoo directors themselves pushed these institutions to phase out shows that seemed more like entertainment than education. Snakes remain an ambassador animal that some zoos take on the road or hold shows to educate people about, but the force feedings and the venom extraction demonstrations were ended.

It is clear that snakes commanded intense attention from audiences. Exotic and horrifying, snakes could draw crowds most anywhere and made money for a variety of professions. Newspaper stories focusing on snake-related accidents served to keep their dangerous reputation alive, a reputation upon which entertainers depended. The fairly regular reports of snake attacks reprinted in newspapers across the nation assured that the public was ready to accept the sensational promises of circus barkers, sideshow banners, and zoo-keepers.

5

On Screen

Snakes in the Movies, Reality Television and Documentaries

Snake movies, reality TV shows, and documentaries explore many of the themes that run throughout the history of antivenin in the United States. There, the danger of living with snakes is undisputed, the audience is not at all cynical, and the movies and shows exaggerate the potential violence or document it in various ways. Snakes are an undeniable favorite among television viewers if one looks at the number of possible movies, documentaries, and reality TV shows about them. One rough way of gauging their popularity as a topic is to compare eco-horror genre movies about animals. When we count up the most popular animals, snakes come in behind sharks and dinosaurs as the preferred scary creatures of the animal world. This makes a fair amount of sense since all three are admittedly much more frightening than, say, frogs, even when they are featured in a film called *Hell Frog Warrior*, or beavers, who made their appearance in *Zombeavers* (2014). Even spiders are no match for the reptiles with film titles like *Big Ass Spider* (2013) or *Eight Legged Freaks* (2002). And clearly, they trump other benign kinds of non-animal, eco horror threats like tomatoes as a possible danger, even with an intriguing title like *Killer Tomatoes Eat France* (1981). When we examine the narrative of three snake eco-horror movies, we can see that the themes that emerge in them echo the scariness that people have faced with snakes in real life in the United States. The themes and style of the movies are, in turn, picked up by the reality TV shows that return us to many of the dilemmas and struggles faced in the past with snakes in the United States. To illustrate this pattern, a review of three snake movies will illustrate how they capture the fears that people have about snakes and then set the structure for the reality TV shows and documentaries. Recent reality TV shows highlight the clashes between Americans and snakes and bring American audiences up-to-date, to a certain extent, about the struggles of living with one another. As we shall see, however, they still leave us with questions and hide the ongoing problems with snake and human interactions as well. There are also circus-like elements to the shows that echo earlier times. Instead of a traveling circus, this is a fixed one brought into the TV viewers' homes. They do not need to go see the freak or geek show, they can watch it while sitting comfortably on their couches. They too have paid a fee to see snakes, but now it is to the cable company rather than the circus or zoo. Much of the same entertainment is now happening—we are still watching snake milking for example, but now the shows have a mass audience rather than a local one. Production companies are now facilitating the killing of snakes on a mass scale, which is disturbing because circuses and zoos did not engage in the wholesale capture of venomous snakes for slaughter or sale.

Snake Eco-Horror Films

Snake eco-horror cinema draws from the same themes as other eco-horror genre films. Sometimes a particular kind of animal violates the separation of the species and attacks humans, as in the case of *Jaws* (1975), for example. Other times, humans are responsible for harming the animal, either directly or through habitat destruction, and this leads to revenge attempts by the animals.[1] In animal horror films, we see how easily the boundary between humans and animals can be violated. We perceive ourselves as the dominant species, but they intrude on our lives in countless ways in the films. Human characters often find themselves face-to-face with the animals, unwittingly giving access to them somehow, or stumbling into their world. Inevitably it is a dangerous world in which the animal controls the environment, and the humans who exist among them are either complicit with the animals, surviving and not telling the newcomers, or worshipping them in pagan-like ways. Civilization always seems a long way away in the very remote jungles, deserts, and mountains where the animals reside. The people from civilization who go into the animals' habitats and incur their wrath are also supposed to be punished in some cases because of their greed (they are hunters), like the ship captain in *Jaws* who knows where to find the shark because he has hunted sharks for so long. In the end, these characters are typically killed, and the innocent and naïve central characters from cities (read: civilized places), learn their lesson about transgressing the boundaries of the animals' homes or bringing about the habitat destruction that caused the animals to multiply, change, or increase in vast numbers. The animals are sometimes presented as monstrous, either because they are hybrid monsters and animals, or more frequently, because their size has been dramatically exaggerated to make them seem more dangerous. They also have a sense of evil and are consciously motivated to kill humans, rather than flee, as most of them would in reality. This justifies the brutal violence against them because the humans are represented as the victims. Animals are not actually harmed in the making of the film, but they are always killed and often mutilated as characters so that humans can reassert their dominance and take control of nature. Three movies that nicely capture the genre of snake eco horror are *Anaconda* (1997), directed by John Masters; *Curse II: The Bite* (1981), directed by Jill Schoelen; and *Snakes on a Plane* (2006), directed by David Ellis.

In *Anaconda*, a researcher (Eric Stoltz) and his production crew are cruising up the Amazon to document and study a little-known tribe. The group includes a few other researchers and a camera crew. On the way, they pick up a snake hunter, played by Jon Voight, who offers to show them where the tribe is located. The tribe worships giant snakes, as the research team can see when they cruise into the tribe's territory and see a snake-shaped totem pole on the riverbank. For various reasons, the travelers have to get off the boat and are eventually attacked by enormous anacondas who bite people in the face and wrap themselves around them to kill them. The snake hunter's real motive is money. He wants to capture a snake for the large amount of cash it would make him. As they go up the river, their ultimate encounter with the largest snake is foreshadowed by smaller snakes that seem to drop into the boat along the way. People get hurt when they get off the boat because the vessel is their safety and there are other animal dangers that are lurking in the water. Voight's character is the knowledgeable, skilled hunter. He is also a male predator himself, and we see the theme of gender in the movie both by the fact that the snake hunter, who has the real expertise, is male, but also when he tries to sexually attack Jennifer Lopez, a member of the production team. Sexuality also runs through the movie because the production crew are attracted to one another and express that at various points. In this fictional version of a snake story, the snakes are sinister, sneaky, and calculating.

They invade people's space by crawling onto the boat. They intentionally surprise them and spend large amounts of time stalking them. Voight's character opines that "anacondas are the perfect killing machines." He educates and scares the audience by sharing how they kill their prey. The "power of their embrace causes your veins to explode," he tells his fellow travelers. When other characters realize that he is really just a coldly calculating capitalist who is willing to ruin everyone's life on the boat to get what he wants, his shipmates accuse him of being the devil. He replies that "there is a devil inside everyone." He is simply acting out this part honestly and taking what he can. Eventually the biggest anaconda finds them and tries to kill them when they have gotten off the boat and are in the most remote area in which they can find themselves. Ice Cube, one of the other cast members, however, vanquishes the snake after a long fight sequence, during which the snake survives explosions and burnings.

We see some of the same themes in *Curse II: The Bite* (1981), but this film is different and captures another eco-horror theme in that it reflects on how human decisions have exacerbated snake problems. In this film, a young couple are traveling through Yellow Sands Nuclear Base in Arizona where the United States government exploded nuclear bombs that caused a genetic mutation of rattlesnakes. As in *Anaconda*, The two main characters, Clark and Lisa, encounter other snakes foreshadowing the really bad snake that they are going to find. In this case, the smaller early snakes sometimes seem to be running away from something scary. As in *Anaconda*, foreshadowing snakes invade the couple's safe space, in this case their car, by getting inside and hiding. They have a flat tire that needs fixing and they pull into a kind of repair shop, that is also partly a ranch, to get help. The man who works there has a southern accent, which in this case seems to suggest that they are a long way from the more urban areas in Arizona. As in *Anaconda*, they are in a very remote area without help, and now they are also among the natives who are vaguely threatening and have learned to survive among the snakes. While there, Clark takes a trip inside the repair shop and does a little investigating when he hears the sound of a dog under a covered crate. When he pulls back the cloth covering, a dog with a rattlesnake's face lunges at him. In this way, we learn that the rattlesnake situation is really bad in this part of Arizona and get a sense of what is to come. Shortly thereafter, Clark is bitten on the hand by a rattlesnake who has hitched a ride in his car. A disreputable local bystander ties a bandana around his arm in the form of a tourniquet, for the ostensible purpose of keeping the venom from spreading, and urges him to get to a hospital quickly to get antivenin. They pull into a hotel, explain what has happened and that they are in need of a doctor. It turns out that a traveling salesman staying at the hotel tells him that he has a vial of antivenin and gives him a shot. This is the wrong antivenin, and the hand begins to slowly mutate into a rattlesnake head as they continue on the rest of their journey. The snake venom invades Clark's body and instead of killing him, eventually turns his whole body into the mutant rattlesnake. In the meantime, however, the audience gets to see the terrible damage that the snake venom has done to his hand by stripping it of skin, turning it bloody, and creating dead tissue. A religious (perhaps Mennonite) farmer takes pity on him when Clark climbs into his truck after he has pulled over at one point. He explains to Clark that "God only asks if his children need help," not what they have done, and takes Clark back to his house with his wife and daughter. Like Eve tempted by the snake in the Garden of Eden, the little girl cannot resist looking under the gauze on Clark's hand, and the hand that is now a snake attacks and kills her. The snake then goes on its final rampage, killing the farmer and simultaneously disgorging small baby snakes that will continue the mutant line. In the end, Clark searches for Lisa and tries to kill her, but he is killed by a back-country sheriff who had pulled the couple over earlier in the mistaken belief that they were drug dealers.

Both films provide us with a *Heart of Darkness* quality. In both cases, the main characters are traveling in a vessel into dangerous territory and no one should "get off the boat," as Chef says in the movie *Apocalypse Now*. If they get away from their life-saving, man-made vessels—the boat or the car—the dangers are too great. The terrible beasts are out there, but so are the people who live among them and have come to coexist with the animals. The people are just as much the feared "other" as the snakes are. They are all dangerous, threatening civilized people, but tempting as well. They too are untrustworthy and motivated by evil. The sexuality that is present in both films ties women to the snakes by subtly suggesting that temptation leads to death. Both the women and the snakes are tempting and cause problems. The people living near the snakes do not have much money, are poorly educated, and are in league with the snakes who are out to get the urban and suburban folks. The message is clear: the closer people get to these kinds of animals, the less civilized they are. These themes recreate the history of snakes and Americans from the perspective now of filmmakers—a new kind of elite.

Snakes on a Plane differs somewhat from typical snake horror films because this time the snakes are intentionally used as weapons by sophisticated gangsters. In the story, a teenager in Hawaii (Sean) witnesses a gangster, named Eddie Kim, kill a man. FBI agent Neville, played by Samuel L. Jackson, is tracking Kim and finds his associates trying to kill Sean. Agent Neville provides witness protection for Sean, but flies him back to Los Angeles to testify against Eddie Kim, who is in jail there. Kim orders his fellow gang members to find the plane that Sean is taking and place venomous snakes on the plane to kill the teen. The gangsters spray pheromones on leis in boxes and place the snakes in boxes in the cargo area. The pheromones make the snakes particularly vicious and ready to attack people. The snakes are released from their boxes through a timer and begin their deadly assault on all passengers. They make their way to the front of the plane where Sean and the FBI agent are seated. All kinds of venomous and nonvenomous snakes are in the boxes, including cobras, rattlesnakes, bushmasters, and even an anaconda. The snakes are extremely aggressive and sneaky as they attack people in the face, hide in their purses, and come up through the toilet to attack. They completely take over the plane, overwhelming everyone in their path. They are an invasive species in our civilized world. When a rattlesnake bites a little boy, one of the other women passengers takes off her earring and uses it to cut open the bite site. After she makes a shallow incision on the bite site, we see the venom come pouring out, showing us that cutting open the incision site really works. A voice on the loudspeaker recommends that people with blisters from the snakebites cut those open as well and (presumably) let the venom flow out. They know that the passengers need antivenin, however, and members of the crew contact a snake expert who tells them what kind they need and helps the FBI track down Kim's associates in a warehouse in a rural area. The bad guy has a list of the snakes on the plane as well as all of the necessary antivenin for the different kinds of snakes. When the plane finally lands at Los Angeles International Airport, paramedics and the snake expert are there to meet them with the antivenin. To help us understand how the paramedics would know which snake antivenin to give each passenger (the old snake identification problem that plagued doctors), the movie has a scene in which one of the boys drew a picture of a cobra who bit his brother on the hand.

This film differs in some ways, yet repeats themes from our history with snakes in others. In this case, the bad people are not rural poor people or people of color in developing nations who live in remote areas. Now the bad guys are sophisticated gangsters. Snakes are still associated with the wrong kinds of people, and these people are still motivated by money, but this time the evil people connected with snakes are smart enough to enter our world rather than the other way around. Unlike the rural bumpkins who are under the control of snakes in their environments, this time, the bad guys control the snakes entirely. Snakes are now weapons and antivenin is the civilized world's method of protecting itself. Most of the people on the plane are completely innocent victims, and we know this because they are placed in the ultimate marker of civilization—an airplane. A variety of kinds of people are bitten on the plane, but we know that they are not poor people because they are on a plane, which costs money, and many of them have spent their vacation in Hawaii, another signifier of wealth. In short, the victims could not possibly have brought this on themselves. Now we see that antivenin works, but we also see the fictional cures of sucking out lots of venom from bites as part of the story as well. In this way we have a kind of medical performance that seems familiar from the past.

All of the themes from the eco-horror movies are repeated in nature documentaries about snakes from science education television companies like the National Geographic Channel and the Discovery Channel. To make these programs more entertaining, rather than simply educational, the snakes are uniformly portrayed as dangerous and many of the people who work with them are poor and from rural areas. The snakes are clashing with people on the remote areas of the United States—on the border lands—but this time it is the snakes who are in trouble.

Python Hunters

National Geographic's *Python Hunters* reality TV show follows the narrative of snake eco-horror movies, and uses their tricks of dangerous sounding music and staged scenes to heighten the sense that snakes are dangerous and bad. Instead of taking over a boat or a plane, this time Burmese pythons have taken over the Florida Everglades. Theories vary on how the "Burms," as the actors call them, have taken over. One possibility is that Hurricane Andrew created this particular invasive species because there was a reptile breeding facility right on the edge of the Everglades at that time that allegedly housed around 600 baby Burmese pythons. The facility was constructed from the same kinds of building materials that one finds in greenhouses and thus it was extremely vulnerable to the wind from the hurricane that ripped it apart. The baby pythons escaped into the Everglades, but it is not clear how many of them survived because small pythons are easily eaten by larger predators like hawks. However, many of them may have made it because surrounding dense foliage, coupled with abundant water and food, provide an excellent habitat for the snakes. Another possibility is that there were enough abandoned pet Burmese pythons that they created a colony in the Everglades. Or perhaps it was a combination of the two problems that created the python invasion. As the narrator tells viewers, this poses two problems: first, the snakes are killing other animals, some of which are endangered species, at an alarming rate; and second, there are so many pythons that they have spread out of the Everglades and into farming and suburban areas. As a result, the Florida Fish and Game Department created a program to hunt the pythons and issued 15 permits to experienced handlers. The three profiled on the show are all exotic snake breeders, and they include biologist Shawn Heflick, policeman Greg Graziani, and Michael Cole. "The snake breeders are defending the Everglades," the narrator tells viewers.[2] This time the pythons are the bad guys because they are an invasive species that is killing our good native species. They are like prosperous immigrants taking jobs from Americans. The show takes place deep in the Florida Everglades, and the distance from civilization is stressed by the spooky music that accompanies the snake handlers as they make their way through the dense foliage. The narrator somberly informs viewers in multiple episodes that the snake is reproducing at a fantastic rate. Rightly or wrongly, the narrator tells viewers the python problem is viewed as a public safety issue. Although the narrator tells viewers that "no Burmese pythons have ever attacked humans," Larry Dunagan, a local farmer, increases the drama of the show by noting that the pythons are "getting closer and closer to homes. Now they are getting rats and rabbits, but when those run out it's going to be small dogs and hopefully not a child."[3]

Because these snakes are killing our own kind, there is no question that they deserved to die. Viewers learn that the hunters must capture and humanely euthanize as many of them as possible. Instead of the rattlesnake bounties of the past, this time the hunters are paid partly by their appearance in the episode. Snakes who are not killed will be used for "further study," the narrator tells viewers.[4] In every show, the men capture snakes, so presumably the other 12 hunters with permits are out doing the same job on a fairly regular basis, although they are not getting filmed doing it. The narrator tells the audience in one episode that "over 600 Burmese have been captured."[5] The spectacle is sanitized and justified by science. These are not just killers, they are men of science who are measuring the snakes, identifying their locations, and taking their temperatures. "Every python they catch," the narrator reassures us, "provides much needed data."[6] The entire emphasis, though, is on the spookiness and danger of the snake hunt and the size of the snakes once they are caught. When they are caught, the men put the snakes in a bag, and we never see what happens to them. Their goal is to catch snakes until the entire invasive species has been eradicated.

The python's monstrous nature is stressed to highlight the good work that the men are doing and make the job seem necessary and exciting. Viewers are told that although the python is not venomous, it has a painful bite in which 100 sharp teeth can dig into prey. Clips of Burmese pythons eating large prey, like alligators and deer, are used to demonstrate the scary nature of the snake's ability to open its mouth extremely wide and squeeze its victims to death. The narrator reminds us that the "bigger the animal, the harder they will strike,"[7] and one episode is dedicated to finding a "monstrous" mother python, who they fear is disproportionately causing an increase in the number of baby pythons in a particular area.[8] Here we have fear of female reproductive power from the immigrant snakes breeding their competitors out. The hunters never find the snake and attribute her absence to the presence of a large alligator who might have eaten her.

The show also walks a fine line between warning us about the pitfalls of exotic reptile ownership, which can lead to the nightmare scenario of escaped snakes on our streets and national parks, and promoting the breeding work of the cast. The breeding operations of the men are shown and profiled in the episodes, providing them with another means of increasing their income by free advertising. The show simultaneously appeals to the ophidiophobes, who are terrified by the snakes, and the snake lovers who want them as pets. We learn, for example, that Michael Cole is an expert in creating new snake colors and has sold his snakes for thousands of dollars. Cole makes a trip to Miami International Airport to show us how exotic snakes arrive and are inspected by Fish and Wildlife Officers. We learn that reptile smuggling is a $20 billion industry and hundreds and thousands of reptiles are smuggled annually.[9] Shawn Heflick's breeding and rescue facility is profiled repeatedly to illustrate his knowledge about exotic snakes. The men attend a reptile exhibition where exotic snakes are for sale, and they are there to serve as experts, but they have brought some of their animals as well. Heflick and his wife also bring their 23-year-old Burmese python, Fluffy, around to schools to teach students that snakes are not as dangerous as people think. The narrator informs viewers that there is a large exotic reptile collecting community in Florida. Between 1996 and 2000, around 100,000 Burmese pythons were legally imported. During that time, there were 13 reported deaths by pet giant constrictors. To place this in perspective, more than 700 people were killed by dogs during the same time frame.[10] And yet, the narrator tells viewers that Burmese pythons are too much pet for most people to handle. They need constant handling to make them docile around humans. Unfortunately people get them when they are small and handle them at that time, but start to lose interest as they get bigger. If they are not handled, they start to strike at people and pose a real hazard, and suddenly they are an unwanted exotic pet that is likely to get released outside. Burmese pythons are also seen as a kind of masculine pet that people can wrap around themselves to look tough. In a presentation to his fellow snake enthusiasts at the reptile exposition, Graziano tells his audience that there have been too many of these unwanted animals, and now politicians in Florida are introducing legislation that would severely regulate their trade.

As in the movies, the show makes it clear that the humans are winning. Despite the premise that the pythons are taking over, the hunters have a harder and harder time finding any snakes to capture, even the small ones. Part of the explanation for the small number is that Florida had some cold winters with frost and Burmese pythons die in that weather. But it is clear that the hunters were very efficient and effective as well at killing large numbers of the snakes. So efficient, in fact, that the show had to turn to other types of invasive reptiles for a continued story. They even, occasionally, come upon a small rattlesnake, but they do not pursue these because that concept is already owned by other shows.

Venom Hunters *and Snake Wranglers*

"The planet faces a worldwide venom shortage," the narrator of *Venom Hunters* soberly tells the audience as he introduces the Discovery Channel's reality TV show. "One hundred thousand people per year are killed each year from snakebite" and thousands of others are injured by snakebite. "Venom is needed for antivenom,"[11] viewers are told, because, as in the past, there is a worldwide antivenin shortage. But what about hospitals? Don't they already keep antivenin on hand? Again, we are reminded that there is not enough. One venom hunter explains, in Episode 3, that "hospitals keep very little antivenin on hand because it's expensive." They might have three vials there, but a big bite can take 48, he explains.[12] There is no Afranio do Amaral to save us this time; now we are on our own. The show gives the impression that we must collect and make the venom ourselves, even while in reality, the major current manufacturer of antivenin is based in the United Kingdom. *Venom Hunters* follows the snake hunting of four professionals who capture venomous snakes, primarily in the United States but also in Australia, for the overriding noble purpose of keeping people alive. They catch snakes for their venom, and also, they admit, for the thrill of the hunt. Other motivating factors are explored in the show (revenge and money are frequently stressed as well), but the justification for the show is capturing the snakes for their venom for medicinal purposes. In the past, venom collecting was only seen in the final stage by zoo guests as they watched the snakes being milked. Now, however, more of the venom-collecting process is used for entertainment. The venom is primarily used for antivenin, the show's viewers are told repeatedly, but as we shall see, the hunters tell us that there are other medical uses as well.

The types of snake hunters the audience meets in the show are the same types who hunted snakes in the past. There is the self-described Oklahoman wild man, Tim Fitzer, and his crew. Fitzer is a backwoods taxidermist who says that he is trying to break into the snake hunting business to supply firms with venom to cure a variety of illnesses and for antivenom (the show calls it antivenom for the sake of its viewers who are unlikely to be familiar with the term antivenin). He tells us that a local lab called him and is looking for all of the western diamondback venom he can find. We learn in a later episode that antivenin is typically created from the venom of four snakes: western diamondback rattlesnakes, eastern diamondback rattlesnakes, Mojave rattlesnakes and cottonmouths. If he can fill this order for western diamondbacks, then the lab might become a regular client.[13] Fitzer is the epitome of the hunter. He is the kind of outdoorsman who used to be portrayed by journalists as dismissive of the problem of snakes. Only this time, the show's more candid emphasis on real human-snake problems uses Fitzer and other characters to show us how dangerous it is to interact with venomous snakes. The show introduces us to him through his home, which is set back in the woods and full of animals that he stuffed as a taxidermist. Almost every open space in the house has a stuffed animal on the wall, including at least one partial rattlesnake with its mouth wide open in a bite mode, and the rest of half of its body coming out of a wooden plaque. Fitzer has long hair, in all episodes wears a skin-tight black t-shirt, some kind of animal claw necklace, jeans, and boots with gaiters to emphasize his toughness, but also his wisdom about walking around near snakes. His team includes Kevin Baker, a kind of rural nice guy who wears a checkered short sleeve shirt and jeans with a cross to illustrate his Christian beliefs, and Hannah Lockhart, who is a tough cowgirl, usually wearing bling-covered cowgirl jeans, a cotton shirt, and the same type of camouflage boots to protect her legs from snakebites in the regional grasses that hide the snakes. In case the viewers could not identify that Fitzer's team is Christian, they pray at one point in a later episode. Lockhart, for example, prays to the Heavenly Father for a "hedge of protection around all of us."[14]

The rest of the teams on *Venom Hunters* harken back to the amateur herpetologist snake hunters we saw previously in this book. Ed Chapman and his apprentice, Justin Bottrell, are the classic snake businessmen. Chapman, who lives in Florida, is well spoken and clearly more suburban. Chapman is typically dressed in a checked shirt, but one that could come from an outdoors store near an upscale mall, and the type of cargo pants that men buy from L.L. Bean or other men's wear stores that cater to the middle class. The audience learns that Chapman was bitten once, and that he had an allergic reaction to the venom as well as the antivenin that almost killed him. His apprentice, Bottrell, resides in Southern California but has been apprenticing with Ed for many years. He hopes to take over the well-established business Chapman created supplying snakes to labs.

In the first episode of *Venom Hunters*, "Bad Ass Labs" has called and needs three cottonmouths. Brian Barczyk and his partner, Chewy, are similar to Fitzer and his group in the sense that they are trying to break into the venom supply market. Barczyk has snake tattoos on his legs and Chewy looks like a typical suburban dad. They hope to be global players, however, so we see them in Australia in all episodes, where they are trying to catch venomous snakes.[15] Dan and Melanie, the final team, are reminiscent of members of the scientific collecting communities like the "Vivarium Society," an amateur herpetological society to which the director of the National Zoo, Thomas Mann, belonged. These two are clearly middle-class collectors who are interested in catching snakes for scientific reasons, and are the most interested in conserving the animals. Dan has a college degree that he got after he lost the lower halves of both his legs to severe pain. He had been in another profession, but realized that a college degree would help him in his next career, so he went back to school, read more about the snakes, and continued collecting them, but his education gave him more knowledge and compassion.

Rattlesnake Republic, Animal Planet's reality TV show about rattlesnake hunters in Texas, focuses primarily on the struggles between humans and snakes and is significantly less conservationist than *Venom Hunters*. These crews are entirely male, and their primary focus is to hunt the snakes to make money and to rid Texans of rattlesnakes on their property. These teams consist of so-called nuisance-control businessmen (the kinds of people who come and remove squirrels, raccoons, and bats from inside houses). Through their profession, they are licensed to kill the animals they collect although they do sometimes indirectly collect animals for venom. One of the central motives on the show is rescuing Texans in distress. The problem, as we have seen in the past, is that there are very distressing situations that do frequently bring humans and snakes into a collision course, and it is helpful to remove the snake from the situation so that children are not bitten, for example. As in the past, moreover, the teams are also motived by money, either as showmen in small local celebrations, as hunters who sell their snakes to a middle man on the show, or as trophy hunters for large snakes.

The show follows four crews of snake hunters that capture the non-scientific snake handling community. Jackie Bibby is a Texas snake legend who calls himself the "Texas Snake Man," and is described as a snake showman. He wears a rattlesnake-skin bowler and drives a white hearse repurposed for his snake-hunting business, nuisance-control business, and showmanship. He is often accompanied by two other men: Mike Herzog and Dougie Dugger. Both wear worn cowboy hats and sunglasses, and one frequently has a toothpick sticking out of his mouth. Their competitors are Robert Ackerman and Shawn Jones. These two are also middle aged, but they are more clean cut. They wear baseball caps and typically are not wearing sunglasses so we can see their eyes. They are in competition with Bibby, however, for a piece of his showman business at fairs, so they are close to his business style, even if they are a more modern looking incarnation. Like Tim Fitzer, the show also has a team led by an experienced, but seemingly economically struggling outdoorsman named Riley Sawyers. Like Fitzer, Sawyers has a long ZZ Top–style beard that seems to mark the American wild outdoorsman who is generally removed from some of the norms of American suburbia or city life, and struggles financially. He too has a hunting partner, Dalton Fritz, who is a complete novice and is trying to learn the business. Although Sawyers is portrayed as struggling, he is actually part of the Sweetwater Jaycees and works on public relations for the Sweetwater Rattlesnake Roundup, the legendary Texas springtime event in which hunters bring in around 5,000 pounds of rattlesnakes that are milked for their venom, weighed, sexed, measured for research purposes, and then slaughtered in a "meat room" for their hides and meat.[16] At the other end of the class spectrum, we have the father and son team of Eric and Rick Timaeus, a respectable, middle-class, small family business that makes money primarily on nuisance control calls and on taking people on trophy hunting excursions for large rattlesnakes. They wear a middle-class outfit of collared polo shirts, cowboy boots, and jeans, and are the kind of businessmen that Texas suburbanites and ranchers call to get rid of problem snakes.

The shows have clear gender messages.[17] They are overwhelmingly male, and their masculinity is a central feature of the show. There are only two female cast members on *Venom Hunters* and there are no permanent female cast members on *Rattlesnake Republic*, which typically showcases women as fearful victims, places them in spectator roles, or uses them for sex appeal. In Episode 1 of *Rattlesnake Republic*, Tim and Eric Timeaus come to the rescue of a pool party with scantily clad women in bikinis who are screaming about a rattlesnake who wanted access to their water. The camera spends a significant amount of time on the cleavage of the women in bikinis and camisole tops. In Season 5 of *Rattlesnake Republic*, Robert Ackerman brings along a woman friend to remove some rattlesnakes from a farm. She is a middle-aged blond woman, named Roxy Edwards, and is in a skin-tight green tank top, cutoff jeans shorts, and cowgirl boots. The narrator informs the audience that his hunting partner, Shawn, objects to her being there because, in his opinion, there are "too many risk factors in bringing a woman like this along." He describes her as a good-looking older woman and insists that "she's going to get her ass bit." In case we did not notice what Edwards was wearing, Shawn points out that she has on "a little bitty pair of shorts," which the narrator informs us could result in a rattlesnake "bite ... above her boots."[18] She insists on pinning the rattlesnake, does a bad job of it, and gets ordered back to the truck by Shawn. The narrator informs us that the men can stick together despite the intrusion of this woman. "The boys have a job to finish, and no fight can stand between them and a hefty pay day."[19] Season 3 features Edna MacDonald as a prop. MacDonald is a 95-year-old who has been catching snakes since she was around 10 years old. Jackie asked her for help finding snakes, ostensibly because he was struggling to find them. Edna meets with Bibby and assures him that she has a den on her property. He is clearly amused by Edna's age and continued enthusiasm for catching venomous snakes, but his business partners do not share his enthusiasm. One of his partners says, "It's too dangerous. We get up there and she gets snakebit, probably wouldn't make it." At "95 years old, a single venomous bite would be fatal. This is just a stunt for you."[20] Viewers are clearly meant to worry about Macdonald hiking up one of the hills on her property in the searing heat looking for a rattlesnake den. Her age and gender are the handicaps that might bring on the much hoped-for bite. But like the woman in the magic show who is cut in half in the box but miraculously appears whole, MacDonald proves them wrong and shows them the den where they find and capture around 20 large rattlesnakes.

There are, however, some exceptions to the gendered message that women are weak and unprofessional. Hannah Lockhart, on *Venom Hunters*, is a strong cast member. Even though he is a wildman, Fitzer has a kind of feminist perspective. He supports Lockhart's tough nature, her independence, and her drive. Viewers watch her catch a large rattlesnake and a coral snake all on her own, a dangerous move as the audience is told repeatedly throughout episodes on both shows. Snake hunting is safest with at least two people. Hunting alone can be fatal if one is bitten and cannot get back for help.

The apprentice men and all other women, however, are treated with disdain on the shows. Apprentice men are portrayed as fearful, naïve, and unfocused. During one hunt, for example, Justin Bottrell is described as "having a hard time staying on task." Chapman, his boss, notes that "he's been screwing around all day long," and "he is out there putzing around looking for the wrong snake."[21] The apprentice's fear is sometimes highlighted through disagreements between team members. Fitzer and Kevin Baker illustrate this dynamic. "I wish Tim would listen to me like he used to," Baker says. "I'm going to suggest that we get the heck out of here" because of the danger and frustrating nature of the hunt. But Fitzer says, "sometimes I felt like I was the only guy out there busting my ass."[22] Similarly, the narrator tells viewers that although Brian has been training Chewy to be an international venom hunter, "his fear of snakes has been his vulnerability."[23] Women, in general, are described disdainfully by the cast members. To take one example, Chapman and Bottrell are hunting for rattlesnakes in Kimball County, Texas, where they are walking through areas with lots of brush and some downed trees. Chapman accidentally brushes his leg against one of them and cuts it on the wood. Bottrell is worried about how much the cut is bleeding and suggests that they need to attend to it. Chapman's response is "we're hunting snakes, we're not out here trying on girls' dresses," and he assures Bottrell that he can stitch it up if he needs to.[24] In another episode, Chapman and Bottrell get separated, and Bottrell confides that he felt like "little red riding hood running through the woods."[25]

Venom Hunters is the most conservationist of the shows, but neither show is particularly concerned about what happens to the snakes or interested in their well-being after they are captured. On *Venom Hunters*, the snakes are typically caught by the collectors, placed in a soft bag, and then put in their backpacks for the trip back to a (sometimes unnamed) lab that has asked them to capture the animals. There are only a couple of episodes in which we actually get to see what the labs look like and what happens to the animals. At their most conservationist, we have Episode 4 of *Venom Hunters*, in which Dan and Melanie are collecting black-tailed rattlesnake venom for the director of the Arizona Poison Control Center at the University of Arizona. This is the only episode where we get an actual representative from the medical community verifying that they need the venom. In this case, a doctor explains that they need the black-tailed rattlesnake venom because they had a recent case in which a man was bitten, and they struggled to keep him alive with the antivenin they had. They knew that he was bitten by a black-tailed rattlesnake and were wondering if perhaps the snake had mutated and its venom was now significantly more potent. The director requested that Dan and Melanie get venom from that same kind of snake in the same area, the Santa Clara Mountains, in Arizona. The director assures the audience that "the work they do helps us further our research of venom and anti-venom research."[26] The couple successfully finds a black-tailed rattlesnake and milks it in the wild, noting that they will not take it out of the wild because the snake's numbers are dwindling and they do not want to further endanger them.

The same concern, however, is not shown to other venomous snakes that are captured and taken on the shows. On *Venom Hunters*, occasionally we see the lab and where the snakes will live the rest of their lives. Just as the rattlesnakes milked by Klauber for their venom lived in his basement, these animals are not in any kind of expansive Butantan-type farm where they will live a decent life. Nor are they in the smaller, but at least glass-enclosed and lighted small space at a zoo. Instead, they spend the rest of their lives in small plastic drawers that are stacked on top of one another for maximum efficiency and safety of the people who work with them. We only occasionally get to know what the labs are called or who staff them. We learn, for example, that George Van Horn has a reptile lab in his Reptile World Serpentarium in Florida. However, some of the other labs are left a mystery, which might be partly to prevent people from breaking in and stealing the expensive antivenin that they have on the property, but the sad state of the snakes' lives also suggests that the labs may want to keep animal welfare protesters away as well.

To prevent us from questioning why the snakes need capturing, the narrator on *Venom Hunters* frequently tells its audience that the animal the hunters caught will produce a significant amount of venom for the rest of its life, but does not say it will do so in a place that has no concern for its welfare other than to keep it alive. Our consciences are assuaged in each capture episode when the narrator explains what the venom collected might do, although there is no discussion of the fact that medical research is not guaranteed to produce results. Sometimes venom has worked very well as a cure for health problems (in addition to snakebites), but other times researchers have hit dead ends with venom.[27] For viewers of this series, the benefits of venom are unquestioned for their scientific necessity. In Episode 2, the narrator informs the audience that Tim Fitzer has been asked by a client to capture copperheads because "a protein in copperhead venom can prevent cancer cells from multiplying."[28] Brian Barczyk goes to Australia for black snake venom that a lab wants for Alzheimer's research, but there is no questioning of this on the show. There may be a scientific researcher doing cancer research with copperhead venom, but there is no discussion of who this is, whether cancer research has been done using the snake venom in the past, and whether the project is likely to succeed. We also learn that an unnamed lab is using taipan venom for blood thinners, but do not get any sense of how this compares to other blood thinners. Are all blood thinners made out of taipan venom? The show does not pursue any of those questions. The cast also plays to this medical use for a sense of urgency and explanation about their work. They are not just doing this for the adrenaline rush and excitement, for money, or to show off how brave they are. This is for scientific research. Hunting copperheads and lamenting how few he has found, Tim notes that "one snake is not going to be enough to cure cancer," so the implication is that he needs to keep hunting more.[29]

Danger

The shows are all about the thrill of the danger involved with snakes even when the danger is sometimes staged for viewers' entertainment. There is a written one-line disclaimer in each episode of *Rattlesnake Republic* that informs viewers that some of the situations have been dramatized, but this is placed at the end with the credits and is easily missed. Both *Venom Hunters* and *Rattlesnake Republic* follow the narrative of eco-horror movies in their setting, their music, the casts' lines, and their foreshadowing. We see that they are in dangerous and remote parts of the United States and the rest of the world, and the shows play that up at every chance. In contrast to the past, the message about venomous snakes is really clear: the places that the snakes live are very remote, and the kinds of people who live in those remote places are different and more wild.

The snakes will bite you, they will kill you, and you may not make it out alive because it is a very long distance to help. Nearly every scene with a snake is a potential bite scene. In case viewers are unable to sense that, the ominous music reinforces the dangers, and the cast typically comments on how dangerous the situation is. There are frequent shots of rattlesnakes striking out at the hunters in both shows as they come upon them or try to put them in bags. There is only one person who seems to be actually struck by a snake during an episode, but it is not clear if he is actually bitten. *Rattlesnake Republic* repeatedly shows the results of a bite that one of the characters received to dramatize their harm. The narrator will frequently note that the snake is curled tightly and ready to strike to heighten the drama. The casts constantly point out to one another how dangerous and erratic the snake is behaving as it tries to defend itself from death or permanent capture for milking purposes. Like viewers at a car race, there is the real potential for injury or death in every episode.

Both shows' emphasis on danger is clearly partly driven by liability reasons. If they claimed (as many have done in the past as we have seen) that snakebites were not that bad, that they were very rare, and we do not need to worry about them, then they would risk having huge numbers of people who watched their show head out into the wilderness to take up collecting for money. The shows' producers could be accused of creating a situation in which people died because they had understated the snakes' dangers. To help prevent that, *Venom Hunters* has verbal and textual warnings that remind us of the educational work that their predecessor snake collectors like the Bronx Zoo Herpetology Curator, Raymond Ditmars, issued in the 1930s and 1940s. It warns viewers, "Do not attempt anything you see," between narrated sections in various episodes.[30] At the start of the show, the text warns that if viewers attempt this on their own "without proper training [they] could die." And if death is not scary enough, the show also warns aspiring amateur hunters that "without a special permit," they could be arrested.[31] The show also informs viewers that the snake hunters are "licensed professionals,"[32] and in that way warns amateurs of the perils of taking up this business without training.

Playing up the danger, however, has the added benefit of making the story riveting. Will they get bitten? Will they die? They are always headed out into dangerous and remote territory in every episode. Snake hunting, and by extension venom hunting, is much different from the movies in which the snakes are everywhere ready to pounce. In fact, the opposite is true. The snakes are typically hidden, trying to stay safe and comfortable, and so they are only found by going into areas that are sometimes remote, as the movies show. In other cases, the horror is that they are right among us without our permission or knowledge. The cast members play up this danger at every opportunity. "Dude this is scaring the [expletive] out of me. Every minute I handle this snake is more of a danger,"[33] one cast member says. "They are just the ultimate killing machine," Chapman tells the audience.[34] The narrator reminds the audience that they are "deep in a Texas forest."[35] Episode 5 of *Venom Hunters*, Season 1, is entitled "Bitten" although no one is actually bitten in that episode. The purpose of the title is to partially explain Ed Chapman's motivation for capturing snakes, which he explains is partly for educational reasons. He was bitten in 1972 by a pygmy rattlesnake in Florida, the kind of snake that he is currently hunting for that episode. It nearly killed him, we learn, because it was a pregnant female, and she was trying hard to defend her herself and pumped a lot of venom into his arm. Sometimes, the names of the places they go capture the danger. Brian Barczyk goes to Savage Crossings, Australia, to capture death adders and taipans. The narrator tells us that Brian and Chewy are "dancing with death in the breeding ground of Australia's most dangerous snakes. One misstep could be fatal."[36] In another episode, the narrator tells the audience that Fitzer is leading his crew "into hostile terrain."[37] *Venom Hunters* emphasizes the bite numbers as well. In the remote Carta Valley of southwest Texas, western diamondbacks bite between 6,000 and 7,000 people per year, the narrator tells viewers.[38]

The snakes' lethality and physicality are also constantly stressed to heighten the thrill of the shows. Before each snake-hunting expedition in *Venom Hunters*, a graphic illustrates what happens when one is bitten by one of these venomous snakes. Their deadliness is always stressed. The narrator also frequently points out the additional ways that the animals are dangerous. The narrator tells us that eastern diamondbacks can strike up to 175 miles per hour.[39] Their size is often stressed as well, as the narrator informs the audience that western diamondbacks can grow in excess of six feet long. When hunting for eastern diamondback rattlesnakes in Appling, Georgia, Fitzer warns his crew that they have a "long strike range. You get too close, you get killed."[40] Riley sends Dalton, his assistant, under one of his client's houses who has at least one rattlesnake in the crawlspace. As we watch Dalton climb laboriously into the hot, small place, the narrator reminds us that "rattlesnakes can slither up to eight feet per second," and it is clear that there is no way that Dalton could be safe if a rattlesnake struck him in that situation.[41] Chapman's bite gives him some authority, and he can vouch for how painful it is. Botrell asks Chapman to tell him what it feels like to be envenomated, and he says, "Put your finger in a fire, hit it with a hammer. That's what it feels like, and that is just in the first few minutes, and then it gets worse."[42] Fitzer was also bitten on the lip by a timber rattler, and this is offered as a motivating factor for his snake hunting. The title of Episode 3 of *Venom Hunters* is "A Score to Settle," and it refers to Fitzer's ostensible desire to revenge his bite. As in the snake eco-horror movies, he's going to fight back and avenge himself. Animal welfare advocates may point out that people are encroaching on rattlesnakes' territory, capturing them, at best turning them into property, and forcing them into what is effectively slave labor, but the shows have no such concerns.

As with the movies, there are foreshadowing dangers along the way. We hear the sounds of birds crying, and Chapman notes that "birds will get in an attack mode and make noise when a snake is around," so it seems like one might be close. Wasps repeatedly attack crews as they pass through the woods looking for snakes. Tim and his crew are attacked as he walks through the woods, and later Chapman, Botrell, and Dan and Melanie are as well as they make their way through the trees and brush looking for snakes. One of the characters is allergic to wasp venom and carries an EpiPen. Chapman and Botrell are drenched by a thunder and lightning storm during one of their hunts, and Botrell points out that there "is no antivenin for a lightning bolt."[43] Tim and his group run into a patch of poison ivy that forces them back to a local hospital when Hannah gets it on her eyelid. Tim Fitzer's crew gets their truck stuck in a stream. The crews also frequently find shed snake skins along the way, portending the possibility of other snakes. We learn in *Rattlesnake Republic* that a shed skin may mean that the snakes are large because snakes that eat well can shed up to four times per year. This foreshadows the presence of large, well-fed snakes.[44] Or, they find a snake that is in the process of shedding its skin and is therefore extra dangerous because it struggles to see, so it will lash out more frequently at perceived danger. They also come upon foreboding and abandoned structures that provide homes for snakes. An abandoned prefab trailer that is ripped apart in the woods is home to a large rattlesnake. "What happened to these people?" Tim asks, in a line that could have come straight out of any eco-horror movie.[45] And members of *Rattlesnake Republic* are repeatedly descending into stone food cellars, structures built in the United States before the age of refrigeration to keep food cool in the west and south. They are dark places without any electricity, and the cast members have to walk into them with flashlights to see if the snakes have taken up residence there.

Another danger both shows stress is climate change, although *Rattlesnake Republic* is a little confusing about its effect. Why talk about rattlesnakes now when Americans have been bitten presumably since they first crossed into the rattlesnakes' territory? The answer, *Venom Hunters'* narrator intones at the start of each episode, is climate change. Like the man-made nuclear testing that creates the mutant snakes in the fictional version in Arizona, or like the man-made agricultural expansion that attracted rattlesnakes to farms, the show acknowledges the fault of humans in creating the snake-human conflict. "Climate change is forcing snakes out of hiding," the narrator says, and this has created more bites as people and snakes come into greater contact.[46] And later, "Record-breaking temperatures are forcing snakes out of hiding."[47] *Rattlesnake Republic* also stresses the climate, but even though they are hunting in the same state, they argue that the heat is making snakes scarce. An odd proposition given that some of the cast members seem to have great success in finding large numbers of snakes. In this way, we see science marshalled to justify entertainment rather than the more complicated truth, which is that money is one of the other motivating factors behind the hunting of snakes.

Business

Just as in the past, capturing snakes is partly about saving people, but also about making money. *Venom Hunters* are in the business of collecting "liquid gold," which is the title of the first episode.[48] To illustrate the profitability of hunting venomous snakes, *Venom Hunters* always stresses how much venom the snake produces once they milk it, and frequently also points out how much the captured snake will produce over its lifetime. In a later episode, the narrator informs the audience that Dan and Melanie are "digging for another kind of treasure: a black-tailed rattlesnake."[49] Tim Fitzer is one of the more articulate voices of the capitalist nature of his work. Snake hunting is a business, and he has to be able to make it work. "I've got orders to fill. I've got deadlines to make."[50] He refers to the venom as "the product."[51] "Let's go get liquid gold," Lockhart says in one episode.[52] "I gave up my financial security to chase a dream. Every hunt has to be a success," Fitzer tells us.[53] Fitzer is new to the business and trying to get it started, so every penny counts. "I've got my whole life savings riding on this,"[54] he reminds the audience. Barczyk tells the audience that "it costs a lot of money to be here."[55] Shawn Jones takes a trip to "Snake Island" in Texas, which he confesses "sounds more like money island to me." There he hopes to find his "money hole," because islands like that can shelter lots of snakes.[56]

The impediments to the business are also stressed to create sympathy for the venom hunters. In one episode of *Venom Hunters*, Fitzer confides that he is having trouble paying his bills. But small problems get in the way of successfully catching snakes. When Hannah Lockhart, his fellow hunter, gets into some poison ivy, the audience realizes that he is going to lose time getting her patched up at the hospital. He confides that he "wasn't prepared for any kind of expense like this."[57] Lockhart is not his daughter, so he would not have been required to pay for her medical bill, but the implication is that he did pay for it, although a trip to an emergency room can cost thousands of dollars, far more, presumably, than the snakes brought in. Luckily, like the men, she's very tough and is ready to go right back out into dangerous territory even though the doctor warns her that the heat could make the poison ivy she has on her eyelid worse. The show promotes sympathy for the characters through their struggles in a capitalist economy. These are just small-time businessmen and women like those in any other occupation.

The pay is typically very small for each rattlesnake, but can increase substantially through trophy hunting. As in the past, these are really bounty hunters, but now money is paid exclusively by a private company owner rather than the state government. *Rattlesnake Republic* has a disposal process that primarily includes selling the snakes to Leroy Higginbottom, a legendary middleman snake dealer who buys the snakes for a top-end amount of $6 per pound, but does not explain where the snakes go from there. Judging from the emphasis on the rattlesnake hides he hangs around the inside of his business, however, many of them are killed. And trophy hunting brings in one of the biggest paydays of all. Rattlesnakes over six feet are rare and collected by hunters. A trophy hunting trip with the Timeauses costs $2,500 per trip.[58]

The entanglement, as Haraway would put it, of snakes on farms and ranches that we have seen from the past is one of the underlying themes of both shows, but it is explored explicitly in *Rattlesnake Republic*. On *Venom Hunters*, the cast hunts snakes on expansive ranch property, although there is no emphasis on that show about how the ranch owners feel about the snakes. In contrast, the writers for *Rattlesnake Republic* explicitly highlight the fact that sometimes ranchers do not want snakes on their property. In one case, Timeaus and his son are called out to catch rattlesnakes on a ranch because they are described by the owner as large and mean. In this particular episode, they struggle to find the large and scary snakes until the night falls, their car dies, and they have to spend the night out among the snakes. Typically, venomous snake hunters are struggling to get out of the area before sundown, because that is when human visibility is lowest and the snakes are the most active, so finding themselves stranded there at night, supposedly without cell phone coverage, heightens the drama of the show. It is not clear why everyone's cell phone coverage died including, for example, the camera operator, but it leads to high drama and echoes the plots of eco-horror movies. According to Timeaus, they will only hunt and remove the male rattlesnakes, however, because "they do serve a purpose. They keep the rodents down, so ranchers want them on their farms."[59] In another case, they are called out for a clearer economic reason. In Episode 3, Timeaus and his son go out to a horse ranch to rid the place of a nest of rattlesnakes. The narrator points out that the owners sell expensive horses, and although they do not discuss their ranch in detail, it seems that this is a quarter horse breeding operation with foals that can easily have a low starting price of thousands of dollars. The last thing that the ranch owner would want is to have either his or her breeding mares, or their foals, bitten and die. As we have seen from the problems in the past, the narrator notes that horses are sometimes bitten on the head as they graze in the grass, and depending upon the location of the bite, they can suffocate and die. There is also a clear class bias in the show, because the two most clean-cut rattlesnake hunters (Timeaus and his son) are the ones who are consistently called out by ranchers to remove snakes. The ranchers want middle-class rattlesnake professionals, not showmen, on their property.

Circus

Other viewers, however, want the showmen, so the television shows give them that as well. *Rattlesnake Republic* offers viewers circus-like performances without their having to leave the living room. Sometimes the show is staged to look like an outdoor hunting expedition and other times they provide viewers a show about a performance. In Episode 1 of *Rattlesnake Republic*, Jackie Bibby and his business associates travel to a rattlesnake den located in a cave on the side of a large hill. They see a rattlesnake at the opening of the cave and feel confident that there are more in there, but the narrator, like the circus ringmaster, heightens the fear. "The highest concentration is often found in the deepest, darkest corner of the den."[60] So the viewers know that he is going to have to go into the den to brave the snakes. The entrance to the cave, however, is very small, so Bibby has to crawl in head first. Once inside the cave on his belly, Jackie finds himself face-to-face with a rattlesnake. We are told that Bibby now needs to carefully extricate himself from that dangerous situation, and the group decides that the best way to do that is by pulling the rattlesnake out of the cave by its tail. This requires that they pull the snake out right next to Bibby while he is lying there. "Any sudden movement can mean a deadly strike to the head," the narrator intones, "his life is literally in his partners' hands."[61] After he is rescued, Bibby adds to the drama by sharing that he was thinking that the cave "might be his final resting place," even though there is no evidence that his partners would have left him there to die. This whole hunting episode seems like an un-staged workday until we see effectively the same stunt performed by Bibby's competitors in a fair.

Each year Flores, Texas, hosts an annual Peanut Fair where there are a variety of festivities, including a parade and sideshows. Bibby and his associates had typically performed in a rattlesnake show at a pit under a tent designed for that purpose. The pit is an enclosed white wooden structure, about adult waist high, with glass panes down near the bottom for children's viewing opportunities. The snakes are placed in the pit with people standing there with snake sticks to push them away when necessary or move them around.

Bibby's competitor Robert Shawn and his associate decide to perform a version of the act we saw in nature by placing a sleeping bag in the middle of the snake pit floor and asking Danielle, a woman assistant, to get into the sleeping bag with over 20 snakes. It is called "Robert Shawn's Death Defying Snake Show." As in the case of the cave, Robert Shawn would go head first into the bottom of the sleeping bag where his male associate places the snakes in the gap between Shawn and the end of the bag. The woman, who is not part of the show in any regular way, but is just a temporary worker (presumably to add some sex appeal to the show), lies with her feet pointed to the bottom of the bag. She expresses some real concern about the stunt, but agrees to do a dress rehearsal. The trick to the show is that Shawn has to stay perfectly still or the snakes will bite. Unfortunately he twitches just the tiniest amount and a snake strikes him on the head. Conveniently it does not bite him, so viewers get the thrill of the attempted bite without the actual disasters that would ensue with a bite to the head. The narrator increases the tension of the moment by reminding viewers that "a rattlesnake strike to the head is the most dangerous strike because it causes swelling to the brain."[62] The woman quits, illus-

Children look at rattlesnakes in a pit designed as a performance venue for snake handlers, often at fairs or rattlesnake roundups (courtesy pixabay.com; https://snappygoat.com).

trating her comparative feminine weakness, and Shawn decides to do the show alone. But it is worth it because he tells viewers, "These shows ain't for fun. We make real money at it."[63]

Rattlesnake Republic uses this as opportunity to stage another snake performance. The premise for the next one is that Bibby is mad about the competition and angry that his venue has been taken away from him, because he will lose money. So, he too decides to stage a show, although it will only get him publicity, not actual revenue. The publicity is worth it, however, because he can get nuisance calls later from the parade attendees, he tells the audience of the TV show, and that will bring in real revenue. Bibby's stunt follows the theme of his hearse vehicle and is very much like the cave stunt as well in its emphasis on proximity to snakes and claustrophobia. He puts on a death-defying snake stunt as he would in a circus. He and his associates drive the hearse through the parade and drape younger women on the hearse, again to get some sex appeal into the show. Then at a certain point in the parade, they stop the hearse to do the show. They bring out a wooden coffin and place Bibby in it. But this time they place wooden blocks around his head, so that the snakes are prevented from getting up to his neck. His associates then drop the rattlesnakes into the bottom of the casket around his leg and genital area, close the casket, and place it back into the hearse. The big question, then, is "will Bibby die" in the coffin in the hearse? Or, at least, will Bibby get bitten on the legs or in the genital area while in a hearse? Bibby notes that the snakes are "getting awful friendly," and just in case the audience is unable to figure out the connection between the hearse and the show, the narrator notes that "we hope the hearse will not be used for what it was designed for."[64] The worst that happens is that he gets really hot in the coffin, but we get the circus-like theatricality of the performance, so the audience does not go away empty handed. The hearse stunt was not enough, however, to appease Bibby, who also decides to reclaim his record of lying in a sleeping bag with the most snakes at the Rising Star Homecoming Festival celebration in Rising Star, Texas. The performance gives his crew the justification for hunting 23 fresh rattlesnakes to bring to the show, break Robert Shawn's new record, and perform the same stunt again for the audience.

The ultimate TV snake circus act, however, is sold as a scientific experiment involving giant green anacondas in Paul Rosolie's *Eaten Alive* documentary. In this film, Paul Rosolie, a researcher of giant anacondas, uses a protective suit that allows a giant green anaconda in the Amazon forest to squeeze him and partially eat his head. Rosolie is rescued, however, from the grasp of the snake by his large expedition team when it is on the verge of breaking one of his arms while squeezing him. This is a millennial documentary complete with an entirely young cast, a drone used for locating snakes, high-tech computer health-monitoring technology, and a *Blair Witch Project* filming style in the scary scenes of the jungle. The stated scientific goal of the documentary is to experience and measure what it is like to be eaten by a giant (20-plus-foot) anaconda and measure the pressure that a victim experiences. One of the sub goals of the show was initially to prove that anacondas do eat people. As with the early American shows that faked relationships between black snakes and small girls, this show also draws our attention to snake myths that are now circulated via doctored Internet videos. The show notes that most of the stories of large snakes eating people are faked, but sometimes, they note, the stories are true. In 1995, a Malaysian rubber plantation worker went on an errand into the woods and was attacked by a python. His brother found him dead in the grasp of a python who was devouring his head. The narrator informs the audience that the central problem that large snakes face in eating people is that they are unable to get their jaws around the widest part of the body: the shoulders. People, then, are defined as adult men, because presumably the snakes would have no trouble getting their jaws around male or female children, and, one would assume, a small woman. Equating men with all people who must be saved, allows us to follow the documentary's logic that it makes sense to test the idea scientifically that an adult man can be eaten by a 20-plus-foot anaconda.

Rosolie has a special high-tech suit constructed for this purpose that consists of several protective layers and built-in measuring devices designed to relay biological data. The show uses all of the same tricks of foreshadowing that eco-horror and reality TV shows use to heighten the thrill of the forthcoming stunt. The narrator notes that the team is "300 miles from civilization and any medical assistance they might need," a fact that fits awkwardly with the fact that we later learn that the team has a physician along on the trip to monitor Rosolie's vital signs during the stunt. The audience is told soberly that the river is "teeming with deadly aquatic life," including caiman and venomous snakes. They are going to the "darkest corner of the Amazon," and like the rattlesnake hunters in *Rattlesnake Republic*, they come across the shed skin of, in this case, a "monster anaconda," foreshadowing their later meeting.

Rosolie's stated purpose is also conservationist. "The Amazon is in crisis," the audience learns, from "rampant deforestation, and illegal logging." Studying these enormous anacondas, the show implies, might help slow this down if only more viewers knew that the snakes were there. Somehow, just the knowledge of their presence would translate into the hard political activism needed to save the Amazon rainforest. At one point, the show quickly shows a link about a conservationist site for anacondas, but unless one knew to stop the show or had purchased the show, it is unlikely that most people watching it would translate their new knowledge into political advocacy. Somehow, the fact that there are scientists on the show suggests that the animals will be protected. Rosolie tells us that they are an international team of explorers and experts, and they are chosen for their scientific expertise, but also their loyalty to him as friends who he can trust to save him from the snake if necessary. Their mission, the audience is informed, is scientific in that it is partly to understand the population distribution and breeding behavior of anacondas that travel the river before they get to the Floating Forest—a large pond surrounded by a dense forest—where they breed. "Any data collected by the team will be invaluable to herpetologists around the world," the narrator informs viewers.

This is science, not a circus stunt, although it seems very much like the stunt of lying in the bag with the snakes. In this case, however, the snake wrangler is lying inside the snake rather than inside the bag. Like fiction and reality TV, Rosolie is looking to break a record. This time it is the largest anaconda ever seen. Rosolie tells the viewers that the "Amazon is the greatest natural battlefield on earth," and he is looking for an "anaconda of truly monstorous proportions" that he had seen during one of the ten years he had lived previously in the Amazon studying anacondas. As with reality TV shows or eco-horror films (or great whale stories), Rosolie has had a personal experience with this animal who he believes measured about 24 feet, 7 inches. During a previous expedition, the audience is told, the snake appeared next to him in the water while he was in a boat on the Amazon. Rosolie and his co-researchers jumped on the snake, and it dragged all six of them into the water and eluded them by diving down to the bottom of the Amazon and escaping. This documentary, then, was a circus stunt designed to educate a larger number of people than circuses had in the past. Our hero this time was willing to put himself in the jaws of the beast, just like a circus lion tamer. Other snake documentaries take the danger even further for viewers' entertainment by showing us people who self-immunize against venom.

Self-Immunizers

Like Martin Crimmins, there are still men who make themselves immune to venom, but now they are subjects of documentaries and provide the public with entertainment. These men go way beyond the circus snakes with their fangs extracted or the man partly eaten by an anaconda with a large team to bail him out. Now we get to see the actual bites and the venom injected into real people. Finally, the audience can watch real and repeated bites, even if the results are significantly less disastrous than they would be if the person bitten had not already developed an immunity to the venom. To make sure that the gore is still there, befitting the snake eco-horror genre, however, the audience gets to see blood. When the self-immunizer uses a real snake to bite him (rather than injecting pre-collected venom with a syringe), then at a minimum the audience gets to see the bloody bite and perhaps a bit of swelling. When the documentary shows the self-immunizers using needles to inject pre-collected venom, the horror is maintained in the same way that reality TV shows do it, which is that they show pictures of previous bites to which the cast members did not prove immune. Bloody and grotesquely swollen hands and arms with skin that has been removed are shown to illustrate what happens to snakebite victims, but also to entertain the audience.

There are around a dozen self-immunizers around the world who work with snake venom. Four of them—Steve Ludwin, Ray Hunter, Norman Benoit, and Tim Friede—are Americans. Among this group, only Ray Hunter has a doctoral degree in herpetology. The rest are amateur herpetologists, but all of them, including Hunter, have collected and owned snakes since they were young. Although he is an American, Ludwin lives in London, where he keeps venomous snakes in plastic storage boxes in his apartment. He milks the snakes then injects the full amount of venom that he just milked without diluting it with water. In the BBC documentary *Man Who Injects Venom* (2009), he tells viewers that he is "exercising [his] immune system" by making his "white blood cells charge the venom."[65] He claims that he was born to work with venomous snakes and knows the risks. All of the medical experts on the documentary (and others) agree that people can build up an immunity to venomous bites by injecting themselves a little at a time with the venom, just as pharmaceutical companies do with horses and sheep, and as Martin Crimmins did. The problem is that there are serious risks, including death. Ludwin had an allergic reaction to one of his injections and discussed it with Wolfgang Wuster, a zoologist at Bangor University, who pointed out to him that if the venom does not kill him, then the allergic reaction could by closing off his airways until he is unconscious and unable to breathe. Ludwin tells viewers, however, that he thinks of what he does as like owning a motorcycle. He is aware that it is risky, but he is willing to take the chance. In London, he works with immunologist Dirk Budka, who screens Ludwin's blood for ways in which it could be used to treat illnesses. He offers that there is a possibility that some day we all may be asking why we did not inject snake venom because of the range of possible bacterial infections it can attack. By the end of the documentary, we learn that Ludwin's blood does actually have properties from the venom that attack the bacteria from MRSA, pneumonia, and E. coli.

Like circus entertainments and reality TV shows, these self-immunizer documentaries are all about excitement and men's love of snakes. They love them so much that they literally come to replace other relationships, leading to failed marriages. Ludwin travels to Florida to meet Ray Hunter (known as Cobra Man) and Norman Benoit, whose wife has forced him to move his self-immunization work to a commercial storage center. While on his trip to Florida, we see the adrenaline rush that all snake hunters get by visiting a reptile breeding facility and searching for snakes in the

Florida Everglades. At the breeding facility, Ludwin holds a king cobra for the first time and tells the audience that "that was the most exciting thing I've ever done." He's excited by the fact that the snake handler at the facility "almost got bit," but he tells viewers that he "wanted to kiss" the cobra because it "looked [him] in the eyes" and has "an intelligence." This documentary gives the viewers the tantalizing prospect that they can watch someone inject themselves with a toxic substance and then have a terrible effect. There are several scenes of the men injecting themselves with venom and then waiting to see if it will have any impact. The Cobra Man explains that he injects himself with a cocktail of venom that comes from snakes including (among others) the black mamba, cobra, coral snake, boomslang, Egyptian cobra and the West African green mamba. The audience watches with concern as Ludwin injects coral snake venom, which we are told is 2.8 times more toxic than cobra venom when measured drop for drop. It is also neurotoxic, and Ludwin had been immunizing with hemotoxic venom, so the drama of the moment is that the audience does not know whether this particular injection will cause a catastrophic physical reaction.

All of the men insist that they are doing their work for the sake of science, even as the viewers wonder if they secretly want to die. In discussing his immunizing with the film's narrator, Ludwin assures his viewers that he is not "flirting with death," and he does "not want to die," even though this is exactly what he is doing. Tim Friede, another self immunizer, in the short documentary by Barcroft TV called *Venom Man Lets Deadliest Snake Bite Him*, very casually tells viewers, "If I die, bury me. Piece of cake."[66] These men place multiple types of venom together in injections to see what, if any, reaction they get, and they seek out the deadliest kinds of snakes the way that a drug addict would look for the next big high. It is difficult not to wonder whether, at a minimum, they are addicted to the adrenaline rush of not knowing whether they will live or die with each injection.

They all claim, however, that they are doing their work for science. Ludwin is ecstatic when Dr. Budka tells him that his immunized blood attacked the pathogens in MRSA, E. coli, and pneumonia cultures, and killed around 95 percent of them. He tells viewers that this is the goal he has been working for all of his life, and now it looks like it might actually help people. Ray Hunter does not self-immunize for the sake of using his blood to help others, but he tells viewers that his collection of 350 venomous snakes is partly for exotic pet collectors, but also for venom milking. He sells their venom to universities where medical researchers are working on various cures. Tim Friede's wife makes a guest appearance on his documentary, and they discuss his failed marriage. He says that he wishes that he was not "so selfish" about injecting the venom, but that the tradeoff of losing his wife and son was worth the possibility that he could save millions of lives if his scientific work pays off. The problem, however, at least at the time of the documentary, was that there was no lab or group of doctors clamoring to use his blood to cure even one person, let alone millions.

All of the snake reality TV and documentaries are exactly like the early attempts by amateur and professional snake enthusiasts to entertain and enlighten people about snakes at the same time. They, in turn, draw their narrative from the snake eco-horror genre to keep the audience watching. Zoos have been criticized for many years as simply entertainment, not really educational institutions, but their herpetology focus does not even come close to the circus-like and extremely violent nature of reality TV and its snake education. The wholesale slaughter of rattlesnakes by the hunters on *Rattlesnake Republic* is not filmed directly, but it is implied as we see the snakes' skins hung up at the middleman's store. The only bad guys in the documentaries are exotic pet owners who let their snakes go. The massive capture and slaughter by the cast members, even some with scientific credentials, is accepted as necessary for science or human preservation. Hundreds of Burmese pythons are quietly taken away and killed for our entertainment. The animal abuse of jumping on an anaconda or of setting the animal up to eat a person in a fake suit is accepted as education simply because it is shown to viewers as reality TV or as a documentary sponsored by National Geographic, and because there are few legal animal-welfare protections for snakes in the United States, or elsewhere, unless they are endangered. The message is clear: they are all nuisance animals, and we are at war with them. They are property, and they are money makers, complete with scantily clad women and death-defying men as we see in the snake eco-horror movies. Circuses have been corporatized. And instead of small traveling acts, we now have only a few staged by big companies making significantly more money off the same types of performances.

6

In Jesus' Name

Holiness and the Handling of Serpents

There is very little mystery as to why snakes inspire fear. The obvious danger posed by venomous snakes, as elaborated in the preceding chapters, and the potential damage that can be caused by snakebite alone, are reason enough to steer clear of snakes in every situation. But what of nonvenomous snakes? Why do harmless garter snakes, milk snakes, or rat snakes have the potential to cause a fear response in many? Or the reason why untrustworthy types are called "snakes in the grass," or accused of speaking with a "forked tongue." The obvious answer is found in the Book of Genesis, and the story of Adam and Eve. The beginnings of Western Judeo-Christian culture are rooted in the image of the snake as an embodiment of Satan himself, the quintessential tempter, driving the denizens of the Garden of Eden to eat from the forbidden Tree of Life.

Combine the Biblical reputation of snakes with the evidence of danger presented by the litany of dangerous reptiles discussed in this book—the timber rattlers, cottonmouths, copperheads, diamondbacks—and it makes for a potent formula for fear and disdain. In fact, the entire section of Genesis devoted to this part of the story of Adam and Eve, and the eventual sin that leads to the downfall of man, depicts the snake as a natural-born deceiver. Chapter 3, verses 1 through 6 begins, "Now the serpent was more crafty than any other wild animal that the Lord God had made," setting the groundwork for the ultimate temptation. It continues, "He said to the woman, 'Did God say, "You shall not eat from any tree in the garden?"' The woman said to the serpent, 'We may eat of the fruit of the trees in the garden, but God said, "You shall not eat of the fruit of the tree that is in the middle of the garden, nor shall you touch it or you shall die."' But

153

the serpent said to the woman, 'You will not die; for God knows that when you eat of it your eyes will be opened, and you will be like a God, knowing Good and Evil.'"[1]

This infraction of God's will came, obviously, with consequences, thus setting the groundwork for man's perpetual battle with snakes. God's punishment of man is well known in the form of original sin, and thus the reason man was cast out from the garden and for human suffering in general (most specifically the suffering women endure during childbirth). Here, however, we are primarily concerned with God's punishment of the snake himself:

> Because you have done this, cursed are you among all animals and among all wild creatures; upon your belly you shall go, and dust you shall eat all the days of your life. I will put enmity between you and the woman, and between your offspring and hers; he shall strike your head, and you will strike his heel.[2]

The operative phrase here being, of course, the last, where God puts enmity between the snake and the offspring of man, as man shall strike at the snake's head while the snake strikes at man's heel. Although much of the evidence we have explored points more to snakes striking at the hands of man (or even more specifically the fingers),[3] the symbolism still holds true. Man is the upright master of the land, while the snake hides in its burrow, waiting for the opportunity to strike.

In the previous chapters of this book, this battle can be seen played out in multiple ways with man and snake fighting for territory in the wilds of the United States and in other areas throughout the world, fearing the inevitable snakebite and trying desperately to find a cure. With the battle between man and snakes as a backdrop, we have explored the social and economic variables that also are at play: wealthy city dwellers were able to remain safe and unconcerned about the ever-present danger of snakebite, while poor, rural folk had to stay vigilant and on guard. This chapter diverges slightly from the dangers presented in previous chapters, and instead looks back to the origins of the man/snake divide. We will be looking specifically at the Biblical and religious relevance of snakes in American society and, thus, at a group of worshippers who, rather than fearing snakes and looking to get rid of them (or profit from them), instead seek to keep them and place them as an essential part of their relationship with God and His word. The fear of snakes that is so important to cultural examples such as the reality TV shows *Venom Hunters* or *Rattlesnake Republic*, or films such as *Anaconda*, here is replaced with a sense of jubilation and celebration. Timber rattlers and cottonmouths are not avoided or killed, they are instead held as one of the most important symbols of religious achievement, proof of baptism by the Holy Spirit.[4] Although the fear has been replaced by joy, this chapter still seeks to investigate the key social and economic issues explored throughout this book. Snakes still serve to act as a point of separation between the bulk of society and those on the fringes, between the haves and the have-nots, and between the "urban" and the "rural."

This chapter looks deeply into the history, culture, and spiritual belief of a sect of Christianity commonly referred to as the "signs following faith."[5] Rather than being linked to a strict hierarchical structure or a specific spiritual leadership as are many other Christian churches, those who consider themselves "sign followers" are bound by a simpler and more loosely structured ideal, which is based on what are known as the Markan Signs, found at the very end of the Gospel of Mark, chapter 16, verses 15–19 (and specifically verses 17–18), in which Jesus, upon his return from death, tells his disciples to go forward into the world to preach His word and gives them a list of signs that will prove baptism in the Holy Spirit to identify those who are believers, and those who are not. Some sign followers also refer to the Gospel of Luke, chapter 10, verse 19, as a benchmark of salvation, and both references to the Gospels teach a very important lesson to those who believe these passages fundamentally— snakes are no longer to be feared.

Before we explore the signs following faith more deeply, there are a few distinctions that need to be drawn in the way certain things or concepts will be detailed in this chapter. First of all, when referring to religious figures and concepts, and especially when referring to God or the Lord directly (but also in the abstract such as He or His), capitalization will be used. Much of the source material for this chapter will be taken from verbal testimony in the forms of television programs and documentary films, so these words are not inherently capitalized, however it is common to see them presented as always capitalized in written materials, and in verbal testimony, there is a distinct emphasis given to them by the speakers. Therefore, this emphasis will be given when using quoted written or spoken materials. Second, the word "serpent" will primarily be used in place of "snake," as the Biblical reference is to the serpent and thus, snakes in these religious contexts are also referred to almost always as serpents. It can also be seen in some of the source material that the serpent/snake distinction is very important in determining context. When speaking of the use of snakes in religious ceremonies, calling them serpents is a way of encapsulating all of the historical and religious iconography, i.e., it was a serpent that approached Adam and Eve in the Garden of Eden, not a snake. However, outside of the religious milieu, a snake is something that you might find under a rock near your home and thus try to capture. Finally, as much of the source material is taken from film or video recordings of interviews with the congregants of these signs following churches, and these churches are primarily found in rural Appalachia, much of the quoted material will be written in colloquial English to preserve the linguistic nature of these exchanges.

The bulk of the source material for this chapter, along with textual sources such as old newspaper articles, journal articles, etc., is taken from a number of documentaries and the National Geographic TV reality series *Snake Salvation*. The three main documentaries used in this chapter span a time period from 1967 to 1991: *Holy Ghost People* (1967) is a documentary filmed by Peter Adair at a church in Scrabble Creek, West Virginia; *People Who Take Up Serpents* (1974) is a short (36-minute) film, by Gretchen Robinson and Stan Woodward, of church services in Greenville, North Carolina, and Newport, Tennessee; and *In Jesus' Name: Taking Up Serpents* (1991) is a 47-minute documentary, filmed by Al Clayton, about churches in Scottsboro, Alabama, and Kingston, Georgia. We also use a more modern take on serpent handling in the form of *Snake Salvation*, which was a reality TV show that aired in 2013 and followed Pastor Jamie Coots, of the Full Gospel Tabernacle in Jesus Name, in Middlesboro, Kentucky, and Pastor Andrew Hamblin, of the Tabernacle Church of God, in LaFollette, Tennessee. Each of the documentary films are unique because, unlike *Snake Salvation* (and as also illustrated in other reality TV shows such as *Rattlesnake Republic* and *Venom Hunters*), there is almost no editorial narration. The documentaries are simply footage of the church services and some interviews with the congregants, thus giving us a clear view of how little fear plays a part in these ceremonies. Alternatively, *Snake Salvation* includes the type of narration and sinister music found in similar reality TV series in an attempt to build suspense, but the interviews with Coots, Hamblin, and their congregants belies the suspense and discounts fear as well. In other words, they are very much not afraid of serpents, no matter how suspenseful the network tries to make the situation. All of these examples, as well, serve to highlight the "otherness" of the members of these churches, both economically and socially. Before digging deeper into the documentary evidence, first we will give some history and background of the signs following faiths in the Appalachian Mountains and the American south, as well as what it means to be a signs following faith in the first place.

The Markan Signs and a Brief History of Serpent Handling

The signs that are referred to in the name signs following faith are found in two books of the New Testament: the Gospel of Mark and the Gospel of Luke. The context for the signs in both the Gospel of Luke and the Gospel of Mark is in reference to Jesus sending his followers out into the world to spread His word, and in both Gospels, Jesus gives those who truly believe power over serpents. The passage from the Gospel of Luke, chapter 10, is a bit abstract, but conveys a clear message of power given over to his followers, as we can see in verses 16–19: "'Whoever listens to you listens to me, and whoever rejects you rejects me, and whoever rejects me rejects the one who sent me,' The seventy returned with joy saying, 'Lord in your name even the demons submit to us!' He said to them, 'I watched Satan fall from heaven like a flash of lightning. See, I have given you authority to tread on snakes and scorpions, and over all the power of the enemy; and nothing will hurt you.'"[6] So those who believe in the Word and accept God are given power over their enemies symbolically through the power to tread on snakes and scorpions with no harm coming to them. Again, this is a relatively abstract reference, but it gives power to the notion that followers of Christ can tread on danger without fear of harm (and in more fundamental interpretations, literally stepping on snakes), and calls to mind the above-referenced section in the Book of Genesis that sets snakes to striking at the heels of man and points to the new covenant with Jesus as removing that danger.

The signs found in the Gospel of Mark (also referred to as the Markan signs), and those to which the sign followers most closely adhere, are much more specific and prescriptive. At the end of the Gospel of Mark, Jesus is again preparing his followers to go out and spread His word, this time in reaction to the disciples' doubt that he had actually risen from the dead: "Later he appeared to the eleven themselves as they were sitting at the table; and he upbraided them for their lack of faith and stubbornness, because they had not believed those who saw him after he had risen. And he said to them, 'Go into all the world and proclaim the good news to the whole creation.'"[7] In the passage following this, Jesus describes to his disciples a series of signs that would identify the true believers, as well as another statement that those who believe are saved and those who don't will suffer condemnation: "'The one who believes and is baptized will be saved; but the one who does not believe will be condemned. And these signs will accompany those who believe: by using my name they will cast out demons; they will speak in new tongues; they will pick up snakes in their hands, and if they drink of any deadly thing, it will not hurt them; they will lay their hands on the sick, and they will recover."[8] As can be seen in this last passage, the message is much less abstract than that in the Gospel of Luke, and the signs are prefaced by the word "will." In the fundamentalist interpretation of this passage by those who follow the signs, if one believes in anything in the Bible, one must believe all of it.[9] Therefore, the handling of serpents is no more optional than any of the Ten Commandments—thou shalt not kill, and thou shalt handle serpents.

Even though this chapter will focus more on the handling of serpents than the other signs, this is not to argue that serpent handling is in any way more important than, say, speaking in tongues or casting out demons. In fact, when congregants are interviewed in the documentaries reviewed in this chapter, many of them make sure to mention that although there is undoubtedly a unique quality to the phenomenon of serpent handling, it usually doesn't occur until the other signs are achieved. Many congregants don't even consider handling a serpent until they have proven they have "taken on the spirit" through a number of other signs, such as speaking in tongues or healing through the laying on of hands. Indeed, many churches that follow the Markan signs don't even participate in serpent handling, choosing to read that passage more as symbolic rather than literal (similar to the interpretation of Luke 10:19), and it is this debate about whether or not to read the handling of serpents as literal that contributes to the outsider status of those who do.[10]

Historically, the signs following faiths began around the turn of the century from the 1800s to the 1900s, and can be traced back to early evangelical ministers seeking what was the indisputable proof of one being baptized with the Holy Spirit. Charles Fox Parham asked a number of his Bethel Bible School students about this problem in Topeka in December of 1900, which was to figure out indisputably what it would look like if someone was indeed experiencing Holy Spirit baptism.[11] The students came back with the response that the proof was in the Apostles speaking in tongues. From there, early Pentecostals also began to look at the Book of Mark, Chapter 16, as a "kind of litmus test for the authenticity of their experience. The text's 'unrivaled' position in the early movement guaranteed that the embodied signs it enumerated would become essential symbols of one's status ... as a follower of Christ."[12]

As the idea of following the Markan signs made its way to the American south, a preacher by the name of A.J. Tomlinson became interested in achieving spiritual baptism through these signs at his Church of God, in the Unicoi Mountains in Tennessee.[13] Tomlinson viewed the signs as an important part of the development of a southern Pentecostal movement that fought against the changing social and economic landscape of the south. Because his church was located in the rural Unicoi Mountains, many of his congregants were poor whites on the fringes of society, and "the signs of Mark formed a reservoir of spiritual and social power for the members of the rapidly growing Church of God.... Signs separated them from the market and industrial forces reshaping Appalachia and highlighted their divergence from the long-established religious bodies in the region."[14] This push to help the poor, rural inhabitants of the Appalachian region establish a religious identity against the backdrop of the developing economies in the more urban areas of the south cemented the Markan signs as an integral way of life and religious practice.

Although the practice of serpent handling had been discussed in a number of news stories that predated Tomlinson's adoption of the signs by about a decade, serpent handling started to gain a much stronger foothold in the Pentecostal movements when Tomlinson wrote in the Church of God's *Evangel* newspaper, in September of 1914, about a revival being held by another preacher named George Hensley. In his article about the revival, Tomlinson wrote that Hensley was holding a revival at the Church of God Tabernacle, in Cleveland, Tennessee, and that "twice during the meeting Serpents have been handled by the Saints."[15] Hensley himself was what could be considered the target demographic of Tomlinson's Church of God—an illiterate, poor white man who made his living by cobbling together jobs and working as a coal miner, a lumberjack, and a moonshiner—so his revival, and the serpent handling that occurred, caught the collective imagination of the religious community. However, this particular revival might have become a historical footnote like the spotty evidence of serpent handling that preceded it if Tomlinson had not continued to write about, and promote, serpent handling through his leadership of the Church of God. Not to be outdone by other Pentecostal signs following churches, Tomlinson continued to regale the religious community with tales of serpent handling and the following of other dangerous signs, such as the drinking of the deadly thing. At the Church of God's Tenth General Assembly, he made sure to tell the church's leaders that "wild poison serpents have been taken up and handled and fondled over almost like babies with no harm to the saints. In several instances fire has been handled with bare hands without the saints being burned.... I have seen no reports of anybody outside the Church of God performing this miracle."[16]

Once the sign of serpent handling became an established manifestation of Holy Spirit baptism, stories of serpent handling in other non–Church of God publications became more prevalent, and the "miracles" associated with this practice became more prevalent as well. In his article "Take Away the Serpents from Us: The Sign of Serpent Handling and the Development of Southern Pentecostalism," Michael J. McVicar recounts a litany of snakebite stories that, unlike the tales of lost limbs and death in the previous chapters in this book, instead tell of miraculous healing or a complete absence of injury. For example, Ralph C. Burnett of the Assemblies of God Church had recently received the gift of the Holy Spirit when he was bitten by a rattlesnake. Other congregation members prayed over him using Mark 16:16–18, and "the healing virtue of the Lord Jesus went through my body like an electric current and I was instantly healed." In another example, Alice Hannah of Prescott, Arkansas, was bitten by a snake, and while church members prayed over her, Hannah also prayed for "the Lord to leave any sign He wanted, that others might know He could heal the bite of a poisonous snake; so He let my foot swell. I was bitten on Monday and never put my shoe on that foot for five days, yet never failed to play the organ and help in every service." Lucy A. Luttrull of Bruner, Missouri, "reported being bitten by a copperhead while speaking in tongues. She refused medical treatment and allowed a brother and sister to anoint her with oil and pray over her."[17] In the case of Hannah and Luttrull, it is important to note that their prayers accepted the risk of injury or death as the result of the snakebite, and this is quite common in the testimonials given by other practitioners of serpent handling. Many will not accept any form of medical attention, but will conversely accept any injury that results, no matter how severe.

Within a few years of establishing serpent handling as a sign of Holy Spirit baptism in the Pentecostal movement, many of the churches began to distance themselves from the Church of God and the Assemblies of God, and Tomlinson himself was forced out of leadership of the Church of God in 1923. When the Church of God's headquarters moved from the Unicoi Mountains to the more urban Cleveland, Tennessee, the demographics of the church's congregation began to change as well, leaving the poorer, rural whites behind for a congregation with higher income and education levels, and less of a need to distinguish themselves through dangerous practices. Legal troubles also slowed the serpent-handling movement as preachers like Hensley began to face arrest for the possession and handling of snakes because some states, including Tennessee, made the practice illegal. The loss of momentum of Tomlinson's (and others') movement to make serpent handling a prime sign of Holy Spirit baptism further relegated the practice to the fringes of society and the poor, uneducated whites in the Appalachian Mountains the Church of God left behind. As we will see, however, the practice continues to this day, although with much less oversight and organization. The churches that practice serpent handling as one of the Markan signs tend to be much smaller and much more remote than those of the early Pentecostal movement. The churches represented in the documentaries *Holy Ghost People*, *People Who Take Up Serpents*, and *In Jesus' Name: Taking Up Serpents*, and the reality show *Snake Salvation* are examples of these churches. As a footnote to this section, it is important to mention that for all of his promotion of serpent handling, it is dubious as to whether A.J. Tomlinson himself ever handled a serpent, and George Hensley ended up dying of a snakebite in 1955.[18]

Much of the knowledge of these movements reached the eyes of the masses as a result of a series of photographs taken by Russell Lee. On assignment for the Department of the Interior in 1946, photographer Lee took around 4,000 photographs in and around the Appalachian coalfields to document the worsening condition of the coal mines and mining communities around that time.[19] As part of this project, Lee also photographed serpent handling in rural churches of mining communities, and specifically one iconic photograph that was originally captioned, "Handling of serpents, a part of the ceremony at the Pentecostal Church of God. This coal camp offers none of the modern types of amusement and many of the people attend the services of this church more for the mass excitement and emotionalism than because of belief in the tenets of this church. Lejunior, Harlan County, Kentucky, 09/15/1946."[20] This particular image served to cement the "otherness" of the early Pentecostal movement, showing the poverty and low social status of the adherents of this type of faith.

Serpent Handlers and Holy Rollers

Holy Ghost People

Peter Adair's 1967 documentary, *Holy Ghost People*, opens with some outdoor shots of the poor mountain community of Scrabble Creek, West Virginia, with a voiceover from the director describing the type of churches that are found in the community, many of which follow the Markan signs. However, Adair also mentions that these churches, and their congregants, are not necessarily highly esteemed in their communities because of the peculiarities of their religious practices. From the "shrieking and convulsive dancing" that are direct manifestations of baptism by the Holy Spirit (which have earned them the pejorative name "Holy Rollers"), to the handling of serpents, these congregants, according to Adair, "are constantly faced with social pressure and even persecution from other people in the area.[21]" The narration then continues to describe how the congregants catch snakes in the mountainous regions around the church and keep them in their homes for use during church services, and that, as mentioned above, many congregants are bitten, but most invariably refuse medical attention and instead rely on prayer for their healing.

After the opening sequence, there is a series of testimonials given by four members of the Scrabble Creek Church, two men and two women, who all give some account of experiencing the signs of baptism by the Holy Ghost. The first testimonial is from a man who describes his first experience of speaking in tongues, while the last comes from a woman who is actively speaking in tongues while giving her testimonial. The other woman is the only one of the four who mentions anything about handling serpents (which she actively participates in) as well as experiencing drinking of the "deadly thing," which in this case is strychnine.[22] These testimonials support the idea that each of the signs is as important as the other, and that handling serpents is something done as a genuine expression of religious practice and not as a spectacle. Following these testimonials, the rest of the documentary is entirely un-editorialized, in that there is no narration and the cameraman (Adair) is silently observing the service as it unfolds.

The pastor begins the service by calling attention to the fact that there is a camera present and implores the congregation to act as they normally would by saying, "Just be yourself. If you obey the Lord when we don't have photographers around, obey Him when we do. Just be yourself ... but I don't care whether they like it or not. A lot of people won't like the testimony I have. They think it's a disgrace to touch a serpent. I don't want to be highly esteemed among men, I'd rather be just what I am. Glory be to God."[23] This introduction is also an obvious defense of the church's practice of serpent handling, and it is telling that this is the only defense the pastor makes. If his concern was for how outside audiences would view the church's practices in general (it is entirely possible someone would view speaking in tongues as shocking), it seems that his defense may have been expanded outside of serpent handling, but it is not. After the pastor's introductory defense, the service itself begins.

The service unfolds for the next half an hour with music, convulsive dancing, testimonials, speaking in tongues, "falling out," and it isn't until around the 37-minute mark (of a 51-minute documentary) that we see a box of snakes being unceremoniously dumped onto the ground amidst a throng of congregants, and then the contents grabbed by several men. It is at this point that a very distinct lack of fear is noticeable. The snakes (some of which look to be three to four feet in length) are handed from person to person in an alarmingly careless fashion, and the lack of narration to give a sense of suspense (as we see in many of the reality TV shows mentioned in previous chapters) is striking. Nobody in the church shies away from the snakes, and most don't seem to notice or be even remotely concerned. The singing and dancing carries on as handfuls of snakes are passed around, held up above people's heads, or dropped back to the floor. Because there is some amount of film editing, and because the film quality itself is relatively poor, it is hard to tell exactly how many snakes there are in the church, how many people actually handle the snakes, and how long the snakes are out of their boxes. In one exceptionally clear shot, however, a man is holding a smaller rattlesnake whose rattle can be seen, and it is moving vigorously—what would be seen by most as a clear warning sign to put the snake down and back away. Nobody in the church that evening, however, seems to notice or be at all concerned.

In what is probably the most important scene in the entire documentary, the service is winding down, and the pastor takes a snake, holds it for a few minutes while talking to the congregation, and then drops it to the ground. The moment is almost imperceptible, but a second before the pastor drops the snake, it turns its head and strikes him on the hand. What happens after is a stark example of the lack of fear present amongst people who follow the Markan signs as an integral part of their faith. There is no screaming, nobody calls an ambulance, and nobody moves to cut the wound and suck out the venom. Instead, another member of the church calmly picks up the snake and puts it back in its box while the pastor wraps a handkerchief around the wound, which is now noticeably bleeding. He calmly addresses the congregation, after wrapping his hand, and says, "That's God's word, good folks. If I die of this snakebite, it's still God's word just the same.... And you wonder why they bite? Well, I don't know, I would like to know myself sometimes."[24] In the last few minutes of the film, the congregation moves to lay their hands on him to pray while his hand becomes more and more visibly swollen. It is not clear whether the pastor dies from the bite,[25] but it is clear that no immediate medical attention is called for.

People Who Take Up Serpents

The second documentary, *People Who Take Up Serpents* (1974), gives us a much more detailed account of the motivation and rationale behind serpent handling as a part of faith. The film, directed by Gretchen Robinson and Stan Woodward, contains many more interviews with congregants, and delves more deeply into the marginalization of the churchgoers, as well as depicting some of the legal issues that arise from serpent handling. The focus of this documentary is also much more specifically the phenomenon of serpent handling. Whereas *Holy Ghost People* gives the viewer a relatively unobtrusive look into one evening's service of the Scrabble Creek Church (which just happens to capture a snakebite), *People Who Take Up Serpents* focuses its attention on giving the congregants an opportunity to describe the internal motivations and spiritual benefits of practicing serpent handling specifically. The interviewees speak at length about how the anointing (baptism) of the Holy Spirit removes all fear. They also raise another issue that is hinted at, but not overtly dealt with, in *Holy Ghost People*, and that is combatting the misconception that handling serpents is some kind of "test" of faith, i.e., if someone has a strong enough faith in God, then God won't let the snake bite. According to the churchgoers in *People Who Take Up Serpents*, this idea couldn't be more false, as most of the devout practitioners of serpent handling interviewed in the film also had stories of being bitten.

The idea that handling serpents is not a direct test of faith is extremely important in understanding how these congregants experience their faith through this dangerous practice. It can be assumed that many of those interviewed have been approached with the "testing faith" premise before, as they all articulate a very clear argument to the opposite. As they describe it, it's not about "daring" God to let a serpent bite you to show how strong your faith is, it is much more of a "giving over" to the baptism of the Holy Spirit or being "filled" with the Holy Ghost. The congregants surrender to this experience and handle serpents (or speak in tongues, drink poison, etc.) because of this undeniable and overwhelming possession by the Holy Spirit. As one congregant puts it, "It's not something you can do just because you want to…. There is a fear for any man of the serpents … the copperheads and rattlesnakes are very dangerous. But when the anointing comes, the Lord just seems to speak to me and tells me that everything is going to be okay. That I don't have to fear the serpents because His anointing is right. His word is right."[26] It is important to note his lack of subjectivity in the decision to handle serpents—you don't do it because you want to, rather you do it because you are moved to by the Holy Spirit—and thereby comes the ability to release all fear. Almost all of the congregants interviewed for the documentary express some form of this idea that you do it because you are moved and not because you have something to prove. Another congregant describes the anointing as a removal of all fear, and that God speaks to him directly and tells him to handle the serpents. Some even describe that not handling serpents when the anointing comes is a distinct disappointment and a missed opportunity.

Interspersed with the interview segments in the film are the same type of church service shots that we see in *Holy Ghost People*, the churches—one in Greenville, North Carolina, and one in Newport, Tennessee—are absolutely abuzz with singing, dancing, convulsing, speaking in tongues, and praying. However, the presence of serpents is much more extreme. Whereas the Scrabble Creek Church in *Holy Ghost People* had perhaps a dozen snakes, the churches depicted in *People Who Take Up Serpents* have significantly more, and in some scenes, people are holding five or more snakes at once. The depictions of serpent handling in this film are downright breathtaking. Part of this could be attributed to the fact that this documentary is in color, while the other two are in black and white. This way the viewer can see more detail of the snakes themselves, such as being able to see the copper-colored scales on the head of what is obviously a copperhead, bringing a more recognizable and palpable danger to the audience. But part of the breathtaking nature of the serpent handling in the film is undoubtedly the absolute carefree (or careless) nature in which the snakes are handled. To again highlight the differences between the fear-driven narratives of television shows like *Venom Hunters* and *Rattlesnake Republic*, and the absolute absence of fear in the serpent-handling documentaries, is to observe the precautions taken while handling the serpents themselves.

In the aforementioned reality TV shows, an emphasis is placed on the proper handling of snakes to minimize the possibility of getting bitten. Special clothing, such as heavy leather boots or gloves, is worn, and special snake-catching apparatuses are used to mitigate the risk of injury, and the narrative follows with the build-up of suspense—when dealing with venomous snakes, there is *always* the possibility of being bitten, so every possible precaution is taken. One could even assume that off camera, in every instance, there is a medical team standing by with vials of antivenin or other important medical supplies, just in case. The church services depicted in these documentaries could not be more different. Virtually no precautions are taken, as the congregants are wearing normal clothing (some are not even wearing shoes), there are no special snake-catching apparatuses on hand, and when the anointing comes, being snakebitten does not even appear to be a concern. The serpents are not just handled by the congregants, they are shaken, tossed, danced with, handed back and forth, and in one sequence, a man rubs a rather large snake all over his head. In another sequence, the church community is at a funeral for some church members who passed away from drinking strychnine (the deadly thing), when a professional snake handler, named Doc Walls, brings out a cobra. As a voiceover to the scene, the man holding the snake describes how he was so anointed that he didn't even know where he was, and we see him dancing vigorously with an approximately four- to five-foot-long cobra in his hands. He swings the cobra around, wraps it around his hands, gyrates with it, and then hands it to another church member before taking it back again and dancing with it some more. Walls, who as a professional snake handler has an intimate knowledge of how deadly this cobra is, also describes the scene in utter disbelief: "When the guy walked up, he looked at the snake, totally eyes glassed over, totally mesmerized and hypnotized, and was just virtually speaking to the Lord Jesus, 'In Jesus' name ... sweet Jesus,' and he just picked this fella out like a bullwhip. And that's when I ran. When he started swinging him around his head, I ran!"[27] Of course, even though the snake itself was being swung around "like a bullwhip," nobody was injured, and Doc Walls was the only one who felt the need to run. The interiors of the churches, like the scene at the funeral, are also hot, noisy, and full of commotion—all things that, according to the narrators of the reality TV shows, make snakes become aggressive. In fact, with the juxtaposition between the fear and suspense generated in the modern reality TV shows about snakes and what can be seen in these church services, if there are any miracles present, it's that people aren't getting bitten all the time.

Although *People Who Take Up Serpents* doesn't catch a snakebite in action like *Holy Ghost People*, it does still show the consequences of the signs following faith, and how those consequences are absolutely accepted by the congregants without question. As mentioned above, there are two church members who die as a result of following the sign of drinking any deadly thing (in this case, strychnine), and there is also a case of snakebite documented in the film. A female churchgoer gets bitten on the hand, and she is interviewed by the filmmakers as she recovers from the snakebite. When we see her in her living room, she is surrounded by other church members, and her hand is visibly swollen. Rather than admitting a mistake or expressing fear for her health or her life, the woman instead describes the spiritual nature of her actions and how this snakebite only serves to deepen her faith, saying, "When the Holy Ghost speaks, that's when I move. So that's why that I put my hand in that box, to take up that serpent that day. To obey God. For God said obedience was better than sacrifice. So I'd rather obey God and die, and go on and be at rest, as to live and not obey God and die and go to a world of the lost."[28] Her concern was not for her health or safety, but rather in following what she saw as the more important task of adhering to the word of God and expressing her willingness to suffer the consequences, whatever they may be. This woman also supports the claim made by other churchgoers that handling serpents is not a test of faith, saying that she had read the Bible many times over, and that although there is a passage telling believers to handle serpents, she has never found anything in the Bible that says you won't get bitten. During this part of the documentary, there is also a conversation between two women about the snakebite victim, quoted here at length, that also illustrates a deepening of conviction rather than a judgment over a lack of faith when someone gets bitten, and also shows how deeply held the fundamental interpretation of the Markan signs is to those who follow them:

> WOMAN 1: Well, I hated about her getting bit and all, but it's Bible, and the Bible don't say it doesn't bite you.
>
> WOMAN 2: Now if that part of the scripture is not right, then none of the rest of it's not right. And it's the truth. If that part ain't right, there's no use in foolin' with any of the rest of it.
>
> WOMAN 1: I know it's right to handle them. You might get bit sometimes, and you might even lose your life, but I don't think that it's wrong because it is Bible.
>
> WOMAN 2: You know, this is real, sure as the world. If one dies occasionally, and there will be some die along the way, but we're going to die anyway.... I'd rather die in the service of the Lord ... the Bible say if we die for His sake, if we lose our life for His sake, we'll find it again, but if we seek to save our life, we lose it. And you know, if I couldn't obey the word of God, if knew one of them things would bite me and kill me, I'd still do it, because I'd be doing the word of God.[29]

The deepening of conviction in the face of danger is something that is seen throughout the rest of the documentary as well, when several other church members describe having been bitten multiple times by venomous snakes, such as copperheads and timber rattlers, and although the spectacle of the serpent handling is captivating, they also express time and time again that it is not for show or to "prove" anything. The church member who is shown violently swinging the cobra at the outdoor funeral tells a story of being approached by Doc Walls, the professional snake handler. Walls apparently offered the man and his wife jobs in his touring snake show, promising $400 a week to both of them to take tickets and to work in the rattlesnake pit. The man turned Walls down, saying that he couldn't get anointed in a carnival atmosphere. Again, one could imagine, based on the backdrop of southern poverty against which this documentary is presented, that $400 a week would be a substantial sum of money to turn down. However, his faith and conviction were more important than a paycheck, and the circus-like atmosphere of the snake show was antithetical to his expression of faith.

If this documentary teaches us anything, it is how strongly held the serpent handlers' conviction is to the practice. No matter how many times one has been bitten, or how much pain is suffered from the bite, none of the congregants interviewed show any wavering in their faith. God instructs them to take up serpents, and if a serpent bites, it is also God's will. If someone dies as a result of a snakebite, or from drinking poison, that is also God's will, and nothing will deter them from doing so, no matter how much distance it puts between them and acceptance by society at large.

In Jesus' Name: Taking Up Serpents

The last, and most recent, documentary reviewed here is Al Clayton's 1991 film, *In Jesus' Name: Taking Up Serpents*. This documentary follows much the same format as *People Who Take Up Serpents*, interspersing interviews with congregants and the activities of church services, but it takes places further south and outside of the Appalachian Mountains. The two churches featured in the film are located in Scottsboro, Alabama, and Kingston, Georgia, and the relatively recent time period of the film shows that although larger movements like Tomlinson's Church of God lost momentum near the middle of the 20th century, the tradition and practice of serpent handling in rural churches in the American south lives on. What this documentary adds to the evidence presented in the previous two films is an even deeper look at the acceptance of the dangers of serpent handling, as well as how these traditions are passed down from generation to generation. This particular documentary also wastes no time in focusing its attention on the practice of serpent handling. Within the first five minutes of the film, we see congregants handling large handfuls of snakes, and we see interview footage of a man describing what it felt like the "first time" he got bitten by a snake. The experience almost killed him, but it also made his faith stronger, accepting that "the Bible said that we gotta suffer for his namesake, for the Gospels' sake, and some Christians don't think that a Christian has to suffer. All the apostles had to suffer ... but we have to suffer this place with pain, too."[30]

The acceptance of suffering and the unshakeable nature of the feeling of faith behind the practice of serpent handling can be seen most clearly in the figure of the pastor of one of the churches (nobody in this documentary is ever named, nor is it identified which church they are members of, so it is nearly impossible to identify him more clearly than this). And although these churches typically don't follow a strict hierarchy, it is evident from his representation in the film that he is at least *a* leader of the church, if not *the* leader. This pastor embodies three of the main themes of this chapter: denying serpent handling as a test of faith, identifying the anointing of the Holy Spirit as a command to take up serpents, and accepting the danger and suffering that come with the practice of serpent handling.

The pastor describes in great detail the process of receiving the anointing of the Holy Spirit and gives a pretty explicit account of the thought process that precedes handling serpents:

> When the Lord bids me to take up a serpent, I'll stand back unless I'm absolutely positive that God wants me to reach out and get it.... I want to be careful, I want to make sure it's God, because some people will take up a serpent by faith and say, "My faith is strong enough to keep me from being hurt." Well I don't say that. I'll stand back and say, "God, I'm waiting on you. I know it's your word, but I want to be right in your will." And I will wait on the anointing of God to come up on me before I reach and get it. And when that anointing comes ... total fear leaves. There is no fear.[31]

Obviously it cannot be assumed that this is the mindset of all those who practice serpent handling, but the thought process is in line with the testimony of many others interviewed in these documentaries. The command to take up the serpents comes with the anointing, and simple faith is not enough to save one from being bitten. A serpent handler must take steps to make sure that the anointing is genuine, and make his or her decision from there, even though it is no guarantee that a bite won't happen.

The pastor later claims that he has never been bitten (and is not looking forward to the day that he may be bitten), but that he learned serpent handling from his father, also a pastor, who had been bitten nine times. He then tells the story of his father's tenth snakebite, the one that eventually took his life, saying, "The last time he was bitten, he was bit in the temple. He died approximately ten hours later. Big rattler that bit him. He did suffer, but I feel that he's gone on home to be with Jesus."[32] Not only does he accept his father's suffering and death as the result of a snakebite, he then uses the scripture to defend his continuation of the practice with the familiar caveat that "the scripture doesn't say that they won't bite. In fact, it does say they will. A lot of people comes against me on that because my dad died with a serpent bite, but they wonder why I continue on with it. Well, I continue on with it because it's the word of God,"[33] and if one believes any of the Word, one has to believe all of the Word. The documentary ends with the pastor then admitting that if he "was carried out by a serpent bite, that'd be alright, too. I'm in this thing to stay, there ain't no bite that's gonna make me doubt."[34]

Another common theme that is articulated particularly well in *In Jesus' Name* is the concept of salvation through following the signs, specifically in regard to living a "sinful" lifestyle prior to Holy Spirit baptism and then finding one's way afterward. There is a brief mention of this in one of the testimonials at the beginning of *Holy Ghost People*, and this thread picks up again in *Snake Salvation*, where several characters such as Cody Coots (Pastor Coots' son) and Big Cody (another congregant) have come to the church from paths that have led to drug addiction and other sinful behavior. One of the congregants in *In Jesus' Name* expresses the same type of experience, and how the "quickening spirit" of God replaces any need for a sinful lifestyle, because although "it's hard to describe what it feels like, you know that you've felt something like you never felt before, and you know there's something of it that come down on you ... you feel it in your hands, and you feel it in your feet, you feel it in your face, and it's every bit good.... I've took cocaine, I've smoked marijuana and drunk whiskey, and been high on all that, but this high you get on Jesus? There's nothing greater than that."[35] It is a bit ironic, however, that many have found this type of salvation through something potentially as (or more) life threatening than smoking marijuana or drinking whiskey.

Snake Salvation

The reality documentary series *Snake Salvation*, which ran on the National Geographic Channel in 2013, is one of the most modern depictions of serpent handling available. The series follows the services of the Full Gospel Tabernacle in Jesus Name, in Middlesboro, Kentucky, led by Pastor Jamie Coots, and the Tabernacle Church of God, in LaFollette, Tennessee, led by Coots's protégé, Pastor Andrew Hamblin. Like the documentaries reviewed in this chapter, *Snake Salvation* depicts the services and religious practices of these rural churches in the American south, however, as argued in Chapter 5, the modern audience demands a more circus-like atmosphere, with amped up suspense and the constant possibility of danger. Therefore, much like *Venom Hunters* and *Rattlesnake Republic*, the episodes of *Snake Salvation* are augmented with dark music and a sinister narrator who predicts danger in every situation. Even the series' episode titles are designed to lure viewers into believing that death by snakebite lurks at the end of every commercial break. For example, episodes with titles like "Bitten in Church," "Deadly Legacy," and "Venom in the Veins" promise heart-pounding scenes of danger and suspense in which venomous reptiles constantly attack their human captors.

This is, of course, not at all the case. The reality of this reality series is that because the subject matter is based on a group of believers, for whom an anointing with the Holy Spirit removes all fear, no matter how much suspense is drummed up through narration and ominous music, the absolute lack of fear on the part of the churchgoers renders it useless. This not to say, however, that there is no payoff for the audience. During the one season the series aired, there are multiple incidents of snakebite. In the episode "Bitten in Church," for example, Coots's father, Greg, gets bitten by a copperhead during a church service, but he survives the bite.[36] In another episode, "Swamp Hunt," Coots's son, Cody, gets bitten twice by a cottonmouth on a snake-hunting excursion. The bite is serious, and Cody's arm swells up to many times its original size, but he survives the bite as well.[37] In a third incident, another churchgoer, named Michael, gets bitten by a copperhead that he has captured, ostensibly to bring to Hamblin's church to use during service. Michael tries to pin the snake down with a cane and grab it by the tail, when it slips out and strikes him on the hand. The scene begins with Hamblin holding Michael's hand and praying in tongues while the narrator describes Hamblin as showcasing one of the Markan signs. The footage then cuts to Hamblin and Michael handling yet another serpent, in this case, a rattlesnake, while again praying over Michael's hand. There doesn't seem to be any question of seeking medical attention, while Hamblin, in a separate interview, says, "The Bible say that wherever two or three are gathered in My name, there I'll be in the midst. And there was more than two or three that prayed for him over there," concluding that Michael would "be alright." At the end of the segment, Michael describes the pain from the snakebite, saying that it burns, aches, and feels like someone "beating on your hand and holding a torch there are the same time" (which is actually how almost everyone in these documentaries describes the pain that accompanies a snakebite).[38] In all three cases, Greg, Cody, and Michael refuse to seek any medical attention whatsoever, and instead choose to be healed through prayer. These incidents are, of course, tense and suspenseful, but the lack of fear shown by the church members, as well as the lack of medical attention, both serve to dampen the suspense and the sense of danger. The bottom line is this: serpent handlers are not afraid of being bitten.

The show itself actually focuses on the more mundane issues in the lives of those who attend and lead serpent-handling churches, and the focus of many of the episodes is, simply, on the capture and care of venomous snakes. Because many snakes don't do well in captivity, Coots and Hamblin are constantly searching for and capturing more serpents to use in their services. According to Hamblin, the life expectancy for the snakes he captures is at minimum a few weeks, and at the most, around a year. This constant search for more snakes also leads to legal issues, which begin to pile up as the series progresses. Both Coots and Hamblin run afoul of the law either by possessing and housing the snakes in an unlawful manner, or by transporting them illegally across state lines. In the episode "Venom in the Veins," Coots, Hamblin, and a crew of other congregants, including Cody Coots, have to pull a *Dukes of Hazzard*–style caper on their way home from a snake-hunting trip because they have to illegally transport the snakes through the state of Tennessee. Even the narration strikes a *Dukes of Hazzard* note in an effort to make the scene more suspenseful, telling the audience that the "boys are on the lookout for the Tennessee police. If Pastor Andrew is caught transporting venomous snakes, he could be facing jail time and the closure of his church."[39] They learn that the police might be on the lookout for them because it has been leaked to the news that someone from Hamblin's church has been bitten (in reality it is the news of Cody Coots's recent cottonmouth bite).

Hamblin and Coots both later get charged for various crimes in relationship to their practice of serpent handling, prompting Coots to write an opinion piece for the *Wall Street Journal* in October of 2013, in which he compares serpent handling to other "overlooked" and potentially harmful religious activities, such as children fasting during Yom Kippur, or receiving sacramental wine while under the legal drinking age during a Catholic Mass. Coots roots his argument in the uncommon and unpopular nature of using venomous snakes in exercising his faith.[40] Hamblin, after the cancellation of *Snake Salvation,* was evicted from his church space because the landlord felt that too many people had been injured or had died from venomous snakebites, and was later forced to turn over dozens of his illegally held snakes to the Tennessee Wildlife Resources Agency.[41]

The biggest story surrounding the short-lived *Snake Salvation*, however, and that which brings us back to the idea of fear and otherness as discussed in this chapter, is the death of Jamie Coots. Coots passed away on February 15, 2014, from a snakebite that hit an artery in his hand. An article written a few days later in the *Lexington Herald-Leader* tells the story of Coots's death, but the story is an absolutely familiar one in the context of the signs following faith. The faithful were worshipping in Coots's church when serpents were handled.[42] In a split second, while he was holding a rattlesnake, the snake turned and bit his hand. Nobody was afraid. Coots's son, Cody, describes the situation in inevitably the same way that these situations are always described. Coots had been bitten many times before and had always been okay. This time, of course, he would also be okay. However, this time he wasn't. Medical attention was refused, and prayers were said, but Jamie Coots still passed away from the bite of a venomous snake. Since Jamie Coots's death, Cody Coots has also been bitten several more times, and each time he has been okay, until, perhaps, he is not.

No Matter What, Snakes Are Still Deadly

This chapter has taken a bit of a turn away from the fear-based narratives of previous chapters and explored a misunderstood community that practices an uncommon and misunderstood form of religious expression. Significantly, those who follow the Markan signs have reached a point where fear of serpents, something that has plagued mankind since the Book of Genesis, is replaced by a Holy Spirit–driven exuberant embrace of these venomous reptiles. Throughout each of these documentaries and reality TV episodes, practitioners of serpent handling not only challenge the fear of snakes that is experienced by most, they carelessly and gleefully (and some could say recklessly) grab handfuls of snakes and dance with them, pray with them, and even toss them in the air. This practice separates these worshippers from society at large, as many see them as religious lunatics and "holy rollers," further compounding their already-established otherness as predominantly poor, under-educated, rural whites. But they find comfort in this practice nonetheless. However, no matter how hard they pray or how much joy they find in their worship, one fact is undeniable: venomous snakes are dangerous and, at times, deadly. If someone gets bitten and refuses medical attention, sure, he or she might survive, but it is guaranteed there will be suffering in it.

Conclusion
Has Anything Changed?

Snakes and humans in the United States, and particularly rattlesnakes, have lived in constant tension and remain so today, the short answer to "has anything changed?" is not that much. Both sides have been opportunists to their peril. The snakes have used us for their well-being, drawn to the food we keep, the shelter we offer, and the water we need. Humans in turn have used them for profit. All along, uninformed voices more interested in promoting themselves as paragons of wisdom have claimed that the battles have not been really been happening, but unfortunately they have. The two sides sometimes occupy each other's spaces, clashing with one another in their efforts to keep themselves alive. The rattle on the rattlesnake only occasionally protects either it or humans. Rattlesnakes and other venomous snakes have killed far more people in the United States than any of the apex predators, like grizzly bears and mountain lions, who Americans wiped out, they claimed, for safety reasons. Like mosquitos, who are tiny and have killed even more Americans, snakes are small, have large numbers, and can hide more easily than large animals. Most of the time they strike quickly to defend themselves, and the person quickly succumbs. If all of rattlesnake victims had been warned graciously by the rattlesnakes and had been given time to back away, as self-proclaimed experts repeatedly insist they do, it seems likely that many of the people who have died from bites would not have done so. Similarly, the rattle does little to keep determined humans away who are working for their own livelihood. If anything, it helps them find the snake to bag it, capture it, place it in a plastic box its entire life for scientific use, or kill it. The result is that when it comes to rattlesnakes, we live with an animal that has the power of death and has killed many people and domesticated animals over the course of our history. We clash with that animal as well as other snakes, including black snakes, water moccasins, and now pythons, on the margins of civilization as both sides seek something in each other's world. A few people straddle that world and live on both sides, but they are backwoodsmen, charmers, snake handlers, nuisance-control men, religious zealots, and zoo people. Even today, rattlesnake experts seem determined to separate people into those who are bitten accidentally, which means that they were undeserving on their bites, and those who deserved to get bitten because they touched the snake. This is an ongoing and noble attempt to protect the snake by pointing out human fault, but it does not erase the bite. It just marginalizes the people who spend time around snakes in a way that we would not distance ourselves from the many people who are bitten by dogs. Large numbers of Americans are bitten by dogs every year, and yet we are not warned to avoid dogs the way that we are asked to stay away from venomous snakes. They were too far into nature and out of our safe, civilized world. The real fear, then, is not just about the snakes, it is also about the loss of civilization that the snakes represent. The descent into a barbaric, brutal world of bites and death.

Ironically, in their effort to portray themselves as civilized, columnists and so-called wildlife experts who wrote about snakes for urban audiences in the past contributed to the death toll among rural people in most states outside of New England. A review of historical newspapers reveals the constant presence of death notices about people, often children, who were killed by rattlesnakes in particular, even as the economic elite in cities like New York and Washington were telling one another that fear of rattlesnakes was entirely unwarranted. They were shy, retiring animals who never killed anyone, they insisted, so it was up to the humans to avoid killing them and to be brave about heading out into the wilderness. The goal of wilderness recreation for the elite was more compelling than any need to take seriously the significant problems and often death that followed a bite. A careful reading of their travels into the wild, moreover, illustrates that they typically did not actually go off on real hiking trips alone into the actual wilderness, they went to hotels in the hilly or mountainous areas nearby and took small day hikes in the surrounding areas. There were people who resided in those areas who already patrolled them for rattlesnakes so that they could sell the urban elite rattlesnake hides as a souvenir from their visit to the countryside. In contrast, there was no such help for people who were in the middle of, or on the border of, the actual countryside. The snakes could simply come into the house chasing a rat, sit in a row of cotton and bite a hand that startled it, take shelter in a farmer's ditch that he was trying to irrigate, or hide out in a rabbit hole and bite the man when he tried to pull out the rabbit that he was killing for dinner. They waited among the berry patches for mice and bit the pickers who were putting the berries onto the tops of desserts for the elites somewhere else.

The fact that a few men who went hunting did not see many rattlesnakes is not particularly surprising. Rattlesnakes, like any animal, are drawn to food sources, and all of their food sources are small. They dine on rodents, who typically are not around large game animals like western elk or buffalo. Hornaday may have seen a few in the wild, but it was likely that they were far fewer in number than he might have seen right under a berry patch. As a result, these elites who did actually head into real wilderness on trips were probably less likely to run into the animals, particularly when they were hunting big game like buffalo stampeding across open country in large numbers. This would likely have been compounded by the fact that they had horses and a group of other men making a fair amount of noise on their way down a trail and giving the snakes plenty of time to hide for safety.

Poor people in rural areas, in contrast, really were bitten a lot. They suffered terribly and frequently died or experienced very long-term consequences. The destructive nature of hemotoxic venom was agonizing for the people who were bitten as their capillaries exploded, their tissues died, and their organs collapsed. There are also stories spread throughout the newspapers of the 18th and 19th century about "lucky" people who survived the bites, but then spent a lifetime in pain from its initial damage. These stories remain today and people reach out to one another looking for answers. Trying to find answers to his chronic health problems that began after his bite, "Naity" (a username in an online conversation on a scientific site about reptiles) confesses that he or she is trying to gain information about the long-term effects of rattlesnake bites. Naity was bitten when s/he was three years old by a western diamondback and was fully envenomated. From that point on s/he has had multiple health problems, including "chronic phlebitis (swollen legs), arthritis, nerve pain/twitches and muscle pain that ... all developed slowly since then." Naity's doctors were also beginning to suspect "possible heart issues." Similarly AshRN reports that he or she was also bitten by a rattlesnake as a child, and by age 28 had multiple medical issues, including "shoulder pain ... numbness down both arms, and fibromyalgia that effects both legs, hips" and also faces heart problems.[1] Another writer, from Tehema County, California, who was bitten shared that he too finds that his heart races at the slightest provocation after he was treated for a rattlesnake bite, and that his neighbor's son, who was bitten at age 14 in southern Oregon, six years after the bite was seeing a cardiologist who felt that the ongoing heart problems were from the snakebite.[2] Now, people can reach out to one another through the Internet to search for answers. In the 18th and 19th centuries, however, people who were bitten communicated through the newspaper if a writer was interested in their story.

Newspapers being nearly the only form of communication partly explain the slow efforts to take bite victims seriously. Elites in large cities who had the money and ability to look for cures were not reading local newspapers, other than their own, of the time. They would not have been able to get them. They did not see the constant death notices found in Arizona, New Mexico, Missouri, Kentucky, South Carolina, North Carolina, Montana, and North and South Dakota newspapers, among others. The *New York Times* regular column "Bitten by a Snake" that started in the late 1800s was designed to remedy that somewhat, but the small number of stories they ran under that title failed to illustrate the magnitude of the problem. If anything, it likely provided readers with the mistaken impression that bites happened rarely because there were so few stories. This was true for stock and domestic animals as well, and its particularly surprising because of the large economic loss that this group of farmers endured. Again, however, they were in the wrong geographic location, so their stories and needs were not getting back to an East Coast elite who might have taken the problem much more seriously if it was happening to them, their children, or their animals. As a result, they likely had no real idea how many people or domestic animals died of snakebites.

Another explanation for the long time it took to get a reliable cure in the United States was the medical practice of writing about single cases for medical journals and textbooks at a time when physicians really did not seem to understand that not all rattlesnake bites have venom in them. It is almost certain that most of the people chronicled in this book who survived without antivenin likely were not actually envenomated by the rattlesnakes or other venomous snakes who bit them. They were bitten, and it no doubt hurt terribly, and probably swelled up and may even have become somewhat infected because of the bacteria in the snake's mouth, so it would likely have seemed that the person had been bitten by a snake who discharged venom when they really had not. The snake might just have eaten and or just decided to send a warning and not actually kill this particular threat to them. Physicians in the 1800s clearly did not understand that and wrote about every bite as though it contained venom. As a result, each physician claimed that his cure worked. As we might expect from the larger culture of "heroic medicine" of the time, the more violent and painful the treatment, the better. Who could stand up to the most painful slicing, cauterizing, and shooting of body parts? If they wanted to be cured, they had to take the treatment or they deserved to die for failing to listen to the wisdom of the doctors who wanted to cure them.

We see this heroic medicine, and the bad advice, translate all the way into our own time period, but now the advice is skewed by class. In the past, doctors and other scientific writers generally recommended cures based upon race and gender. African Americans were not to be trusted to receive whiskey, because they were likely faking a bite, and young girls should not be given either whiskey or razors, because that did not fit with ideals of femininity. But in our online world of advice in which anyone can now share their perspective, we see clear class divisions between medical information in which those that are aimed at the middle and upper-middle class give accurate scientific advice, while peer conversation in places like survivalist online chat groups continue to offer scientifically faulty and questionable advice. The same poor people living in the wilderness without easy access to good health care remain the most vulnerable to snakebite deaths if they take the advice of their peers on survivalist sites seriously. In contrast to the past, however, when Americans' livelihoods placed them in direct contact with snakes, now their politics are placing them in danger. Survivalists in particular have decided that they do not want any part of the U.S. governmental system, so they have retreated to the wilderness to live a life as free of governmental intervention as possible.[3]

Unfortunately this means that survivalists in online chat sites are the new best source for bad information about snakebites, although there are the occasional rational and intelligent voices on these sites who disagree and try and educate their peer group. "The Hog," a writer who contributed to survivalistsboard.com, recommended that his peers avoid antivenin altogether because "in untrained hands" they were "likely to suffer the same as not treating the bite." He recommended taking a stretch crepe bandage and winding it the length of the limb, not too tightly, but just enough to constrict the capillaries under the skin.[4] Another participant, with the user name "armyranger1," recommended against antivenin because it would "only work for a specific snake," so he or she recommended that people lie down and not move, "allowing the poison to move slowly" in their blood. Another survivalist shared the following radio story with his peers: Chad Cross was bitten by a 6-foot timber rattler while hunting turkey in Alabama. The snake bit through his hunting pants and Muck boots. The bite was excruciatingly painful, and began to swell immediately. Luckily (he claims), he carried a product sold by Amazon.com, among other sources, called a "Venom Extractor," which is the modern incarnation of the snakebite kit. Where the previous antivenin kits used to come with antivenin itself, a syringe, a razor, and a tie of some kind for a ligature, most of that (with the exception of a tie for a ligature in the deluxe model of the kit), is now gone. As a result, the only venom extraction help that people can now purchase is a device that claims to extract all venom, including from a mosquito bite. It is highly questionable whether it is possible to extract snake venom in this way given this very rudimentary technology, but Chad claimed that he got "3 or 4 cups" of venom from his bite wound. This in itself illustrates that he was not telling the truth, because at most a rattlesnake only releases a tablespoon of venom in any bite.[5] Chad urged other hunters to immediately go to a sporting goods store and buy a kit as soon as possible. They were only around $10, he assured his fellow hunters, so they could buy a few and leave them in various places, like their trucks, where they could get to them easily after they were bitten. Others were not so sure. One writer, asking for advice from a wilderness survival, hiking, and camping forum, inquired about putting together a snakebite kit. He pointed out that the "experts" say that the snakebite kits you see in the stores "don't work," and they all say the "same thing," which is to get to the hospital as quickly as possible. But, he wanted to know, what can you do if you are so remote that you can't get to a hospital quickly? "What am I supposed to just shoot myself in the head to make my death easier?" he wanted to know.[6] His fellow survivalists sympathized and offered this information: Well, it was true that antivenin was also expensive (another reason to feel like they needed different treatment), and if they lacked health insurance, this would be a large problem. The writer claimed that "negative pressure venom extractors" that people can buy in the store are 35–40 percent effective, and the kinds of kits that include mouth suction are 25 percent effective, contrary to all expert advice. So, if they could suction out 40 percent of the venom they could increase their survival rate by 85 percent, which in terms of actual survival rate would give them a 95 percent survival rate. Most medical personnel, the writer insisted, insist on antivenin because the "controlled nature of the environment," which was code for the idea that doctors can control your health. In the end, the writer insisted that the person get a snakebite kit, learn to use it, and "pray it never is needed."[7]

Later, the person who asked the initial question claimed that he had used his kit "a whole lot," even for "insect bites and such," and claimed it had worked.[8] This is clearly not true, and if he had read the review by a herpetologist and medical practitioner named Jordan Benjamin on the product's site, he would have seen that the actual experts do not recommend this product. Benjamin points out that the "short answer to the question of whether or not the Sawyer Extractor can effectively remove venom from the site of a bite is a resounding no: the Sawyer Extractor and all of the other 'snakebite kit' variations employing suction, incisions, electricity, heat, cold, and so forth have been repeatedly shown to be utterly ineffective at the job they are designed to market and accomplish. They simply do not work!" He notes that there is a caveat, which is that they do work for removing flesh-eating botfly larvae.[9] He points out that there are several possible reasons why these extractors do not work. One is that the fangs of the snakes are curved, so they do not make holes that go straight down but rather curve away from the initial opening. The tunnels the bites make also collapse very quickly making sucking out the venom next to impossible. The venom diffuses very rapidly into different tissue compartments rather than sitting in a pool, straight down from the bite site where it could be easily removed. Providing a link to an actual medical study about the extractors he notes that "evidence based medicine and all studies to date suggest that they are at best ineffective and at worst harmful."[10]

Undeterred by science, some survivalists also continue to make claims about other painful treatments. Dr. Daryl Neans, a veterinarian in Pflugerville, Texas, had his story about a cure reprinted in a survivalist online site about snakebites. A rancher brought his dog to Dr. Neans 30 minutes after the dog had been bitten on the face by a rattlesnake. The dog's face started swelling, so Neans decided to use a unusual technique. He brought the dog out to his truck, "connected a wire to one of the spark plug wires of his truck then grounded another one to the frame and used the two wires to shock the 'dog's face half a dozen times around the bites.'" The treatment seemed to "relieve the dog's pain." He supposedly then gave the dog antivenin, but he was "convinced that the shock had already effected the cure." His explanation was that "body tissue is negatively charged, snake venom is slightly positive, and unlike charges attract." And perhaps the "ionization of the venom molecules" was "altered by electrical shock so that they 'couldn't attach themselves to animal tissue and destroy it.'"[11] Just in case readers were left with the impression that only dogs were getting this treatment, the article clarified that this is a treatment tried on people today as well. Dr. Markus Kryger had read about the treatment in an unnamed medical journal and decided to use it on a courthouse employee in southwestern Missouri who was bitten by a copperhead near the courthouse. He gave her a tetanus shot, and then used jumper cables attached to the spark coil of his car to treat the wound. Within an hour she was back to work, so Dr. Kryger became convinced that electrical shock "could deactivate snake venom because of the chemistry of the poison." His theory was that snake venom has trace metals in it "whose properties could be easily set by high-voltage shock, thereby possibly uncoupling what makes the venom work."

Dr. Ronald Guderian, a missionary doctor from Seattle, is credited as the first to use this technique on people from the Esmeraldas Province of Ecuador. He had initially used the ignition systems of outboard motors and chainsaws, but later went to a portable battery-powered "buzzer and coil" setup that he got from a friend in Indiana. Then the same friend sent him some stun guns to try instead. He claims that if people are shocked within 15–20 minutes of the bite, the pain stops and no swelling will occur. Or the swelling and pain will stop if they both started. He typically uses a Nova Technologies stun gun on his patients with the "electrodes modified so that the current can be passed directly through the limb by placing an electrode on each side." The patients receive "20,000 to 25,000 volts or more" in DC voltage.[12] Dr. Guderian felt that this was the only safe way to jolt people with electric shocks. He claimed that an ignition system might scramble a pacemaker. There had, however, been "some trouble with reproducing the effect of the treatment in the laboratory." Supposedly the treatments in the laboratory did not work because they were using cheap imitation stun guns from Taiwan and South Korea. And besides, they did not test the treatment on humans, just small animals. To drum up business for his stun gun product, Jim Scroggins, the vice president of Nova Technologies, took a trip to Ecuador to verify the claims of Dr. Guderian. On a hike through the jungle, he was bitten by a conga ant and used the stun gun to shock his wound, and miraculously, within 30 to 60 minutes it was gone, he claimed.

Just like the prohibitionists did a hundred years ago, survivalists face a dilemma. Whiskey once upon a time was used as one of the cures for snakebite, but prohibitionists did not believe that anyone should have whiskey, so what then should they say to people? The answer was to deny that there was a problem or tell people to avoid going anywhere near snakes. The problem for survivalists is that, by definition, they are out in the wilderness and making the conscious decision to have as little to do as possible with modern society, its scientists, and its government. Or they are "preppers" who believe that the end is near. Some kind of collapse is going to happen that is so huge that we will not have access to modern medicine. So, what do they do besides hook themselves up to their car battery or buy a stun gun? The answers vary according to survivalists. Like the prohibitionists, one suggests that you can simply avoid the problem. He or she recommends "close supervision of our children": no play at night in snake habitats, wearing gaiters and thick boots, watching where people put their hands, and letting the snake go its way rather than trying to catch it.[13] Although this is all generally true, as we have seen, the problem is that lots of people are bitten in surprising ways even under close supervision. And most of them were not trying to catch the snakes. Another prepper lays out a stark vision of the future. Sam Coffman, of the American Prepper Network, argues that we are likely going to face a disaster involving water and medicine. And then once the disaster happens, animals will start to come out in force, which means that venomous snakes will increase their numbers and be a threat to everyone, not just people who currently live in the wilderness. Antibiotics and antivenin will be limited or nonexistent. So what should we do for treatment? Look to plants, he proposes. But, this will entail taking his many online courses that he sells to teach people how to use herbal medicine.[14]

In contrast, informative sites aimed at the middle and upper-middle class are almost unanimous in the scientific accuracy and simplicity of their advice. News stories about bites and treatment techniques give us up-to-the-minute bite stories from around the country rather than sad stories of dead children. The stories are typically accompanied with accurate medical advice and an emphasis on getting to a hospital quickly. And cell phones have made an enormous difference in how fast medical help can arrive. The very day we write this conclusion, a man from Temecula, California, was bitten by a rattlesnake at 1:30 p.m. and summoned help immediately. The paramedics tried to give him aid, but he needed more help than they could give, so he was taken to a higher-level trauma center.[15] A 20-year-old man was hiking in the Chico Hill State Park in California and was bitten as well. He was flown out of the park to a local hospital for treatment. The newspaper reporting the bite spent more time telling readers what to do when bitten than it did about the actual bite experience, and its advice paralleled that of do Amaral and his fellow antivenin advocates many years before others seemed to grasp their wisdom. The article recommended loosening any clothing that was constrictive (rather than tying a ligature), staying calm, and calling 911 for help.[16]

Backpacker.com, a professional hiking site, shared this story and we can see the stark difference with the survivalists' conversations. Fifty-year-old Lorraine Johnson was doing her daily workout hike, for its stress relief and health benefits, on April 13, 2010. She was hiking in Franklin Canyon Park, a 605-acre green space between Los Angeles and the Santa Monica Mountains. She was only about 100 feet into the trail when she inadvertently stepped right on a rattlesnake that she did not see. It never rattled, it simply bit her on her inner ankle before moving away. She was not wearing hiking boots because it was 80 degrees that day. She wanted exercise and had never seen a rattlesnake in that area, so she had no fear of running into one of them. At only 5'4" and about 100 pounds, however, the rattlesnake venom spread quickly through her system. This particular rattlesnake, it turned out, also possessed the new hybrid type of venom that included both neurotoxic and hemotoxic properties. As a result, she had to fight to stay conscious as her oxygen was cut off and she was in acute pain as the hemotoxic part of the venom was starting to destroy her body tissue. Although she had her cell phone with her, the large cliffs in the park blocked most cell phone transmission, so she stumbled back down the path. Luckily a passing car stopped, picked her up, and took her to a park ranger who called an ambulance. She went to a hospital and was given 116 vials of antivenin that eventually saved her life. Her advice, like the sound advice from other newspapers, was to remove tight clothing, clean the bite area, and get to a hospital immediately. Unlike the survivalists, she specifically recommended not doing anything else to the bite.[17] Now the middle class and elite get good advice because they share honest and accurate information about bites with one another. But she was also a member of a demographic that listens to scientific advice and seeks its help.

Nevertheless, we sometimes still see a clear desire, among the medical profession, to blame the person bitten. Somehow, they insist, the bite victim was doing the wrong thing and thus, on some level, deserve their bite. Writing for *The Journal of Emergency Medical Services*, a doctor provides pre-hospital treatment advice to first responders. To familiarize responders with the ways in which a person might get bitten, the doctor provides a hypothetical scenario. "While hiking with friends, a 20-year-old man encounters a rattlesnake. Curious, he attempts to touch the reptile and is bitten on the right index finger. The man and his friends hike two hours back to their car before they can call for help." He offers, without evidence, that "alcohol is frequently involved" in snakebite cases, and that bite victims can "pose a treatment problem if extremely inebriated." If the message is not clear enough that people who are bitten bring it on themselves, he adds this point as well: at times "facial or tongue bites have occurred from handlers attempting to kiss a snake."[18] As we can see from the many cases that we reviewed, as well as actual demographic data in the United States, people were typically not bitten because they were drunk and played around with the snake or kissed it. Although there are no current rattlesnake bite studies in the United States, the ones in the past clearly indicate that the plurality of bites occurred among children, the vast majority of whom were bitten in chance encounters as they played in areas that they did not realize had a rattlesnake nearby. Similarly, people working, not drinking, were the most likely to get bitten, including woodsmen, common laborers, highway workers, and farmers.[19] The results of demographic bite studies in other snake-rich countries parallel this finding. A scientific study of the demographics of snakebites in India showed that exactly the same kinds of people remain the most likely to be bitten. In India, Russels vipers were the most common venomous snakes who bit people and they were most likely to bite men from "the working class, who worked in outdoor occupations, without adequate protective footwear in monsoon season." They were also overwhelmingly likely to be bitten in rural areas.[20]

It is certainly true, however, that snakes remain a source of entertainment and income for many people (including this book). Although some rattlesnakes are protected by the Endangered Species Act, some of them are not, and so they are used for commercial reasons in all kinds of ways. As in the past, snakes in the United States and around the world are used for entertainment. Today, however, that entertainment is often sold as scientific education. The Discovery Channel and National Geographic Channel offer shows that are at least in part designed to educate the audience about the potential deadly toll of bites or suffocation, where snakes live, their size, and so on. Unlike circus performers who did not kill snakes for money (in fact it was in their interest to keep them alive), many of the modern shows about rattlesnakes and pythons have massive amounts of snake death and capture as their purpose. It is difficult to imagine similar shows about other animals that included that much slaughter on the same kinds of television networks. Can we imagine a show on National Geographic that praises the work of people who slaughter even non-endangered species, like deer, by the thousands every spring? Even hunting shows do not emphasize the mass slaughter of animals. But because of who they are and what they can do to protect themselves, even some of our most animal welfare-conscious media has offered us images of massive death that glorify the killers and kidnappers in the name of health and science.

To be sure, however, snakes are still entertaining people in person, as we could see by the snake nuisance-control workers on snake-hunting and venom-hunting shows. Snake charmers also remain in countries around the world (India, Pakistan, Egypt), and so on. But we use snakes as in-person entertainment now as well. The difference is that we do not call them snake charmers, we call them educators. It is not okay to have fun with snakes unless you can claim to educate people as well. Partysnakes.com is a company that will bring snakes to your child's birthday party in the United States. They tell prospective parents that they bring "hands-on education and entertainment to any function." They send "expert reptile educators to entertain your party guests while they learn about the world" in a "safe and educational way." The snakes are "docile and well-mannered," so children can hold them and drape them around themselves for pictures as party souvenirs.[21] Snakehead Ed, a retired science teacher living in Indiana, offers snake entertainment to children's parties and schools around his state as well. He promises entertainment, but people will learn more about "nature, reptiles, biomes and science through interactive, close encounters with exotic snakes." He brings a variety of snakes to kids' parties, starting with corn snakes and ending with large boas and pythons. All party attendees are allowed to touch the snakes if they want to, but he does not force them. They can also have their picture taken holding a snake. What's changed, then, is that unlike the circus charmers who performed for others, or zoos whose herpetologists did not let people have any physical contact at all, private companies are now giving people the ability to physically interact with the animals directly, all in the name of education and science.[22] Even the rattlesnake roundups offer educational shows, even though thousands of them are killed as part of the roundup. The famous snake entertainers and hunters star in these shows as educators. Jackie Bibby, for example, appeared in an educational snake pit show at the annual rattlesnake roundup. Using several assistants standing in the pit with him, he shows that if people move slowly or stand still, they are less likely to get bitten, but if they move quickly, the snakes will strike. They tend to strike when they are startled. To illustrate the point to his audience, he placed one of his assistants in the center of the raised, glass-enclosed pit, and had his assistants pile rattlesnakes around the man's feet. The audience watched as the snakes tried to bite the handlers who move toward them, but left the man standing still right in the middle of them alone. However, these shows always offer the possibility of the bite (unlike the snake birthday parties), and this educational demonstration did not disappoint. One of Bibby's helpers is bitten on the hand and rushed to the hospital for antivenin.[23]

Snakes are also used in entertainment in western Europe. There, women are hired as snake charmers by a company called Hafla Entertainment, which offers "entertainment from around the world," but is based in the United Kingdom. The charmers perform for children's parties, or they can be more "adult oriented" if requested. They have a variety of themes, including circus and side show, Middle Eastern, rock/matrix, fetish/dominatrix, showgirl, Rio Carnival, Venetian Masquerade, Indiana Jones, and the Wild West. Pictures of the particular snake charmers and scenes from their acts are placed on the website so that customers can select which one they would like to have come and perform. Although the website says that they perform for children's parties, the women are all in either bikinis or belly dancing outfits, or some other form of sexy costume. The snakes are posed next to the women's breasts so that the camera captures both in the picture. In short, these are the same kinds of sexy snake charmers that we saw in circuses, but now they work for entertainment

A cowboy working at a rattlesnake roundup (courtesy pixabay.com; https://snappygoat.com).

companies and personalize their services for their clients, rather than conducting one mass show for their circus audience.[24]

Not everyone is entertained by snakes, however, and so they remain a feared animal. Psychiatrists estimate that one-third of humans have ophidiophobia (fear of snakes). The phobia tends to develop when people are children, and as we might expect from this book, it often happens because of a personal encounter with a snake, in which it tried to defend itself by hissing, rearing, or biting the child.[25] This leads to a lifelong fear of the animals that can be debilitating for people with severe symptoms, as they will avoid places such as beautiful outdoor scenery just in case they might encounter one. There is also, however, a mass hysteria about them as the well. New Englanders exterminated most of their timber rattlesnake population through hunting and habitat destruction. In an attempt to bring them back, Tom French, assistant director of the Massachusetts State Division of Fisheries and Wildlife Natural Heritage and Endangered Species Program, attempted to create a protected preserve for them on an uninhabited (by humans) island, called Mount Zion, in the Quabbin Reservoir, in the center of the state. His plan was to introduce ten timber rattlesnakes per year on to the island. Nearby residents from Ware, Massachusetts, killed the plan through protests, although French pointed out that rattlesnakes had not killed people in the state for many years, and the Republican governor, Charlie Baker, endorsed the plan for species preservation and environmental protection reasons. As in the past, experts assured people in written editorials that rattlesnakes were not really dangerous and that they rarely bit people.[26] People adjacent to the island, however, who might actually come into contact with them, were not happy with the idea of having these kinds of new neighbors. They pointed out that snakes are excellent swimmers and that there was a land bridge in any case that connected the "island" to the surrounding land.[27]

Other attempts at protecting rattlesnakes have been more successful and they depend upon the stealth of the experts who protect them. In Glastonberry, Connecticut, we find a model of how humans and rattlesnakes can coexist. In that community rattlesnake experts have quietly kept developers from destroying the rattlesnake population and protected humans at the same time. In addition to preventing housing developments in rattlesnake den areas, a local rattlesnake expert has educated the public through information given to potential home buyers and created a rattlesnake emergency removal crew that relocates the rattlesnake rather than kill it or send it to a research lab as we see in the documentaries.[28]

The two different responses of communities in New England illustrate the ongoing tensions between people and snakes. The response that people have to them is visceral and protective. People are in favor of reintroducing endangered species to the wild in theory, but that frequently clashes with the fact that there are very few completely wild places left, which means that we have to find some way for both species to co-exist. People in surrounding communities who face possible negative effects from reintroduced animals are ardent critics that wildlife agencies have to take seriously when they reintroduce animals. Unlike the past when people were moving into the rattlesnake's homes, now animal protection groups and herpetologists have to find a way to move rattlesnakes back near people's homes, and they face a skeptical public. Kyle Whitcombe, a policeman and resident of Ware, for example, confessed to the *Boston Globe* that he was "terrified of snakes" and did not want them near his home.[29]

In many ways, aside from professional herpetologists, other scientists, or collectors (people that tend to have a more rational, scientific relationship with snakes rather than the more common fear-based interactions many have with them in the wild), the only group of people in this text who desire a closer relationship with snakes are the religious communities that practice the handling of serpents as a part of their daily expression of faith. However, this relationship, as we have seen, is not without its significant problems. Even though the practitioners of serpent handling live without a fear of snakes, those in their surrounding communities (as well as law enforcement and animal regulation agencies) don't feel the same way, viewing serpent handlers as religious zealots on the fringes of society and sanity. This is compounded by the problem that although they don't fear snakes like the rest of society, they are still subject to the same types of injuries and deaths that plague people who live in areas where venomous snakes are in abundance. Only the bites that happen in serpent-handling church services are far from accidental. The Biblical nature of serpent handling also works, in many ways, to reestablish the fear that society at large has in regard to snakes because, as it says in the Book of Genesis, the serpent is bound by God to strike at the heel of man, while man strikes at the head of the serpent—the beginning of a relationship that was never meant to be friendly to begin with. So although serpent handlers could feasibly function as ambassadors of goodwill between man and snakes, their misunderstood, mistrusted, and outright dangerous practices serve only to make people fear snakes more.

Sadly the carnage of humans killing snakes continues. Canadian-born journalist, author, and screenwriter Ryan Knighton shared his experience as a blind man at the Sweetwater Rattlesnake Roundup. The Sweetwater Roundup was started in the 1950s as a way to keep the population of rattlesnakes down because a local doctor was treating many bites a year, and local ranchers wanted a way to lose fewer cattle to death from rattlesnake bites to the nose.[30] Roundups started in the 1930s by ranchers in Oklahoma, Georgia, Texas, and Alabama to create an economic incentive for people to clear their property of animals that were dangerous to themselves and their livestock, and in Sweetwater the local chamber of commerce turned it into an annual money-making opportunity for the town. Some states, like Pennsylvania, have moved to humane roundups that are essentially educational events in which no snakes are collected from the wild. Other states like Texas, however, continue to catch snakes from the wild in an inhumane manner, including by pouring gasoline or chemicals down their burrows. Once the snakes arrive at the roundup, they are either killed, used for other roundups, or have their mouths sewn shut for photo opportunities with people. To sew a snake's mouth shut, it is placed in a freezer to make it easier to handle with a needle. The snake typically dies after the photo opportunity.[31] Going to the roundup was part of Knighton's journey of testing his senses in various ways and experiencing the world of sound in particular. At the Sweetwater Roundup, rattlesnake hunters go to the surrounding cattle acreage and gather up one and a half tons of rattlesnakes, so this, he tells us, is the "grand canyon of sound," the "only downside is a ton and a half of rattlesnakes." He takes his brother with him because they both "love everything cowboy." They get into the stadium, and his brother, who is guiding him, "freezes in terror." His brother says, "I don't mean to exaggerate, but it's all snake." For example, "ten feet in front of us there is an old man, and currently he's shaking a rattlesnake at a baby." The journalist felt every manner of thing rattlesnake for sale: belt buckles, skins, chaps. He heard "rattles going by everywhere" and repeated phrases like, "Oh [expletive]"; "back up, back up, back up"; and "yeah, that's how fast it can happen." The brothers registered for a hunt to catch their own rattlesnake and drove out to a 9,000-acre ranch with their guide, Jeb, the next day. They had a snake hook, a garbage can, and a hand mirror. They were told that the rattlesnakes "are everywhere," so they should keep their "eyes down at all times" whereupon his brother leaned over to him and said, "You are so screwed." They were told that when they found a rattlesnake they should wave their stick at it, to make the snake strike at their boot and then use the stick to pin it down. Knighton hung on to his brother's elbow and took "large, soft astronaut steps into a desert full of snakes." A fellow participant on the tour, that

Knighton nicknamed Mr. Coors because he was drinking beer at 8:30 in the morning, said, "Can I ask you something, are you blind?" When Knightly said yes, he said, "God damn, you are the bravest son of a bitch I've ever met," and brought his family over for a photo. Finally, he finds a snake who rattles right in front of him and then goes silent because "it was busy leaping up trying to take [another participant's] face off." The snake then turned and hid under a shack. Knighton's response was unique. At this point he "became so disgusted" with himself. Why? Because he explained, "here's this creature that has evolved over millennia and it only can say one thing, which is 'leave me alone.'" Back at the Sweetwater Festival, he ironically gets asked to judge the festival's beauty contest. The women, with their big hair, wore white paper hazmat suits and skinned rattlesnakes as their talent. When they were done, they took their bloody hands and made a handprint on a wall behind them, signed their names in blood, and put cutesy hearts next to their signatures. He relates that when he was holding his first snake and skinning it, a person helping him put a small thing in my hand that was twitching: it was a heart. He was struck by the sadness of what he had done and the barbarity of the whole event. When he was finished, he too put his "bloody palm to the wall," because he says in a way that sums up much of the human-snake interaction experience in the United States, "the world is just that horrifying and strange and loud."[32]

The violence of the rattlesnake roundups, that are ultimately, primarily money makers for the local citizenry, rather than a real means of reducing snake numbers in the area, is staggering. Animal welfare philosopher Peter Singer's crucial question, "can they suffer?" is not asked at these brutal style roundups.[33] But this question needs to be asked about everyone involved: both the poor, rural man or child who gets bitten by the snakes, and the snakes themselves. And then, if we sincerely ask that question of both sides, like author Donna Haraway, we believe that there "is a chance for getting on together with some grace" and respect.[34]

Chapter Notes

Preface

1. For examples of biological studies, see Ted Levin, *America's Snake: The Rise and Fall of the Timber Rattlesnake* (Chicago: University of Chicago Press, 2016); Harry W. Green, *Snakes: The Evolution of Mystery in Nature* (Berkeley: University of California, 1997); Mark O'Shea, *Boas and Pythons of the World* (Princeton, NJ: Princeton University Press, 2007). For snake field work examples, see Richard Lapidus, *Snake Hunting on Devil's Highway: Humorous Tales from the Glory Days of Snake Hunting* (Indianapolis: Dog Ear Publishing, 2006) or professional biologists such as D. Bruce Means, *Stalking the Plumed Serpent and Other Adventures in Herpetology* (Sarasota, FL: Pineapple Press, 2008); Leslie Anthony, *Snakebit: Confessions of a Herpetologist* (Vancouver: Greystone Books, 2008); and the story of Joe Slowinski's ill fated collecting trip to Burma in Jamie James, *The Snake Charmer: A Life and Death in Pursuit of Knowledge* (New York: Hyperion, 2000).

2. Bryan Christy, *The Lizard King: True Crimes and Passions of the World's Greatest Reptiles Smugglers* (New York: The Hachette Book Group, 2008).

3. See, for example, Chen Yuan-Lee, ed., *Snake Venoms* (New York: Springer-Verlag Berlin Heidelberg, 1979); Jean-Philippe Chippaux's *Snake Venoms and Envenomations* (Malabar, FL: Krieger Publishing, 2006); Henry Parrish's *Poisonous Snakebites in the United States* (Vantage Press, 1980) and Russell E. Findlay's medical textbook, *Snake Venom Poisoning* (Great Neck, NY: Scholium International, 1983) that also has a chapter that focuses on a few of the pre-antivenin cures for snake bite. Also Laurence M. Klauber's *Rattlesnake: Their Habits, Life Histories, and Influence on Mankind* (Berkeley: University of California Press, 1997).

4. Drake Stutesman, *Snake* (London: Reaktion Books, 2005).

5. Donna Haraway, *When Species Meet* (Minneapolis: University of Minnesota Press, 2008), 5.

6. Haraway, *When Species Meet,* 10.

7. See for example "An Epidemic of Snakes," *New York Times,* 24 Aug. 1890, 20.

8. See for example "Bee Stings" in *British Bee Keeper Journal and Bee Keeper-Advisor,* Volume 26 (1898): 335.

Chapter 1

1. Samuel Hopkins Adams, "The Poison Bugaboo," *Everybody's Magazine,* Vol. 28, (July-December 1910): 518–19, 519.

2. "Rattlesnake," *The New North-west* (Deer Lodge, MT), 13 Nov. 1896. *Chronicling America: Historic American Newspapers.* Lib. of Congress. http://chroniclingamerica.loc.gov/lccn/sn84038125/1896–11-13/ed-1/seq-8. Accessed 2 May 2017.

3. Adams, "The Poison Bugaboo," 518.

4. William Temple Hornaday, *The American Natural History* (New York: Charles Scribner's Sons, 1914), 348, 349, 518.

5. *Dodge City Times* (Dodge City, KS), 25 May 1878. *Chronicling America: Historic American Newspapers.* Lib. of Congress. http://chroniclingamerica.loc.gov/lccn/sn84029838/1878–05-25/ed-1/seq-1/. Accessed 28 March 2017.

6. "Killed by a Snake Bite," *New York Times,* 29 Sept. 1886, 3.

7. Jun Noak, "A Case of Snake Bite," *United States Medical Investigator,* Vol. 7, No. 1 (1869): 66–67.

8. "Killed by Rattle Snake Bite," *The Wenatchee Daily World* (Wenatchee, WA), 17 June 1909. *Chronicling America: Historic American Newspapers.* Lib. of Congress.

http://chroniclingamerica.loc.gov/lccn/sn86072041/1909–06-17/ed-1/seq-1/. Accessed 2 May 2017.

9. "Death from Rattlesnake Bite," *The Copper Era* (Clifton, Graham County, AZ), 6 Aug. 1908. *Chronicling America: Historic American Newspapers*. Lib. of Congress. http://chroniclingamerica.loc.gov/lccn/sn89053851/1908–08-06/ed-1/seq-4/. Accessed 2 May 2017.

10. "Boy Handles Snake: Supposed to Be Harmless, but Proves Fatal to Boy," *The Lakeland Evening Telegram* (Lakeland, FL), 19 Oct. 1912. *Chronicling America: Historic American Newspapers*. Lib. of Congress. http://chroniclingamerica.loc.gov/lccn/sn95047222/1912–10-19/ed-1/seq-2/. Accessed 12 April 2017.

11. Robert Marshall, "Snake Bites," *United States Medical Investigator*, Vol. 21 (1885): 569.

12. "Fatally Bitten By a Snake," *New York Times*, 3 August 1889, 2.

13. "Snakes!" *The Tacoma Times* (Tacoma, WA), 29 June 1909. *Chronicling America: Historic American Newspapers*. Lib. of Congress. http://chroniclingamerica.loc.gov/lccn/sn88085187/1909–06-29/ed-1/seq-3/. Accessed 12 April 2017.

14. "Rattlesnakes," *Eclectic Magazine of Foreign Literature, Science, and Art*, Volume 16 (1872): 723–28, 725.

15. *Snips & St. Johns Herald* (St. Johns, AZ) 12 September 1903. https://chroniclingamerica.loc.gov/lccn/sn95060581/1903–09-12/ed-1/seq-1/. Accessed 8 September 2018.

16. "What Happened Outside of Chicago," *The Day Book* (Chicago, IL), 9 October 1912.

17. "Cure of Rattlesnake Bite," *Holbrook Argus* (Navajo County, AZ), 11 June 1907. https://chroniclingamerica.loc.gov/lccn/sn94051342/1907–06-11/ed-1/seq-5/. Accessed 8 September 2108.

18. Martin Lalor Crimmins, "Snake Bites and the Saving of Human Life," *The Military Surgeon*, Vol. 73, No. 3 (1934): 125–132, 128.

19. "Bark Peelers," *The Fairmont West Virginian*, 07 Aug. 1905. *Chronicling America: Historic American Newspapers*. Lib. of Congress. http://chroniclingamerica.loc.gov/lccn/sn86092557/1905–08-07/ed-1/seq-8/. Accessed 12 April 2017.

20. "Rattlesnakes," *Eclectic Magazine of Foreign Literature, Science, and Art*, Volume 16 (1872): 723–28, 726.

21. Laurence Klauber, Venom, Vol. 111, Account of a Snakebite, 23 August 1923 sent to Klauber. Author Unknown. Miscellaneous Folder, San Diego Natural History Museum.

22. Letter from Martin Crimmins to Laurence Klauber, 4 September 1946, Crimmins Folder, Box 76, Laurence Klauber Correspondence, San Diego Natural History Museum.

23. "Bitten by a Snake," *New York Times*, 1 August 1888, 3.

24. "Bitten by a Rattlesnake," *Edgefield Advertiser* (Edgefield, SC), 20 July 1893. *Chronicling America: Historic American Newspapers*. Lib. of Congress. http://chroniclingamerica.loc.gov/lccn/sn84026897/1893–07-20/ed-1/seq-4/. Accessed 12 April 2017.

25. "Has Brand of Serpent," *Omaha Daily Bee*. (Omaha, NE), 19 Oct. 1913. *Chronicling America: Historic American Newspapers*. Lib. of Congress. http://chroniclingamerica.loc.gov/lccn/sn99021999/1913–10-19/ed-1/seq-4/. Accessed 12 April 2017.

26. "Lubbock Farmer Bitten by Rattlsnake Last Week," *Lubbock Avalanche*, 6 June 1922. https://chroniclingamerica.loc.gov/lccn/sn86088055/1922–06-06/ed-1/seq-9/. Acessed 12 April 2017.

27. "Rattlesnakes, " *Eclectic Magazine of Foreign Literature, Science, and Art*, Volume 16 (1872): 723–728, 726.

28. "An Epidemic of Snakes," *New York Times*, 24 Aug. 1890, 20.

29. "Bitten by a Snake," *New York Times*, 8 July 1887, 2.

30. Letter from Warren Lee Brazelton to Laurence Klauber, 8 July 1948, Brazelton, W.L., Folder, Box 76, Laurence Klauber Correspondence, San Diego Natural History.

31. Laurence Klauber to Warren Lee Brazelton, 13 July 1948. Brazelton, W.L., Folder, Box 76, Laurence Klauber Correspondence, The San Diego Natural History Museum, hereafter referred to as SDNHM.

32. Warren L. Brazelton to Laurence M. Klauber, Brazelton, W.L., Folder, Box 76, Laurence M. Klauber Correspondence, SDNHM.

33. Ada Meling to Laurence Klauber, 25 April 1935, Meling Folder, Box 77, Laurence Klauber Correspondence, and Klauber to Ada Meling, 20 April 1933, Meling Folder, Box 77, Laurence Klauber Correspondence, SDNHM.

34. Ada Meling to Laurenc Klauber, 25 April 1935, Meling Folder, Box 77, Laurence Klauber Correspondence, and Klauber to Ada Meling, 20 April 1933, Meling Folder, Box 77, Laurence Klauber Correspondence, SDNHM.

35. Edwin D. Mckee to Laurence Klauber, 14 September 1931, Edwin D. Mckee Folder, Laurence Klauber Correspondence, SDNHM.

36. "Deadly Snake Bite," *Daily Capital Journal* (Salem, OR), 10 August 1905, 3.

37. "Too Many Snake Bites," *The Farmer's Magazine*, Vol. 57 (Jan. to June 1880): 62.

38. "Deaths from Snake Bites," *New York Times*, 11 Aug. 1895, 9.

39. "Deaths from Snake Bites," *New York Times*, 11 Aug. 1895, 9.

40. "Hindoo Zoohily and Snake-Bites," *The Journal of American Medical Association*, Vol. 36, No. 14 (April 1901): 1048–1049. See also Catherine C. Hopley, *Snakes: Curiosities and Wonders of Serpent Life* (London: Griffith and Farran; New York: E.P. Dutton, 1882). Hopley has the same racist views.

41. Prairie Illinois Farmer, "Snakes," *The Working Farmer*, Vol. 9 (1858): 165.

42. Prairie Illinois Farmer, "Snakes," *The Working Farmer*, Vol. 9 (1858): 165.

43. See Martin Lalor Crimmins, "Snake Bites and the Saving of Human Life," *The Military Surgeon*, Vol. 73, No. 3 (1934): 125–132, 129.

44. Jesse T. Palmer, "The Banana in Caribbean Trade," *Economic Geography*, Vol. 8, No. 3 (July 1932): 262–273, 263.

45. Jesse T. Palmer, "The Banana in Caribbean Trade," *Economic Geography*, Vol. 8, No. 3 (July 1932): 262–273, 266.

46. Jesse T. Palmer, "The Banana in Caribbean Trade," *Economic Geography*, Vol. 8, No. 3 (July 1932): 262–273, 264.

47. "Judge Williams Dead," *Arizona Republican* (Phoenix, AZ), 25 May 1899. *Chronicling America: Historic American Newspapers*. Lib. of Congress. http://chronicling america.loc.gov/lccn/sn84020558/1899–05–25/ed-1/seq-4/. Accessed 13 April 2017.

48. Raymond L. Ditmars, *Confessions of a Scientist* (New York: Macmillan, 1934), 70–71.

49. Thomas McCreary, M.D., and Harold Wurzel, M.D., Philadelphia, "Poisonous Snake Bites: Report of a Case," *Journal of the American Medical Association*, Vol. 170, Issue 3 (May 1959): 268–272, 268–269.

50. Letter from Roger Conant to Laurence Klauber, 29 July 1952. Miss C667 Roger Conant Collection, Box 54, Folder 23, American Museum of Natural History.

51. Laurence Klauber to Afranio do Amaral. Do Amaral Folder, Box 76, Laurence Klauber Correspondence, SDNHM.

52. David Kulcyzk, "The Snake Woman—Cypress Orange Country—July 20, 1948," Posted 25 June 2012, http://www.dkulczyk.com/. Accessed 3 November 2012.

53. Today's Program. Ross Allen's Reptile Institute. Miss C667, Roger Conant Collection, Box 46, Folder 1. American Museum of Natural History.

54. Letter from Gladys Marnhout to Roger Conant, Miss 667, Roger Conant Collection, Box 46, Folder 1. American Museum of Natural History.

55. See for example, George A. Otis, *A Report of Surgical Cases: Army of the United States From 1865 to 1871*, War Department, Surgeon General's Office, Circular No. 3, 1871. In this case they recorded three snakebites.

56. Lieutenant W. Culbert Lyon, "Venomous Snakes of the United States, Their Bites and Treatment," *The Military Surgeon*, Vol. 27, No. 1 (July 1910): 383–385, 383.

57. John Chalmers Da Costa, *Modern Surgery, General and Operative*, Fifth edition (Philadelphia: W.B. Saunders and Co., 1908), 264–65.

58. J.V.D. Middleton, Memorandum of a Case of Snake Bite. George A. Otis, *A Report of Surgical Cases: Army of the United States From 1865 to 1871*, War Department, Surgeon General's Office, Circular No. 3 (1871), 164.

59. A.B. Campbell, "Memorandum of a Recovery from a Rattlesnake Bite," J.V.D. Middleton, Memorandum of a Case of Snake Bite. George A. Otis, *A Report of Surgical Cases: Army of the United States From 1865 to 1871*, War Department, Surgeon General's Office, Circular No. 3 (1871), 164.

60. Jules Le Carpentier, "Report of a Case in which a Bite from a Rattlesnake Proved Fatal." George A. Otis, *A Report of Surgical Cases: Army of the United States From 1865 to 1871*, War Department, Surgeon General's Office, Circular No. 3 (1871), 165.

61. "Bite of the Rattlesnake," *The Herald and News* (Newberry, SC), 16 December 1904.

62. Martin Crimmins to Laurence Klauber, 30 September 1946, Crimmins Folder, Box 76, SDNHM. This letter is describing a book about a Texas camp from the latter 1880s.

63. Letter from Martin Crimmins to Laurence Klauber, 11 June 1945, Martin Crimmins folder, Box 76, Laurence Klauber Correspondence, SDNHM.

64. Martin Crimmins to Laurence Klauber, 4 November 1941, Martin Crimmins File, Box 76, Laurence Klauber Correspondence, SDNHM.

65. "A Chapter on Rattlers," *News and Citizen* (Morrisville, VT), 29 Sept. 1887. *Chronicling America: Historic American Newspapers*. Lib. of Congress. http://chronicling america.loc.gov/lccn/sn97067613/1887–09–29/ed-1/seq-1/. Accessed 12 April 2017.

66. "Mortality from Snake-Bites in India," *The Latter Day Saints' Millennial Star*, Vol. LI (1889): 814–15, 814. Newspaperarchive.com. Accessed 11 November 2016.

67. "The Game and Game Laws of India," *Quarterly Review*, Vol. 167 (1888): 94–95.

68. Afranio do Amaral, "The Snake Bite

Problem in the United States and in Central America," *Bulletin of the Antivenin Institute of America*, Vol. 1, No. 2 (July 1927): 31–35, 32.

69. A.W. Chase, *Dr. Chase's Recipes or Information for Everybody: An Invaluable Collection of About Eight Hundred Practical Recipes* (Ann Arbor: Published by the Author, 1864), 154.

70. Vickers T. Atkinson, William Dickson, William Heyser Harbaugh, and James Law, *Special Report on Diseases of Cattle* (Washington, D.C.: Government Printing Office, 1904), 15–16.

71. *Second Annual Report of the Bureau of Animal Industry for the Year 1885, U.S. Department of Agriculture* (Washington, D.C.: Government Printing Office, 1886): 335–36, 336.

72. Pierre A. Fish, *Journal of the American Veterinary Medical Association*, Vol. 61, No. 14 (1922): 362.

73. Oswaldo Vital Brazil, "History of the Primordia of Snake-Bite Accident Serotherapy," *Memorias do Instituto de Butantan*, Vol. 49, No. 1 (1987): 7–20, 12.

74. E. Clive Webb, Lieutentent, A.V.C., Veterinary Officer, "Snake-Bite in Horses," *Journal of Comparative Pathology and Therapuetics*, Vol. 20 (1907): 100–104, 101–103.

75. Sidney Smith, Jr., "Snake Bite," *American Veterinary Review* Vol. 44 (1911–1912): 162.

76. "Whisky Saves a Snake-Bitten Horse," *New York Times*, 2 Aug. 1896, 2.

77. W.H. Watts, "The Bite of the Rattlesnake," *Monthly Homeopathic Review*, Vol. 17, No. 7 (1 July 1870): 442–43.

78. "Rattlesnakes," *Eclectic Magazine of Foreign Literature, Science, and Art*, Volume 16 (1872): 723–728.

79. "Rattlesnake Bite (Stock)," *The Gazette Times* (Heppner, OR), 8 October 1914, pg. 9. Newspaperarchive.com. Accessed 4 November 2016.

80. Theodore Roosevelt, *Through the Brazilian Wilderness* (New York: Charles Scribner's Sons, 1914), 17–20.

81. Letter from Ray Ditmars to Roger Conant, 17 March 1927. Miss 667, Roger Conant Collection, Box 50, Folder 3. American Natural History Museum.

82. Harry Dunn, "Snakes Battle to Death for Science," *Illustrated World*, Vol. 27, No. 5 (July 1917): 779.

83. "Something About Snake-Root—The First Legislative Grant for a Medical Discovery, North Carolina," *North Carolina Medical Journal*, Vol. XV and XVI (1885): 185–186.

84. Pennsylvania State Department of Agri-

culture, *The Monthly Bulletin of the Division of Zoology*, Vol. 11, No. 3 (July 1904): 165.

85. "Rattle Snake Near Hinsdale," *The Daily Gate City and Constitution-Democrat* (Keokuk, IA), 18 Aug. 1920. *Chronicling America: Historic American Newspapers*. Lib. of Congress. http://chroniclingamerica.loc.gov/lccn/sn87057262/1920–08-18/ed-1/seq-6/. Accessed 13 April 2017.

86. Henry Mushinksy and Alan H. Savitsky, "Position of the American Society of Icthyologists and Herpetologists Concerning Rattlesnake Conservation and Roundups," Position Paper on the American Society of Ichthyologists and Herpelogists Organization site. http://www.asih.org/sites/default/files/documents/resources/pprattlesnake.pdf. Accessed 27 April 2017.

87. Jenks Cameron, *The Bureau of Biological Survey: Its History, Activities and Organization* (Baltimore: Johns Hopkins Press, 1929), 171–185.

88. Afranio do Amaral, "The Anti-Snake-Bite Campaign in Texas and the Sub-Tropical United States," *Bulletin of the Antivenin Institute of America*, October 1927: 77–85, 77.

89. "Large Snakes Killed by Women. Some Club or Stone the Reptiles. Others Behead Them," *New York Times*, 9 Aug. 1894, 12.

90. "Large Snakes Killed by Women. Some Club or Stone the Reptiles. Others Behead Them," *New York Times*, 9 Aug. 1894, 12.

91. "The Tragic Story of a Snake," *New York Times*, Sept. 1888, 6.

92. *Richmond Democrat* (Richmond, Ray County, MO), 27 Sept. 1883. *Chronicling America: Historic American Newspapers*. Lib. of Congress. http://chroniclingamerica. loc.gov/lccn/sn86063662/1883–09-27/ed-1/seq-2/. Accessed 13 April 2017.

93. "A Real Snake Story," *Arizona Weekly Citizen* (Tucson, AZ), 7 Sept. 1895. *Chronicling America: Historic American Newspapers*. Lib. of Congress. http://chronicling america.loc.gov/lccn/sn82015133/1895–09-07/ed-1/seq-1/. Accessed 13 April 2017.

94. "Snakes for Barrooms. How a Connecticut Genius Finds a Living by Hunting Serpents," *New York Times*, 24 March 1886, 4.

95. "Snake-Killing Record Broken," *New York Times*, 6 Sept. 1891.

96. Letter from Roger Conant to Laurence Klauber, 1 December 1962, Roger Conant Collection, Miss C667, Box 52, Folder 2, American Natural History Museum.

97. Laurence Klauber to Afranio do Amaral, 28 June 1928, Do Amaral Folder, Box 76, Laurence Klauber Correspondence, SDNHM.

98. Laurence Klauber to Roger Conant, 4 Nov. 1947, Miss C667, Roger Conant Collec-

tion, Box 54, Folder 23, American Museum of Natural History.

99. "Notes Based on Interview with Asa Pitman, Summer 1947," Mss C667, Roger Conant Collection, Box 54, Folder 23, American Natural History Museum.

100. "Notes Based on Interview with Asa Pitman, Summer 1947," Mss C667, Roger Conant Collection.

101. Raymond Ditmars, "Poisonous Reptiles of the United States," *The World To-Day*, Vol. 11, No. 1 (July 1906): 1044–1051, 1045.

102. Raymond Ditmars, "Poisonous Reptiles of the United States," *The World To-Day*, Vol. 11, No. 1 (July 1906): 1044–1051, 1045, 1046.

103. "Snakes and Wild Honey," *Edgefield Advertiser* (Edgefield, SC), 5 Feb. 1919. *Chronicling America: Historic American Newspapers.* Lib. of Congress. http://chronicling america.loc.gov/lccn/sn84026897/1919–02-05/ed-1/seq-7/. Accessed 14 April 2017.

104. "A Snake Battle," *Jamestown Weekly Alert* (Jamestown, Stutsman County, D.T. [N.D.]), 26 July 1888. *Chronicling America: Historic American Newspapers.* Lib. of Congress. http://chroniclingamerica.loc.gov/lccn/sn85042405/1888–07-26/ed-1/seq-4/. Accessed 13 April 2017.

105. "Killed Huge Rattler," *Crittenden Record-Press* (Marion, KY), 29 May 1913. *Chronicling America: Historic American Newspapers.* Lib. of Congress. http://chroniclingamerica.loc.gov/lccn/sn86069460/1913–05-29/ed-1/seq-5/. Accessed 13 April 2017.

106. *The Oasis* (Arizola, AZ), 5 Sept. 1896. *Chronicling America: Historic American Newspapers.* Lib. of Congress. http://chroniclingamerica.loc.gov/lccn/sn85032933/1896–09-05/ed-1/seq-2/. Accessed 13 April 2017.

107. *The Holt County Sentinel* (Oregon, MO), 25 Sept. 1914. *Chronicling America: Historic American Newspapers.* Lib. of Congress. http://chroniclingamerica.loc.gov/lccn/sn90061417/1914–09-25/ed-1/seq-3/. Accessed 12 April 2017.

108. *The Laurens Advertiser* (Laurens, SC), 28 Sept. 1897. *Chronicling America: Historic American Newspapers.* Lib. of Congress. http://chroniclingamerica.loc.gov/lccn/sn93067760/1897–09-28/ed-1/seq-2. Accessed 13 April 2017.

109. *The Adair County News* (Columbia, KY), 17 June 1914. *Chronicling America: Historic American Newspapers.* Lib. of Congress. http://chroniclingamerica.loc.gov/lccn/sn86069496/1914–06-17/ed-1/seq-8/. Accessed 13 April 2017.

110. *Marble Hill Press* (Marbel [sic] Hill, MO), 3 July 1913. *Chronicling America: Historic American Newspapers.* Lib. of Congress. http://chroniclingamerica.loc.gov/lccn/sn89066695/1913–07-03/ed-1/seq-1/. Accessed 13 April 2017.

Chapter 2

1. M.G. Ellzey, in H. H. Soule, *Hints and Points for Sportsmen* (New York: Forest and Stream Publishing Co., 1889), 163.

2. "Snake-bites and Their Treatment," *American Medico-surgical Bulletin*, Vol. 12, No. 21 (10 Nov. 1898): 1031. This is a review article of this work, no author given: Dr. B.M. Rickets (Cicin Lanc.-Clinic, Vol. XLI no. 9, 1898).

3. Elaine Breslaw, *Lotions, Potions, Pills and Magic: Health Care in Early America* (New York: New York University Press, 2012), 47.

4. Elaine Breslaw, *Lotions, Potions, Pills and Magic: Health Care in Early America* (New York: New York University Press, 2012), 48.

5. Elaine Breslaw, *Lotions, Potions, Pills and Magic: Health Care in Early America* (New York: New York University Press, 2012), 35.

6. It's not always clear who authored an article about snakebite treatment. When it is clearly noted that the author was a physician we note that fact. In other cases there are no author names noted at all. We describe them as medical science writers to identify their purpose of illuminating (from their perspective), the public about the best treatment.

7. For a clear quick review of the effects of rattlesnake venom see "What Is the Venom Type in a Western Diamondback Rattlesnake and What Chemicals in the Venom Cause the Body to Practically Breakdown," no author, University of California, Santa Barbara, Science Line, http://scienceline.ucsb.edu/getkey.php?key=2100. Accessed 11 December 2017. For general biological properties of venom, see Harry W. Green, *Snakes: The Evolution Mystery in Nature* (Berkeley: University of California Press, 1997), 86–91.

8. "For Rattlesnake Bite, First Chicken and then the Snake Applied to the Wound," *New York Times*, 20 July 1885, 2.

9. F.W. Hambleton, "Pueblo Colorado," *Recreation, American Canoe Association and League of American Sportsmen*, Vol. X, No. 1 (Jan. 1899): 218.

10. C.E. Hobbs in his *Botanical Handbook* (Boston, 1876) gives twenty-six species of snakeroot (165).

11. Charles Lynch, *American Red Cross*

Abridged Text-Book on First Aid, Police and Firemen's Edition (Philadelphia: P. Blakiston's Son & Co., 1914), 66.

12. H.T. Peck, The International Cyclopaedia, Vol. 13 (New York: Dodd, Mead & Co., 1900), 599.

13. John King and Robert Newton, The Eclectic Dispensatory of the United States of America (Cincinnati: H. W. Derby, 1852), 38.

14. P.L. Simonds, The Journal of the Society of Arts, No. 216, Vol. V (9 January 1857): 101–105, 101.

15. P.L. Simonds, The Journal of the Society of Arts, No. 216, Vol. V (9 January 1857): 101–105, 103.

16. P.L. Simonds, The Journal of the Society of Arts, No. 216, Vol. V (9 January 1857): 101–105, 105.

17. "Remedy for Hydrophobia" Scientific American,, Vol. XLII, No. 1 (3 January 1880): 264.

18. Catherine C. Hopley, Snakes: Curiosities and Wonders of Serpent Life (London: Griffith and Farran; New York: E.P. Dutton & Co., 1882), 537.

19. C.E. Hobbs in his Botanical Handbook (Boston, 1876), 165–166.

20. "How They Cured a Snake Bite." New York Times, 4 July 1895.

21. A Methodist Preacher (no real name given), "Saliva as an Antidote to Poison," Southern Cultivator, Vol. 11, No. 1 (1853), 91.

22. A Methodist Preacher (no real name given), "Saliva as an Antidote to Poison," Southern Cultivator, Vol. 11, No. 1 (1853), 91.

23. A Methodist Preacher (no real name given), "Saliva as an Antidote to Poison," Southern Cultivator, Vol. 11, No. 1 (1853), 91.

24. A Methodist Preacher (no real name given), "Saliva as an Antidote to Poison," Southern Cultivator, Vol. 11, No. 1 (1853), 91.

25. Catherine C. Hopley, Snakes: Curiosities and Wonders of Serpent Life (London: Griffith and Farran; New York: E.P. Dutton & Co., 1882), 542, 543.

26. No Author, The Plantation, Series I, Vol. 11, 660.

27. Afranio do Amaral, A General Consideration of Snake Poisoning and Observations on Neotropical Pit-Vipers (Cambridge: Harvard University Press, 1925), 19.

28. Captain G.R.G. Fisher, "Be a Helpful Bystander," The Bemidji Daily Pioneer (Bermidji, MN) 9 September 1920, 8.

29. "Care for the Bite of a Rattlesnake," Scientific American, Vol. 3, No. 27 (25 March 1848): 192, 132.

30. George Bacon Wood and Franklin Bache, The Dispensatory of the United States of America, Eleventh Edition (Philadelphia: J.B. Lippincott and Co., 1858), 432.

31. Dr. A.S. Byne, "Carbonate of Ammonia in the Bites of Poisonous Reptiles," Boston Medical and Surgical Journal, Vol. 48 (1858): 248.

32. J.A. Kirkpatrick, "Ammonia for a Rattlesnake Bite," Southern Journal of Homoeopathy, Vol. 11, No. 3 (1893): 117–118.

33. Catherine C. Hopley, Snakes: Curiosities and Wonders of Serpent Life (London: Griffith and Farran; New York: E.P. Dutton & Co., 1882), 547.

34. "Injection of Ammonia for Snakebites," Pacific Medical and Surgical Journal, Vol. 16, No. 10 (March 1875): 507.

35. "Antidote Against Snake-Bite," The Natal Agricultural Journal, Vol. 11 (1908): 217.

36. Morris R. Rice, "Snake Poison and Its Treatment," Medical Brief, Vol. 32, Issue 2: 795–796.

37. Catherine C. Hopley, Snakes: Curiosities and Wonders of Serpent Life (London: Griffith and Farran; New York: E.P. Dutton & Co., 1882), 544.

38. George Shipman, The United States Medical and Surgical Journal, Vol. 3 (1867–8): 210.

39. H.K. Gilman, The Naval Brigade and Operations Ashore: A Hand-Book for Field, U.S.M.C, Bureau of Navigation, Navy Department, Naval Professional Papers, No. 20 (Washington, D.C.: Government Printing Office, 1884), 270.

40. John Chalmers Da Costa, Modern Surgery, General and Operative, Fifth Edition (Philadelphia: W.B. Saunders and Co., 1908), 264–265.

41. Blanche Swainhardt, Ray Cyrus Yeoman, Carlos Grant Williams, Leo Leavitt Rummell, Zeno Payne Metcalf, George Colvin Humphrey, and Florence Forbes, The Rural Efficiency Guide (Cleveland: The People's Efficiency Publishing Co., 1918), 184.

42. "An Antidote for Snake Bite," The National Druggist, Vol. 38 (1908): 281.

43. M.D. (Assistant Surgeon General, United States Public Health Service), Prevention of Disease and Care of the Sick: How to Keep Well and What to Do in Case of Sudden Illness 1918, Miscellaneous Publication No. 17, Third edition (Washington, D.C.: Government Printing Office, 1919), 201.

44. Prentiss Willson, "Snake Poisoning in the United States: A Study Based on an Analysis of Seven Hundred and Forty Cases," Archives of Internal Medicine, No. 1 (January 1908): 516–570, 562. This is an AMA publication.

45. Catherine C. Hopley, Snakes: Curiosities and Wonders of Serpent Life (London: Griffith and Farran; New York: E.P. Dutton & Co., 1882), 545–546.

46. John Collins Warren, *Surgical Pathology and Therapeutics* (Philadelphia: W.B. Saunders, 1894), 501.

47. F.W. Hambleton, "Pueblo Colorado," *Recreation, American Canoe Association and League of American Sportsmen*, Vol. X, No. 1 (January 1899): 218.

48. S.B. Higgins, "Snake Poison and Its Antidote," *Monthly Homeopathic Review*, Vol. 14, No. 7 (1 July 1887): 440–442, 422.

49. Drill Regulations and Outlines of First Aid for the Hospital Corps, United States, Medical Department, Army, The War Department (Washington, D.C.: Government Printing Office, 1908), 160.

50. P.L. Simonds, *The Journal of the Society of Arts*, Vol. V, No. 216 (9 January 1857): 101–105, 102.

51. Martin Lalor Crimmins, "Snake Bites and the Saving of Human Life," *The Military Surgeon*, Vol. 73, No. 3 (1934): 125–132, 127.

52. Dudley Jackson, "Treatment of Snake Bite," *Southern Medical Journal*, Vol. XXII, No. 7 (July 1929): 605–607, 606.

53. Martin Crimmins to Laurence Klauber, 18 July 1946, Crimmins Folder, Box 76, Laurence Klauber Correspondence, SDNHM.

54. Afranio do Amaral, "The Brazilian Contribution Towards the Improvement of the Specific Snake Bite Treatment," *Proceedings of the New York Pathological Society* (1923): 89–98, 96.

55. Dudley Jackson, "Treatment of Snake Bite," *Southern Medical Journal*, Vol. XXII, No. 7 (July 1929): 605–607, 606.

56. "Snake Bite," Staten Island Zoological Society, *Animaland*, Vol. XI, No. 3 (July-August 1944): 3–4. Staten Island Zoological Society Archives.

57. "Snake Bite," Staten Island Zoological Society, *Animaland*, Vol. XI, No. 3 (July-August 1944): 3–4. Staten Island Zoological Society Archives.

58. "Snake Bite," Staten Island Zoological Society, *Animaland*, Vol. XI, No. 3 (July-August 1944): 3–4. Staten Island Zoological Society Archives.

59. Raymond Ditmars, "Snakes," *Field and Stream*, January 1927, St. Louis Zoo Records, 1910–1940, Roll 6, Western Historical Manuscript Collection, University of St. Louis–Missouri.

60. Robert Hellman, "An Account of a Bite by a Prarie Rattlesnake and the Treatment Which Followed," Laurence Klauber Miscellaneous Folder 1951–52, Laurence Klauber Venom, Vol. 111, SDNHM.

61. S.B. Higgins, "Snake Poison and Its Antidote," *Monthly Homeopathic Review*, Vol. 14, No. 7 (1 July 1887): 440–442, 441.

62. H.K. Gilman, *The Naval Brigade and Operations Ashore: A Hand-Book for Field*, U.S.M.C, Bureau of Navigation, Navy Department, Naval Professional Papers, No. 20 (Washington, D.C.: Government Printing Office, 1884), 207.

63. "The Snake Bite Case, William Gore Very Low, But Whisky May Save Him," *New York Times*, 16 May 1888, 3.

64. Catherine C. Hopley, *Snakes: Curiosities and Wonders of Serpent Life* (London: Griffith and Farran; New York: E.P. Dutton & Co., 1882), 551.

65. "Poisonous Snake Bites: Result of Dr. Allen's Experiment Made Known," *New York Times*, 24 April 1882, 17.

66. Catherine C. Hopley, *Snakes: Curiosities and Wonders of Serpent Life* (London: Griffith and Farran; New York: E.P. Dutton & Co., 1882), 549–550, 548.

67. Charles L. Dulles, ed., *Medical and Surgical Reporter*, Vol. 48 (January–July 1888): 754–755, 754.

68. "Ophidians, No. 3—Their Evils," *The Dublin University Magazine*, Vol. LXXXVII (March 1876): 344–360, 352.

69. *Evening Star* (Washington, D.C.), 18 April 1909. *Chronicling America: Historic American Newspapers*. Lib. of Congress. http://chroniclingamerica.loc.gov/lccn/sn83045462/1909–04-18/ed-1/seq-24/. Accessed 12 April 2017. No author, *Puck*, Vol. 18, No. 461 (6 January 1886): 301.

70. *Evening Star* (Washington, D.C.), 18 April 1909. *Chronicling America: Historic American Newspapers*. Lib. of Congress. http://chroniclingamerica.loc.gov/lccn/sn83045462/1909–04-18/ed-1/seq-24/. Accessed 10 April 2017.

71. James Henry Potts, *Black and White or the Saloon Versus Temperance: The Greatest Problem Facing Our Nation Today* (Detroit: F.B. Dickerson and Co., 1908), 350, 352.

72. "The Texas Rattler and the Whiskey Bottle," *The Farmer and Mechanic Volume* (Raleigh, NC), 24 Feb. 1903. *Chronicling America: Historic American Newspapers*. Lib. of Congress. http://chroniclingamerica. loc.gov/lccn/sn99061556/1903–02-24/ed-1/seq-1/. Accessed 12 April 2017.

73. Ino F. Hill, "Popular Idols Broken," *The Assembly Herald, Presbyterian Church in the U.S.A. Office of the General Assembly*, Vol. 7, No. 1 (July 1902): 130.

74. *Belmont Chronicle* (St. Clairsville, OH), 2 Aug. 1855. *Chronicling America: Historic American Newspapers*. Lib. of Congress. http://chroniclingamerica.loc.gov/lccn/sn85026241/1855–08-02/ed-1/seq-1/. Accessed 3 April 2017.

75. *The Ward County Independent* (Minot, Ward County, ND), 15 Feb. 1905. *Chronicling*

America: Historic American Newspapers. Lib. of Congress. http://chroniclingamerica. loc.gov/lccn/sn88076421/1905–02-15/ed-1/seq-4/. Accessed 28 March 2017.

76. The St. Johns Herald (St. Johns, Apache County, Arizona Territory), 19 Dec. 1889. Chronicling America: Historic American Newspapers. Lib. of Congress. http://chroniclingamerica.loc.gov/lccn/sn94051692/1889–12-19/ed-1/seq-1/. Accessed 4 April 2017.

77. Ernest Thompson Seton's The Woodcraft Manual for Boys was more of an advocate of knives, perhaps because boys would be using knives to do woodcraft and hence it was presumed they would be safe. He recommend cutting open the wound and actually leaving it open for a week. He also recommended antivenin and strychnine. He noted that whisky was recommended, "but plenty evidence that many have been killed by such remedies, and little that they have every saved anyone, except perhaps when the victim was losing courage or becoming sleepy" (340). The boys were to "send as fast as [they could] for a doctor" (340). The author recommends Ray Ditmars' The Reptile Book, and his Reptiles of the World for further reading. Ernest Thompson Seton, The Woodcraft Manual for Boys (Garden City, NY: Doubleday, Page & Co., 1917), 340–341.

78. "Boy Scouts," New York Times, 7 August 1921, 71. ProQuest Historical Newspapers. Accessed 2 October 2016.

79. Lina Beard and Adelia Belle Beard, On the Trail: An Outdoor Book for Girls (New York: Charles Scribner's Sons, 1915), 171, 177.

80. G.H. Halberstadt, A.F. Knoefel, W.A. Lynott, W.S. Roundtree, and M.J. Shields, Advanced First-Aid Instruction for Miners, Department of the Interior, Bureau of Mines (Washington, D.C.: Government Printing Office, 1917), 201.

81. Lieutenant W. Culbert Lyon, "Venomous Snakes of the United States: Their Bites and Treatment," The Military Surgeon, Vol. 27, No. 1 (July 1910): 383–385, 385.

82. E.H. Winston, "Snakes Good and Bad," Hospital Corps Quarterly, United States Navy Department Bureau of Medicine, Vol. 5, No. 1 (Jan. 1921): 22–25, 23, 24.

83. Wilson G. Harger and Edmond Bonney, Handbook for Highway Engineers, 3rd Edition (New York: McGraw Hill, 1919), 383, 385, 464.

84. William J. Parks, "Venomous Reptiles," Medical Council: A Practical Journal for the General Practitioner, Vol. 27 (1912): 228.

85. "Snake Poison Cure," American Notes and Queries, Vol. 8 (19 March 1892): 237.

86. M.D. (Assistant Surgeon General,

United States Public Health Service), Prevention of Disease and Care of the Sick: How to Keep Well and What to Do in Case of Sudden Illness 1918, Miscellaneous Publication No. 17, Third edition (Washington, D.C.: Government Printing Office, 1919), 202.

87. Prentiss Willson, "Snake Poisoning in the United States: A Study Based on an Analysis of Seven Hundred and Forty Cases," Archives of Internal Medicine, No. 1 (January 1908): 516–570, 569. This is an AMA publication.

Chapter 3

1. Oswaldo Vital Brazil, "History of the Primordia of Snake-Bite Accident Serotherapy," Memorias do Instituto de Butantan, Vol. 49, No. 1 (1987): 7–20, 9.

2. See Moyer S. Fleisher and Leo Loeb, "Action of Calmett[e]'s Cobra Antivenin upon the Venom of Heloderma," in Leo Loeb and Carl Alsberg, eds., The Venom of Heloderma (Washington, D.C.: Carnegie Institute of Washington, 1913), 201–203; Joseph McFarland, A Text-Book upon the Pathogenic Bacteria and Protozoa, Seventh Edition (Philadelphia: W.B. Saunders Co., 1912); Hideyo Nochughi, "Snake Venoms," Modern Medicine, Vol. 1 (1907): 247–265.

3. Frances Gow Smith, "Snakes Are Safe if You Know," Popular Science Monthly, Vol. 108, No. 1 (January 1926): 20–21, 136–38, 21.

4. Barbara J. Hawgood, "Pioneers of Anti-Venomous Serotherapy: Dr. Vital Brazil (1865–1950)," Toxicon, Vol. 30, No. 5/6 573–579, 575, 576.

5. Barbara J. Hawgood, "Pioneers of Anti-Venomous Serotherapy: Dr. Vital Brazil (1865–1950)," Toxicon, Vol. 30, No. 5/6 (1992): 573–579.

6. Raymond Ditmars, "Treatment of Our First Case of Snake Bite," New York Zoological Society Bulletin, Vol. 24, No. 1 (January 1916): 1358–1364, 1361.

7. Frank G. Carpenter, "City of Snakes," Moderator-Topics, Vol. 36, No. 1 (9 September 1915): 350–352, 350.

8. Frank G. Carpenter, "City of Snakes," Moderator-Topics, Vol. 36, No. 1 (9 September 1915): 350–352, 351.

9. Afranio do Amaral, "The Brazilian Contribution Towards the Improvement of the Specific Snake Bite Treatment," Proceedings of the New York Pathological Society (1923): 89–98, 91.

10. Frank G. Carpenter, "City of Snakes," Moderator-Topics, Vol. 36, No. 1 (9 September 1915): 350–352, 351.

11. Frank G. Carpenter, "City of Snakes,"

Moderator-Topics, Vol. 36, No. 1 (9 September 1915): 350–352, 352.

12. Afranio do Amaral, *Serpientes em Crises*, 47.

13. Raymond Ditmars, "Treatment of Our First Case of Snake Bite," *New York Zoological Society Bulletin*, Vol. 24, No. 1 (January 1916): 1358–1364.

14. Afranio do Amaral, "Announcement," *Bulletin of the Antivenin Institute of America*, Vol. 1, No. 1 (March 1927): 1–2, 2.

15. Afranio do Amaral, No title, two page description of the antivenin, Do Amaral Folder, Box 76, Laurence Klauber Correspondence, SDNHM.

16. Afranio do Amaral to Laurence Klauber, 15 April 1926, Do Amaral Folder, Box 76, Laurence Klauber Correspondence, SDNHM.

17. Laurence Klauber to Afranio do Amaral, 30 April 1926, Do Amaral Folder, Box 76, Laurence Klauber Correspondence, SDNHM.

18. Laurence Klauber to Afranio do Amaral, 30 April 1926, Do Amaral Folder, Box 76, Laurence Klauber Correspondence, SDNHM.

19. Afranio do Amaral, "The Snake Bite Problem in the United States and in Central America," *Bulletin of the Antivenin Institute of America*, Vol. 1, No. 2 (July 1927): 31–35, 32.

20. Afranio do Amaral, "The Snake Bite Problem in the United States and in Central America," *Bulletin of the Antivenin Institute of America*, Vol. 1, No. 2 (July 1927): 31–35, 32.

21. Louis Galambos and Jane Eliot Sewell, *Networks of Innovation: Vaccine Development at Merck, Sharp & Dohme, and Mulford, 1895–1995* (Melbourne: Cambridge University Press, 1995), 1–32.

22. Doris Cochran, Meeting Minutes, 15 January 1926, Box 1, Vivarium Society, RU 7163, Smithsonian Institution.

23. Martin Lalor Crimmins, "Snake Bites and the Saving of Human Life," *The Military Surgeon*, Vol. 73, No. 3 (1934): 125–132, 126.

24. Martin Lalor Crimmins, "Poisonous Snakes and the Antivenin Treatment," *Southern Medical Journal*, Vol. XXII, No. 7 (July 1929): 603–605, 604.

25. Afranio do Amaral, "The Snake Bite Problem in the United States and in Central America," *Bulletin of the Antivenin Institute of America*, Vol. 1, No. 2 (July 1927): 31–35, 33.

26. Raymond L. Ditmars, *Strange Animals I Have Known* (New York: Harcourt, Brace and Company, 1931), 194.

27. Afranio do Amaral, No title, two page description of the antivenin, Do Amaral Folder, Box 76, Laurence Klauber Correspondence, SDNHM.

28. Afranio do Amaral to Laurence Klauber, 11 July 1927, Do Amaral Folder, Box 76, Laurence Klauber Correspondence, SDNHM.

29. Laurence Klauber to Thomas S. Githens, 6 December 1935, Thomas Githens File, Box 76, Laurence Klauber Correspondence; Laurence Klauber to Thomas S. Githens, 17 December 1935, Thomas Githens File, Box 76, Laurence Klauber Correspondence; Thomas Githens to Laurence Klauber, 21 October 1938, Thomas Githens Folder, Box 76, Laurence Klauber Correspondence. All from the SDNHM collection.

30. Thomas S. Githens M.D., and I.D. George, "Comparative Studies on the Venoms of Certain Rattlesnakes," a paper presented at the Fourteenth Annual Meeting of the American Society of Ichthyologists and Herpetologists, Philadelphia, 12 May 1931. Thomas Githens File, Box 76, Laurence Klauber Correspondence, SDNHM; Afranio do Amaral to Laurence Klauber, 25 May 1927, Do Amaral Folder, Box 76, Laurence Klauber Correspondence, SDNHM.

31. Afranio do Amaral to Laurence Klauber, 28 May 1927, Do Amaral Folder, Box 76, Laurence Klauber Correspondence, SDNHM.

32. Laurence Klauber, Venom 111, 1935, Box 77, pages 7–9, SDNHM.

33. Klauber to Do Amaral, 8 September 1926, Do Amaral Folder, Box 76, Laurence Klauber Correspondence, SDNHM.

34. Klauber to Do Amaral, 8 September 1926, Do Amaral Folder, Box 76, Laurence Klauber Correspondence, SDNHM.

35. Afranio Do Amaral to Laurence Klauber, 8 September 1926, Do Amaral Folder, Box 76, Laurence Klauber Correspondence, SDNHM.

36. Laurence Klauber to Afranio do Amaral, 3 January 1927, Do Amaral Folder, Box 76, Klauber Correspondence, SDNHM.

37. Afranio do Amaral to Laurence Klauber, 9 May 1927, Afranio do Amaral Folder, Box 76, Laurence Klauber Correspondence, SDNHM.

38. Laurence Klauber to Afranio do Amaral, 22 March 1927, Box 76, Laurence Klauber Correspondence, SDNHM.

39. Laurence Klauber to Afranio do Amaral, 22 March 1927, Box 76, Laurence Klauber Correspondence, SDNHM.

40. Laurence Klauber, Venom 111, 1935, pages 12–15, Box 77, SDNHM.

41. Thomas Githens to Laurence Klauber, 31 January 1935, Thomas Githens Folder, Box 76, Laurence Klauber Correspondence,

SDNHM; Thomas Githens to Laurence Klauber, 3 November 1932, Thomas Githens File, Box 76, Laurence Klauber Correspondence, SDNHM.

42. Laurence Klauber to Paul Breese, 17 August 1943, P.L. Breeze Folder, Box 76, Laurence Klauber Correspondence, SDNHM.

43. Laurence Klauber to Afranio do Amaral, 9 May 1927, Do Amaral File, Box 76, Laurence Klauber Correspondence, SDNHM.

44. Laurence Klauber to Afranio do Amaral, 10 March 1927.

45. Do Amaral to Laurence Klauber, 16 March 1927, Do Amaral Folder, Box 76, Laurence Klauber Correspondence, SDNHM.

46. Do Amaral to Laurence Klauber, 16 March 1927, Do Amaral Folder, Box 76, Laurence Klauber Correspondence, SDNHM.

47. Laurence Klauber to Afranio do Amaral, 3 May 1927, Afranio do Amaral Folder, Box 76, Laurence Klauber Correspondence, SDNHM.

48. Laurence Klauber to Afranio do Amaral, Do Amaral Folder, Box 76, Laurence Klauber Correspondence, SDNDM.

49. Afranio do Amaral to Laurence Klauber, 25 May1927, Do Amaral Folder, Box 76, Laurence Klauber Correspondence, SDNHM.

50. Afranio do Amaral to Laurence Klauber, Do Amaral Folder, Box 76, Laurence Klauber Correspondence, SDNHM.

51. Raymond L. Ditmars, *Strange Animals I Have Known* (New York: Harcourt, Brace and Company, 1931), 209.

52. Martin Lalor Crimmins, "Snake Bites and the Saving of Human Life," *The Military Surgeon*, Vol. 73, No. 3 (1934): 125–132, 127.

53. Harry Goldberg, "Robbing the Snakes' Fangs of their Poison," *Fresno Bee*, 14 August 1927, http://www.newspaperarchives.com, accessed 5 June 2009.

54. Raymond L. Ditmars, *Strange Animals I Have Known* (New York: Harcourt, Brace and Company, 1931), 210.

55. Jesse Donahue and Erik Trump, *American Zoos During the Depression: A New Deal for Animals* (Jefferson, NC: McFarland, 2010), 130–131.

56. Afranio do Amaral to Laurence Klauber, 4 May 1927, Do Amaral Folder, Box 76, Laurence Klauber Correspondence, SDNHM.

57. Laurence Klauber to Afranio do Amaral, 20 June 1927, Do Amaral Folder, Box 76, Laurence Klauber Correspondence, SDNHM.

58. Laurence Klauber to Afranio Do Amaral, 7 June 1927, Do Amaral Folder, Box 76, Laurence Klauber Correspondence.

59. Laurence Klauber to Afranio Do Amaral, 8 August 1927, Do Amaral Folder, Box 76, SDNHM.

60. Afranio Do Amaral to Laurence Klauber, 2 August 1927, Do Amaral Folder, Box 76, Laurence Klauber correspondence, SDNHM.

61. Roger Conant to Laurence Klauber, 21 June 1945, Mss. C667, Roger Conant Collection, Box 54, Folder 23, American Museum of Natural History.

62. Gladys Marnhout to Roger Conant that contained a letter from Ross Allen to Marnhout, 17 July 1944, Miss 667, Roger Conant Collection, Box 46, Folder 1, American Museum of Natural History.

63. Laurence Klauber to Roger Conant, 14 May 1945, Miss C667, Roger Conant Collection, Box 54, 23, American Museum of Natural History.

64. Letter from Roger Conant to Laurence Klauber, no date, Miss 667, Roger Conant Collection, Box 54, Folder 21, American Museum of Natural History.

65. Frances Gow Smith, "Snakes Are Safe if You Know," *Popular Science Monthly*, Vol. 108, No. 1 (January 1926): 20–21, 136–38, 138.

66. E.H. Winston, "Snakes Good and Bad," *Hospital Corps Quarterly*, United States Navy Department Bureau of Medicine, Vol. 5, No. 1 (Jan. 1921): 22–25, 24.

67. See for example, William W. Hoback M.D., and Thomas W. Green M.D., "Treatment of Snake Venom Poisoning with Cortisone and Corticotropin," *The Journal of American Medicine* (1953): 152 (3)236–237, doi:10.1001/jama.1953.63690030016006g. Accessed 11 September 2016.

68. Newton C. McCollough M.D. and Joseph F. Gennaro, Ph.D., "Treatment of Venomous Snakebite in the United States," *Clinical Toxicology*, 3(3) (1970): 483–500, 491.

69. Newton C. McCollough M.D. and Joseph F. Gennaro, Ph.D., "Treatment of Venomous Snakebite in the United States," *Clinical Toxicology*, 3(3) (1970): 483–500, 483.

70. See for example, H.A. Reid and R. D. Theakston, "The Management of Snake Bite," *Bulletin of the World Health Organization*, 61 (6) (1983): 885–895. Or see Morgan Stewart, Sander Greenland, and Jerome Hoffman, "First Aid Treatment for Poisonous Snakebite: Are Currently Recommended Procedures Justified?" *Annals of Emergency Medicine*, 10, 6 (1981): 331–335, 334. DOI: http://dx.doi.org/10.1016/S0196–0644(81)80129–1. Accessed 11 September 2016.

71. Henry M. Parrish, *Poisonous Snakebites in the United States* (New York: Vantage Press, 1980), 22–23.

72. For the online antivenin see "Snake-Antivenin.com" at http://www.snake-antivenin.com/. Accessed 13 March 2017.

73. Danny Lewis, "Why a Single Vial of Antivenom Can Cost $14,000," Smithsonian.com, 11 September 2015. http://www.smithsonianmag.com/smart-news/why-single-vial-antivenom-can-cost-14000–180956564. Accessed 19 April 2017.

74. "Rattlesnake Antivenin," RX List.com, http://www.rxlist.com/rattlesnake-antivenin-drug.htm. Accessed 13 March 2017.

75. Texas Poison Control Center, "Venomous Critters," https://poisoncontrol.org/prevention/venomous-critters/. Accessed 13 March 2017.

76. Christopher Ingraham, "This $153,000 Rattlesnake Bite Is Everything Wrong with Health Care," *The Washington Post*, 20 July 2015, www.washingtonpost.com/news/wonk/wp/2015/07/20/this-153000-rattlesnake-bite-is-everything-wrong-with-american-health-care/?utm_term=.506dfc9eda0a. Accessed 18 April 2017.

77. Christopher Ingraham, "This $153,000 Rattlesnake Bite Is Everything Wrong with Health Care," *The Washington Post*, 20 July 2015, www.washingtonpost.com/news/wonk/wp/2015/07/20/this-153000-rattlesnake-bite-is-everything-wrong-with-american-health-care/?utm_term=.506dfc9eda0a. Accessed 18 April 2017.

78. Danny Lewis, "Why a Single Vial of Antivenom Can Cost $14,000," Smithsonian.com, 11 September 2015, http://www.smithsonianmag.com/smart-news/why-single-vial-antivenom-can-cost-14000–180956564. Accessed 19 April 2017.

79. Justin (no last name given), "Justin's Rattlesnake Bite Story," https://rattlesnakebite.org/, no date. Accessed 18 April 2017.

Chapter 4

1. *The Boston Morning Post*, 12 June 1833, Vol. 4. No. 77. Accessed at newspaperarchive.com.

2. *Angelica Allegani Republican* (Angelica, NY), 29 October 1880.

3. *Decatur (IL) Daily Review*, Tuesday, 26 May 1896.

4. "A Wonderful Snake Story," *New Albany (IN) Ledger*, Saturday, 23 October 1853.

5. "Rattlesnake on a Steam Boat: A Leaf from the Life of a Louisiana Swamp Doctor," *Terre Haute (IN) Wabash Courier*, Saturday, 8 July 1848.

6. "The Charmed Girl and the Snake Humbug," *The New York Daily Times*, Friday, 27 July 1855.

7. "The Program for Today," *Athens Daily Banner*, 6 Oct. 1900, 1, reproduced by the University of Georgia's Hargrett Rare Book and Manuscript Library, www.libs.uga.edu/hargrett/pexhibit/athens.html.

8. See, for example, a photo and description of a snake wagon built in 1903 and used by Ringling-Barnum for two decades. Joseph T. Bradbury, "Circus Wagon History File," *Bandwagon*, Vol. 5, No. 6 (Dec. 1961): 3–6, accessed at https://circushistory.org/archive/ringling-bros-snake-den/.

9. "'Step Lively,' Sid the Elephant to the 'Hippo,'" *New York Times*, 18 March 1906, 11, ProQuest Historical Newspapers.

10. "Circus Opens Today 'Better Than Ever,'" *New York Times*, 31 March 1926, ProQuest Historical Newspapers.

11. "Pythons Sold Here at So Much a Yard," *New York Times*, 15 June 1924, ProQuest Historical Newspapers.

12. Lewis Nichols, "Changing, But Unchanged, Is the Circus," *New York Times*, 6 April 1930, 85, ProQuest Historical Newspapers.

13. Both images are available online at the Wisconsin Historical Society, www.wisconsinhistory.org. The date for the Hall photograph is given as 1868, although that seems incorrect.

14. Roger Conant and Joseph T. Collins, *Reptiles and Amphibians: Eastern/Central North America* (Boston: Houghton Mifflin, 1998), 349–50.

15. Slim Price, "Snake Handling," Sideshow World, August 2003, http://www.sideshowworld.com/snakehandling.html, accessed 26 June 2009.

16. "Snake Charming Easy for Those Who Like Sport," *Des Moines Daily News*, 9 May 1909, newspaperarchives.com, accessed 22 Oct. 2009.

17. "Circus Camels Fail to Sir Jersey Boys," *New York Times*, 1 April 1928, 37, ProQuest Historical Newspapers.

18. "Rattlesnakes Drop to 8 Cents a Pound," *New York Times*, 8 Jan. 1922, 33, ProQuest Historical Newspapers.

19. William T. Usher, "That Was the Horseshoe that Made the Ringer," in *Endangered Species*, Sideshow World (1999), http://www.sideshowworld.com/TGOD-Endangered-WFU11.html, accessed 26 June 2009.

20. Walt Hudson, "Snake Show," 7 May 2005, Sideshow World, http://www.sideshowworld.com/tgodWHSS.html, accessed 26 June 2009.

21. Rosemarie Garland Thomson, *Freakery: Cultural Spectacles of the Extraordinary Body* (New York: New York University Press,

1996), 130–32. Davis died in 1927. See obituary, "Bosco the Snake Eater Dead," *New York Times*, 29 Oct. 1927, 17, ProQuest Historical Newspapers. Harry Houdini, *Miracle Mongers and Their Methods: A Complete Expose of the Modus Operandi of Fire Eaters, Heat Resisters, Poison Eaters, Venomous Reptile Defiers, Sword Swallowers, Human Ostriches, Strong Men, Etc.* (no date), available at www.pinkmonkey.com/dl/library1/digi516 pdf and other sites.

22. Brian Schraum, "100 Years of Homecomers: Changes and Constants," *Southeast Missourian*, 20 July 2008, www.semissourian.com/story/1446177.html; Clare B. Cox, "Rasche Hall: A Plain Monument to a Colorful Character," *Virginia Tech Magazine* (Winter 2006), www.vtmagazine.vt.edu/winter 2006/retrospect.html. Bosco also gets a brief mention in Jack London's novel *Martin Eden*.

23. Howard Erickson, "A Boy Acrobat in P.T. Barnum's Circus," *Sunday World Herald*, 27 Nov. 1932, Sideshow World, http://www.sideshowworld.com/tgodLbapt.html, accessed 26 June 2009.

24. "The 'Rattlesnake King of the Rockies,'" *New York Times*, 12 May 1895.

25. *The McCook Tribune* (McCook, NE), 24 Aug. 1888. *Chronicling America: Historic American Newspapers*. Lib. of Congress. http://chroniclingamerica.loc.gov/lccn/sn94056415/1888-08-24/ed-1/seq-6/. Accessed 10 April 2017.

26. "Brownsville Man Supplies Poison from Rattle Snakes for the Use of Scientists," *Brownsville Herald*, 3 June 1923, 4, newspaperarchives.com, accessed 22 Oct. 2009.

27. "Ships Four Tons of Snakes," *New York Times*, 15 June 1908, 1, ProQuest Historical Newspapers.

28. W.A. King Jr. *Rattlingly Yours ... Snake King* (Brownsville, TX: Springman-King Lithograph Company, 1964), 74.

29. For a discussion of the Mexican tax, see W.A. King Jr., *Rattlingly Yours ... Snake King*, 68–69.

30. "Boxes of Great Snakes," *New York Times*, 10 August 1895.

31. "An Astonished Manager," *New York Times*, 10 July 1883, ProQuest Historical Newspapers.

32. "Shed a Tear for This Unhappy Circus Snake," *Morning Avalanche*, 16 April 1937, 1, newspaperarchive.com, accessed 18 Sept. 2009.

33. "Giant the Best Man at Midget Wedding," *New York Times*, 17 April 1916.

34. "Pythons Sold Here at So Much a Yard," *New York Times*, 15 June 1924; "Boom in Wild Animal Market," 29 Oct. 1922, 102;

"Huge Animal Cargo Will Arrive Today," 4 June 1922; "Brings Big Cargo of Wild Animals," 1 June 1922; "Floating Zoo Roars Its Way into Port," 8 April 1922. All from ProQuest Historical Newspapers.

35. "A Chapter About Snakes," *New York Times*, 13 July 1881.

36. "Big Circus Snake Dies," *Washington Post*, 6 Oct. 1906, newspaperarchive.com, accessed 18 Sept. 2009.

37. "Python, Not Sea Serpent," *New York Times*, 1 August 1895.

38. "Elephants, Peanuts, and Freaks Again," *New York Times*, 23 March 1913, ProQuest Historical Newspapers; "The Circus Freak Seen Off Guard as a Human Being," *New York Times*, 6 April 1913, ProQuest Historical Newspapers.

39. "Giant the Best Man at Midget Wedding," *New York Times*, 17 April 1916, ProQuest Historical Newspapers.

40. "Circus Freaks Dine on 'Zip's' Birthday," *New York Times*, 6 April 1914, ProQuest Historical Newspapers.

41. "Snakes Refused Shelter," *Salt Lake Tribune*, 4 June 1933, newspaperarchive.com, accessed 18 Sept. 2009.

42. "Snakes in Bed," *Lincoln Evening News and Daily Call*, 29 Dec. 1898, 7, newspaperarchive.com, accessed 18 Sept. 2009.

43. "Circus Beasts Roar for Radio Audience," *New York Times*, 5 April 1925, 15, ProQuest Historical Newspapers.

44. Paul T. Gilbert, "Reporter Finds Out How It Feels to Cuddle Snake," *Chicago Evening Post*, 23 July 1925, reproduced, with photo, at http://www.bertramstories.com/circus.html, accessed 25 March 2010. In Chicago, Cleo was being played by "Peggy," an illusionist who was also an experienced snake handler.

45. No title, *Ogden Standard Examiner*, 8 August 1937, newspaperarchive.com, accessed 22 Oct. 2009.

46. "Drank Snake Stupefier," *Daily Kennebec Journal*, 19 June 1903, newspaperarchive.com, accessed 18 Sept. 2009.

47. "A Python's Brief Outing," *New York Times*, 10 Oct. 1886, ProQuest Historical Newspapers.

48. "Circus Snake Is Again at Large," *The Bee* (Danville, VA), 15 July 1926, newspaperarchive.com, accessed 18 Sept. 2009.

49. "11-foot Snake Caught," *New York Times*, 7 April 1935, N2, ProQuest Historical Newspapers.

50. "St. Louis People Are Searching for Python," *Daily Capital News*, 23 Aug. 1932, newspaperarchive.com, accessed 18 Sept. 2009.

51. "Escape of the Boa," *Anaconda Stan-*

dard (MT), 20 July 1907, nespaperarchive. com, accessed 15 Jan. 2010.

52. "Kills Circus Snake," *Portsmouth Daily Times*, 14 Sept. 1916, 2, newspaperarchive. com, accessed 18 Sept. 2009.

53. "Patrolman Kills 6-foot Circus Snake," *Syracuse Herald*, 19 Sept. 1919, 6, newspaperarchive.com, accessed 18 Sept. 2009.

54. "Snake Charming Easy for Those Who Like Sport," *Des Moines Daily News*, 9 May 1909, newspaperarchives.com, accessed 22 Oct. 2009.

55. "Circus Worker Seriously Ill from Snakebite," *Piqua Daily Call*, 30 June 1936, 7, Newspaperarchives.com, accessed 22 Oct. 2009.

56. "The Snake Charmer's Burial," *New York Times*, 17 July 1884, ProQuest Historical Newspapers.

57. "In the Embrace of a Snake," *New York Times*, 6 June 1891, ProQuest Historical Newspapers.

58. "Snake, Lady, and Bull: Huge Reptile and Beast Engage in Deadly Combat," *Algona (IA) Advance*, 13 August 1903, www.newspaperarchive.com.

59. "Circus Snake Bites Man's Nose," *Wellsboro Agitator*, 17 Aug. 1910, newspaperarchive.com, accessed 18 Sept. 2009.

60. "Python Bites Two During Circus Act," *New York Times*, 15 April 1932, 16, ProQuest Historical Newspapers; "Huge Circus Snake Wounds 2 Performers," *Cumberland Evening News*, 15 April 1932, 1, newspaperarchive. com, accessed 18 Sept. 2009. The national papers apparently misspelled the performers' names as Luigi Canestrelli and Alfred Carciona.

61. "Hypnotist Continues After Python's Bite," *New York Times*, 3 April 1926, ProQuest Historical Newspapers.

62. "Nearly Crushed by a Snake," *New York Times*, 9 Aug. 1923, 6, ProQuest Historical Newspapers. The circus was performing in Hudson, Massachusetts.

63. It's highly unlikely that the python was this big. For common sizes of different pythons see Mark O'Shea, *Boas and Pythons of the World* (Princeton, NJ: Princeton University Press, 2007), 23.

64. "Capture of a Big Python," *New York Times*, 7 March 1897, 1, ProQuest Historical Newspapers.

65. "Anaconda Attacks Giraffe: Exciting Combat in Circus that Ended in Death," *Waterloo (IA) Daily Courier*, 8 February 1902.

66. "Circus Snake Stampedes Crowd," *Logansport Pharos*, 11 Nov. 1907, newspaperarchive.com, accessed 18 Sept. 2009.

67. Helen Lefkowitz Horowitz, "The Na-tional Zoological Park: 'City of Refuge or Zoo?'" in R.J. Hoage and William A. Deiss, eds., *New Worlds New Animals: From Menagerie to Zoological Park in the Nineteenth Century* (Baltimore: Johns Hopkins University Press, 1996), 126–135, 128.

68. Lucile Quarry Mann Transcript, RU 9513, Box 1, pg. 1, Smithsonian Institution Archives.

69. Lucile Quarry Mann Transcript, RU 9513, Box 1, pg. 33, Smithsonian Institution Archives.

70. Lucile Quarry Mann Transcript, RU 9513, Box 1, pg. 74, Smithsonian Institution Archives.

71. Lucile Quarry Mann Transcript, RU 9513, Box 1, pg. 64, Smithsonian Institution Archives.

72. Lucile Quarry Mann Transcript, RU 9513, Box 1, pg. 65, Smithsonian Institution Archives.

73. Lucile Quarry Mann Transcript, RU 9513, Box 1, pg. 110, Smithsonian Institution Archives.

74. Lucile Quarry Mann Transcript, RU 9513, Box 1, pg. 84, 83, Smithsonian Institution Archives.

75. The initiation process consisted of learning a password, secret signs, and receiving a special name. They also learned about particular healing herbs, none of which were designed to save people from snakebite, but were used for other purposes. They realized that the Smithsonian would like pictures of their experience for Americans' educational benefit so they took them and brought them back.

76. William M. Mann, "A New Home for Reptiles," CBS Radio Address, 19 Dec. 1930, Reptiles, Box 2 RU 7293, Smithsonian Institution Archive. Quoted in Jesse C. Donahue and Erik K. Trump, *American Zoos During the Depression: New Deal for Zoos* (Jefferson, NC: McFarland, 2010), 111.

77. Jesse C. Donahue and Erik K. Trump, *American Zoos During the Depression: New Deal for Zoos* (Jefferson, NC: McFarland, 2010), 111.

78. Jesse C. Donahue and Erik K. Trump, *American Zoos During the Depression: New Deal for Zoos* (Jefferson, NC: McFarland, 2010), 111.

79. *Wonders Among Us: Celebrating 75 Years of the Detroit Zoo* (Detroit: Detroit Zoological Society, 2003), 33, 69.

Chapter 5

1. For a discussion of this genre, see Katarina Gregersdotter, Johan Hoglund, and

Nicklas Hallen, "Introduction," in Katarina Gregersdotter, Johan Hoglund, and Nicklas Hallen, eds., *Animal Horror Cinema: Genre, History and Criticism* (New York: Palgrave: MacMillan, 2015), 1–18; or see Lee Gambin, *Massacred by Mother Nature: Exploring the Natural Horror Film* (Baltimore: Midnight Marquee Press, 2012), 15–27.

2. *Python Hunters*, Season 2, Episode 1. National Geographic. The numbers in the paragraph are taken from this episode as well.

3. Narrator, *Python Hunters*, Season 2, Episode 1. National Geographic.

4. Narrator, *Python Hunters*, Season 2, Episode 1.

5. Narrator, *Python Hunters*, Season 2, Episode 1.

6. Narrator, *Python Hunters*, Season 2, Episode 1.

7. Narrator, *Python Hunters*, Season 2, Episode 1.

8. Narrator, *Python Hunters*, Season 2, Episode 7.

9. Narrator, *Python Hunters*, Season 2, Episode 4.

10. Narrator, *Python Hunters*, Season 2, Episode 1.

11. Narrator, *Venom Hunters*, Season 1, Episode 1, The Discovery Channel.

12. Ed Chapman, *Venom Hunters*, Season 1, Episode 3.

13. Narrator, *Venom Hunters*, Season 1, Episode 5.

14. Hannah Lockhart, *Venom Hunters*, Season 1, Episode 5.

15. Chewy only identified by this name. He does not have a last name on the show.

16. *Rattlesnake Roundup*, National Geographic Youtube clip, https://www.youtube.com/watch?v=U6TfBBN8vqs. Accessed 26 January 2017.

17. They also have a clear racial bias in that everyone on the show appears to be of European descent even though the show is set in Texas where substantial parts of the population are Latino.

18. Shawn and Narrator, *Rattlesnake Nation*, Season 1, Episode 5.

19. Narrator, *Rattlesnake Nation*, Season 1, Episode 5.

20. Mike Duggie, *Rattlesnake Republic*, Season 1, Episode 3.

21. Narrator and Ed Chapman, *Venom Hunters*, Season 1, Episode 3.

22. Kevin and Tim Fitzer, *Venom Hunters*, Season 1, Episode 3.

23. Narrator, *Venom Hunters*, Season 1, Episode 3.

24. Ed Chapman, *Venom Hunters*, Season 1, Episode 4.

25. Justin Botrell, *Venom Hunters*, Season 1, Episode 5.

26. Director of Arizona Poison Control Center, *Venom Hunters*, Season 1, Episode 4.

27. For medicinal venom uses that have worked for a variety of medical problems see Drake Stutesman, *Snake* (London: Reaktion Books, 2005), 104.

28. Narrator, *Venom Hunters*, Season 1, Episode 2.

29. Tim Fitzer, *Venom Hunters*, Season 1, Episode 2.

30. See for example, *Venom Hunters*, Season 1, Episode 2.

31. See for example, *Venom Hunters*, Season 1, Episode 3.

32. Narrator, *Venom Hunters*, Season 1, Episode 5.

33. Tim Fitzer, *Venom Hunters*, Season 1, Episode 1.

34. Ed Chapman, *Venom Hunters*, Season 1, Episode 2.

35. Narrator, *Venom Hunters*, Season 1, Episode 2.

36. Narrator, *Venom Hunters*, Season 1, Episode 2.

37. Narrator, *Venom Hunters*, Season 1, Episode 4.

38. Narrator, *Venom Hunters*, Season 1, Episode 3.

39. Narrator, *Venom Hunters*, Season 1, Episode 2.

40. Tim Fitzer, *Venom Hunters*, Season 1, Episode 4.

41. Narrator, *Rattlesnake Republic*, Season 1, Episode 1.

42. Chapman, *Venom Hunters*, Season 1, Episode 2.

43. Justin Botrell, *Venom Hunters*, Season 1, Episode 5.

44. Narrator, *Rattlesnake Republic*, Season 1, Episode 1.

45. Tim Fitzer, *Venom Hunters*, Season 1, Episode 6.

46. Narrator, *Venom Hunters*, Season 1, all episodes.

47. Narrator, *Venom Hunters*, Season 1, Episode 3.

48. *Venom Hunters*, Season 1, Episode 1.

49. Narrator, *Venom Hunters*, Season 1, Episode 5.

50. Tim Fitzer, *Venom Hunters*, Season 1, Episode 1.

51. Tim Fitzer, *Venom Hunters*, Season 1, Episode 1.

52. Hannah Lockhart, *Venom Hunters*, Season 1, Episode 3.

53. Tim Fitzer, *Venom Hunters*, Season 1, Episode 2.

54. Tim Fitzer, *Venom Hunters*, Season 1, Episode 2.

55. Brian Barczyk, *Venom Hunters*, Season 1, Episode 2.

56. Robert Shawn Jones, *Rattlesnake Republic*, Season 1, Episode 1.

57. Tim Fitzer, *Venom Hunters*, Season 1, Episode 4.

58. Narrator, *Rattlesnake Republic*, Season 1, Episode 6.

59. Eric Timeaus, *Rattlesnake Republic*, Season 1, Episode 2.

60. Narrator, *Rattlesnake Republic*, Season 1, Episode 1.

61. Narrator, *Rattlesnake Republic*, Season 1, Episode 1.

62. Narrator, *Rattlesnake Republic*, Season 1, Episode 2.

63. Robert Shawn, *Rattlesnake Republic*, Season 1, Episode 2.

64. Jackie Bibby and the Narrator, *Rattlesnake Republic*, Season 1, Episode 2.

65. *Man Who Injects Venom*, https://www.bbc.co.uk/programmes/p05m541d.

66. *Venom Man Lets Deadliest Snake Bite Him*, 2016, https://www.youtube.com/watch?v=ucpGlWnq8EE. Accessed 3 March 2017.

Chapter 6

1. *New Oxford Annotated Bible, with Apocrypha* (New York: Oxford University Press, 1991), Genesis 3: 1–6.

2. *New Oxford Annotated Bible, with Apocrypha* (New York: Oxford University Press, 1991), Genesis 3: 14–15.

3. See references to specific snake attacks in chapters 1–3.

4. This reference changes slightly depending on the context in which it is used. The more traditional Biblical references use baptism, while the documentaries reviewed in later sections of this chapter tend to use anointing. Also Holy Spirit and Holy Ghost are interchangeable.

5. W.W. Harmon, "Signboards," *Church of God Evangel*, 25 February 1928, 3.

6. *New Oxford Annotated Bible, with Apocrypha* (New York: Oxford University Press, 1991), Luke 10: 16–19.

7. *New Oxford Annotated Bible, with Apocrypha* (New York: Oxford University Press, 1991), Mark 16: 14–15.

8. *New Oxford Annotated Bible, with Apocrypha* (New York: Oxford University Press, 1991), Mark 16: 16–19.

9. This fundamentalist claim, that if one wants to believe part of the Bible, one must believe all of the Bible, is found in every documentary reviewed in this chapter.

10. Michael J. McVicar, "Take Away the Serpents from Us: The Sign of Serpent Handling and the Development of Southern Pentecostalism," *Journal of Southern Religion* 15 (2013): http://jsr.fsu.edu/issues/vol15/mcvicar.html.

11. Charles F. Parham, "The Latter Rain: The Story of the Original Apostolic or Pentecostal Movements," in Sarah E. Parham, ed., *The Life of Charles F. Parham, Founder of the Apostolic Faith Movement* (1930; New York: Garland, 1985), 51–52.

12. Michael J. McVicar, "Take Away the Serpents from Us: The Sign of Serpent Handling and the Development of Southern Pentecostalism," *Journal of Southern Religion* 15 (2013): http://jsr.fsu.edu/issues/vol15/mcvicar.html.

13. R.G. Robins, *A.J. Tomlinson: Plainfolk Modernist* (New York: Oxford University Press, 2004), 184; and Charles W. Conn, *Like a Mighty Army: A History of the Church of God, 1886–1995* (Cleveland, TN: Pathway Press, 1996), 3–9.

14. Michael J. McVicar, "Take Away the Serpents from Us: The Sign of Serpent Handling and the Development of Southern Pentecostalism," *Journal of Southern Religion* 15 (2013): http://jsr.fsu.edu/issues/vol15/mcvicar.html.

15. *Church of God Evangel*, 12 September 1914, 6.

16. Michael J. McVicar, "Take Away the Serpents from Us: The Sign of Serpent Handling and the Development of Southern Pentecostalism," *Journal of Southern Religion* 15 (2013): http://jsr.fsu.edu/issues/vol15/mcvicar.html.

17. Michael J. McVicar, "Take Away the Serpents from Us: The Sign of Serpent Handling and the Development of Southern Pentecostalism," *Journal of Southern Religion* 15 (2013): http://jsr.fsu.edu/issues/vol15/mcvicar.html.

18. Michael J. McVicar, "Take Away the Serpents from Us: The Sign of Serpent Handling and the Development of Southern Pentecostalism," *Journal of Southern Religion* 15 (2013): http://jsr.fsu.edu/issues/vol15/mcvicar.html.

19. Roger May, "Looking Back at Russell Lee's Appalachia—1946," *Walkyourcamera.com*, 2 January 2013.

20. Michael J. McVicar, "Take Away the Serpents from Us: The Sign of Serpent Handling and the Development of Southern Pentecostalism," *Journal of Southern Religion* 15 (2013): http://jsr.fsu.edu/issues/vol15/mcvicar.html.

21. Narrator, *Holy Ghost People*, 1967.

22. Congregant, *Holy Ghost People*, 1967.

23. Congregant, *Holy Ghost People*, 1967.

24. Congregant, *Holy Ghost People*, 1967.
25. Although in at least one source, it is reported that the pastor died of the snakebite later that evening.
26. Congregant, *People Who Take Up Serpents*, 1974.
27. Congregant, *People Who Take Up Serpents*, 1974.
28. Congregant, *People Who Take Up Serpents*, 1974.
29. Congregant, *People Who Take Up Serpents*, 1974.
30. Congregant, *In Jesus' Name: Taking Up Serpents*, 1991.
31. Congregant, *In Jesus' Name: Taking Up Serpents*, 1991.
32. Congregant, *In Jesus' Name: Taking Up Serpents*, 1991.
33. Congregant, *In Jesus' Name: Taking Up Serpents*, 1991.
34. Congregant, *In Jesus' Name: Taking Up Serpents*, 1991.
35. Congregant, *In Jesus' Name: Taking Up Serpents*, 1991.
36. *Snake Salvation*, Season 1, Episode 7.
37. *Snake Salvation*, Season 1, Episode 4.
38. *Snake Salvation*, Season 1, Episode 1.
39. *Snake Salvation*, Season 1, Episode 5.
40. Jamie Coots, "The Constitution Protects My Snake Handling," *The Wall Street Journal Online*, 3 October 2013.
41. "Snake Handling Pastor and His Congregation Evicted from their Church," *Daily Mail*, 22 June 2014.
42. Bill Estep, "Bitten by a Rattlesnake, Pastor Cried Out to 'Sweet Jesus' Before Collapsing in Church," *Lexington Herald-Leader*, 22 February 2014.

Conclusion

1. Naity, "Long term effects of Rattlesnake bites?" VenemousReptiles.org, 22 September 2012, accessed 19 April 2017; AshRN, "RE: Long term effects of Rattlesnake bites?" VenemousReptiles.org, 19 December 2012.
2. Yetolder, "RE: Long term effects of Rattlesnake bites," VenemousReptiles.org, 25 October 2013.
3. For an example of survivalist politics, see M.D. Creekmore's "Daily Collapse Report," at www.dailycollapsereport.com. Accessed 18 April 2017.
4. "Can You Buy Anti-Venom" discussion thread, Wildness Survival, Hiking and Camping Forum, www.survivalistboards.com. Accessed 14 March 2017.
5. Dom Cosentino, "This is Why You Should Have a Snake-Venom Kit With You in the Woods," Deadspin.com, posted 26 April 2013. Accessed 14 March 2017.
6. "Can You Buy Anti-Venom," Wildness Survival, Hiking and Camping Forum, www.survivalistboards.com. Accessed 14 March 2017.
7. "Can You Buy Anti-Venom," Wildness Survival, Hiking and Camping Forum, www.survivalistboards.com. Accessed 14 March 2017.
8. "Can You Buy Anti-Venom," Wildness Survival, Hiking and Camping Forum, www.survivalistboards.com. Accessed 14 March 2017.
9. Jordan Benjamin, "These are Dangerous for Snakebites," customer review, 17 May 2014, on the Sawyer Products B4 Extractor Pump found on Amazon.com. https://amazon.com/Sawyer-Products-B4-Extractor-Pump/dp/B000AU9PEC/ref=sr_1_1?ie=UTF8&qid=1492543922&sr=8–1&keywords=venom+extractor+kit. Accessed 18 April 2017.
10. Jordan Benjamin, "These are Dangerous for Snakebites," customer review, 17 May 2014, on the Sawyer Products B4 Extractor Pump found on Amazon.com. https://www.amazon.com/Sawyer-Products-B4-Extractor-Pump/dp/B000AU9PEC/ref=sr_1_1?ie=UTF8&qid=1492543922&sr=8–1&keywords=venom+extractor+kit. Accessed 18 April 2017.
11. "A Shock Cure for Snakebite," no author, Wildness Survival, Hiking and Camping Forum, www.survivalistboards.com. Accessed 14 March 2017.
12. "A Shock Cure for Snakebite," no author, Wildness Survival, Hiking and Camping Forum, www.survivalistboards.com. Accessed 14 March 2017.
13. "Can You Buy Anti-Venom" discussion thread, Wildness Survival, Hiking and Camping Forum, www.survivalistboards.com. Accessed 14 March 2017.
14. Sam Coffman, "Venomous Snake Bites, Infections, and Herbal Medicine," 19 November 2013, www.americanpreppersnetwork.com/2013/11/venomous-snake-bites-infections-herbal-medicine.html. Accessed 18 April 2017.
15. "Rattlesnake Bites Man Walking Near Temecula," *Valley News*, 18 April 2017. https://www.myvalleynews.com/story/2017/04/18/news/rattlesnake-bites-man-walking-near-temecula/52421.html.
16. "Hiker Bitten by Rattlesnake in Chino Hills State Park," *Daily Bulletin*, 16 April 2017. http://www.dailybulletin.com/general-news/20170416/hiker-bitten-by-rattlesnake-in-chino-hills-state-park.
17. Kristy Holland, "Out Alive: Survive a

Rattlesnake Bite," Backpacker.com, 30 May 2012. http://www.backpacker.com/survival/out-alive-survive-a-rattlesnake-bite.

18. Anthony F. Pizon, MD, "Snakebites: Prehospital Assessment & Treatment of Envenomations," *Journal of Emergency Medical Services* (31 March 2017). http://www.jems.com/articles/2007/03/snakebites.html.

19. See for example, Henry M. Parrish, MD, "Mortality from Snakebites United States, 1950–1954," Public Health Reports, National Institutes of Health. Vol. 72, No. 11 (November 1957): 1027–1030, 1027–1028. https://www.ncbi.nlm.nih.gov/pmc/articles/PMC2031414/pdf/pubhealthreporig00143–0083.pdf. Accessed 19 April 2017. Later studies by Parrish came to similar conclusions. Most of the people were white, male, children. Henry M. Parrish, James Dikroeger, and Homer Hall, "Counting California's Snakebites," *California Medicine*, Vol. 101, Issue 5 (10 November 1964): 352–357, 354–355.

20. Abin Chandrakumar, T.N.K. Suriyaprakash, P. Linu Mohan, Levin Thomas, and P.V. Vikas, "Evaluation of Demographic and Clinical Profile of Snakebite Casualties Presented at a Tertiary Care Hospital in Kerala," *Clinical Epidemology and Global Health*, Vol. 4, Issue 3 (September 2016): 140–145. Quotes come from the abstract. http://www.sciencedirect.com/science/article/pii/S2213398415000913. Accessed 19 April 2017.

21. "Make Your Next Party Special," Partysnakes.com. Accessed 22 April 2017.

22. Snakehead Ed, "Home," www.snakeheaded.net. Accessed 26 April 2017.

23. Larry Bartley, "Texas Snake Man, Episode 1," a video found on Rising Star Entertainment Network "Good Ol' Boy Videos," https://risingstarentertainmentnetwork.com/texas-snake-man-episode-1. Accessed 26 April 2017.

24. "Snake Charmers," Hafla Entertainment, http://www.haflaentertainment.com/.

25. "How to Overcome Ophidiophobia (Fear of Snakes)," Calm Clinic, http://www.calmclinic.com/phobias/ophidiophobia. Accessed 26 April 2012.

26. Christopher Benfey, "Fear of Rattlsnake Island," *The New York Review of Books*, 18 April 2016. http://www.nybooks.com/daily/2016/08/18/fear-of-rattlesnake-island-massachusetts/. Accessed 26 April 2017.

27. Jess Bidgood, "Rattlesnake Island Colony Gives Small-Town Massachusetts Jitters," *New York Times*, 28 May 2016. https://www.nytimes.com/2016/05/29/us/island-rattlesnake-colony-gives-small-town-massachusetts-jitters.html?_r=0. Accessed 26 April 2017.

28. See Ted Levin, *America's Snake: The Rise and Fall of the Timber Rattlesnake* (Chicago: University of Chicago Press, 2016), 321–354.

29. Christopher Benfey, "Fear of Rattlsnake Island," *The New York Review of Books*, 18 April 2016. http://www.nybooks.com/daily/2016/08/18/fear-of-rattlesnake-island-massachusetts/. Accessed 26 April 2017.

30. Danny Lewis, "Controversial Texas Rattlesnake Roundup Nets Largest Catch to Date," Smithsonianmag.com, 25 March 2016. http://www.smithsonianmag.com/smart-news/controversial-texas-rattlesnake-roundup-nets-largest-catch-date-180958575/. Accessed 27 April 2017.

31. "Educate Rattlesnake Roundups," Errnow, http://errnow.weebly.com/history-of-roundups.html. Accessed 27 April 2017.

32. Ryan Knighton, "You're So Screwed," *The Moth Stories Told Live* http://player.themoth.org/#/?actionType=ADD_AND_PLAY&storyId=551. Accessed 26 April 2017.

33. Peter Singer, "In Defense of Animals."

34. Donna Haraway, *When Species Meet* (Minneapolis: University of Minnesota Press, 2008), 15.

Bibliography

Archives

Laurence Klauber Archives at the San Diego Natural History Museum
Roger Conant Papers at the American Natural History Museum, New York
Staten Island Zoological Society Archives
Western Historical Manuscript Collection, University of St. Louis
William Mann Collection at the Smithsonian Institution Archives

Government Documents

Assistant Surgeon General, United States Public Health Service. "Prevention of Disease and Care of the Sick: How to Keep Well and What to Do in Case of Sudden Illness." Miscellaneous Publication No. 17, Third edition. Washington, D.C.: Government Printing Office, 1919.

Atkinson, Vickers T., William Dickson, William Heyser Harbaugh, and James Law. *Special Report on Diseases of Cattle.* Washington, D.C.: Government Printing Office, 1904.

Drill Regulations and Outlines of First Aid for the Hospital Corps. Medical Department, United States Army. The War Department. Washington, D.C.: Government Printing Office, 1908.

Gilman, H.K. *The Naval Brigade and Operations Ashore: A Hand-Book for Field.* U.S.M.C, Bureau of Navigation, Navy Department, Naval Professional Papers, No. 20. Washington, D.C.: Government Printing Office, 1884.

Halberstadt, G.H., A.F. Knoefel, W.A. Lynott, W.S. Roundtree, and M.J. Shields. *Advanced First-Aid Instruction for Miners.* Department of the Interior, Bureau of Mines. Washington, D.C.: Government Printing Office, 1917.

Le Carpentier, Jules. "Report of a Case in which a Bite from a Rattlesnake Proved Fatal." In George A. Otis, *A Report of Surgical Cases: Army of the United States from 1865 to 1871.* War Department, Surgeon General's Office, Circular No. 3, 1871.

Middleton, J.V.D. Memorandum of a Case of Snake Bite. In George A. Otis, *A Report of Surgical Cases: Army of the United States from 1865 to 1871.* War Department, Surgeon General's Office, Circular No. 3, 1871.

Parrish, Henry M. "Mortality from Snakebites United States, 1950–1954." Public Health Reports, National Institutes of Health. Vol 72. No. 11 (November 1957): 1027–1030.

Second Annual Report of the Bureau of Animal Industry for the Year 1885. U.S. Department of Agriculture. Washington, D.C.: Government Printing Office 1886.

Winston, E.H. "Snakes Good and Bad." *Hospital Corps Quarterly,* United States Navy Department Bureau of Medicine Vol. 5, No. 1(January 1921): 22–25.

Journal and Magazine Articles

"Antidote Against Snake-Bite." *The Natal Agricultural Journal*, Vol. 11 (1908): 217.

"An Antidote for Snake Bite." *The National Druggist*, Vol. 38 (1908): 281.

"Bee Stings." *British Bee Keeper Journal and Bee Keeper-Advisor*, Vol. 26 (1898): 335.

Benfey, Christopher. "Fear of Rattlesnake Island." *The New York Review of Books*, 18 April 2016.

Brazil, Oswaldo Vital. "History of the Primordia of Snake-Bite Accident Serotherapy." *Memorias do Instituto de Butantan*, Vol. 49, No. 1 (1887): 7–20.

Byne, Dr. A.S. "Carbonate of Ammonia in the Bites of Poisonous Reptiles." *Boston Medical and Surgical Journal*, Vol. 48 (1858): 248.

"Care for the Bite of a Rattlesnake." *Scientific American*, Vol. 3, No. 27 (25 March 1848): 192.

Carpenter, Frank G. "City of Snakes." *Moderator-Topics*, Vol. 36, No. 1 (9 September 1915): 350–352.

Chandrakumar, Abin, T.N.K. Suriyaprakash, P. Linu Mohan, Levin Thomas, and P.V. Vikas. "Evaluation of Demographic and Clinical Profile of Snakebite Casualties Presented at a Tertieary Care Hospital in Kerala." *Clinical Epidemiology and Global Health*, Vol. 4, Issue 3 (September 2016): 140–145.

Coots, Jamie. "The Constitution Protects My Snake Handling." *The Wall Street Journal Online*, 3 October 2013.

Crimmins, Martin Lalor. "Poisonous Snakes and the Antivenin Treatment." *Southern Medical Journal*, Vol. XXII, No. 7 (July 1929): 603–605.

_____. "Snake Bites and the Saving of Human Life." *The Military Surgeon*, Vol. 73, No. 3 (1934): 125–132.

Culbert, Lyon W. "Venomous Snakes of the United States, Their Bites and Treatment." *The Military Surgeon*, Vol. 27, No. 1 (July 1910): 383–385.

Ditmars, Raymond. "Treatment of Our First Case of Snake Bite." *New York Zoological Society Bulletin*, Vol. 24, No. 1 (January 1916): 1358–1364.

do Amaral, Afranio. "Announcement." *Bulletin of the Antivenin Institute of America*, Vol. 1, No. 1 (March 1927): 1–2.

_____. "The Anti-Snake-Bite Campaign in Texas and the Sub-Tropical United States." *Bulletin of the Antivenin Institute of America*, Vol. 1, No. 3 (October 1927): 77–85.

_____. "The Brazilian Contribution Towards the Improvement of the Specific Snake Bite Treatment." *Proceedings of the New York Pathological Society*, 1923: 89–98.

_____. "The Snake Bite Problem in the United States and in Central America." *Bulletin of the Antivenin Institute of America*, Vol. 1, No. 2 (July 1927): 31–35.

Donahue, Jesse, and Erik Trump. *American Zoos During the Depression: A New Deal for Animals*. Jefferson, NC: McFarland, 2010.

Dulles, Charles L. *Medical and Surgical Reporter*, Vol. 48 (January–July 1888): 754–755.

Dunn, Harry. "Snakes Battle to Death for Science." *Illustrated World*, Vol. 27, No. 5 (July 1917): 779.

Estep, Bill. "Bitten by a Rattlesnake, Pastor Cried Out to 'Sweet Jesus' Before Collapsing in Church." *Lexington Herald-Leader*, 22 February 2014.

Fish, Pierre A. *Journal of the American Veterinary Medical Association*, Vol. 61, No. 14 (1922): 362.

"The Game and Game Laws of India." *Quarterly Review*, Vol. 167 (1888): 94–95.

Githens, Thomas S., and I.D. George. "Comparative Studies on the Venoms of Certain Rattlesnakes." Paper presented at the Fourteenth Annual Meeting of the American Society of Ichthyologists and Herpetologists, Philadelphia, 12 May 1931.

Greenland, Sander, Morgan Stewart, and Jerome Hoffman. "First Aid Treatment for Poisonous Snakebite: Are Currently Recommended Procedures Justified?" *Annals of Emergency Medicine*, 10:6 (1981): 331–335.

Hambleton, F.W. "Pueblo Colorado. Recreation." *American Canoe Association and League of American Sportsmen,* Vol. X, No. 1 (January 1899): 218.

Harmon, W.W. "Signboards." *Church of God Evangel,* 25 February 1928: 3.

Hawgood, Barbara J. "Pioneers of Anti-Venomous Serotherapy: Dr. Vital Brazil (1865–1950)." *Toxicon,* Vol. 30, No. 5/6 (1992): 573–579.

Higgins, S.B. "Snake Poison and Its Antidote." *Monthly Homeopathic Review,* Vol. 14, No. 7 (1 July 1887): 440–442.

Hill, Ino F. "Popular Idols Broken." *The Assembly Herald, Presbyterian Church in the U.S.A. Office of the General Assembly,* Vol. 7, No. 1 (July 1902): 130.

"Hindoo Zoohily and Snake-Bites." *The Journal of American Medical Association,* Vol. 36, No. 14 (April 1901): 1048–1049.

Hoback, William W., and Thomas W. Green. "Treatment of Snake Venom Poisoning with Cortisone and Corticotropin." *The Journal of American Medicine:* 152, 3 (1953): 236–237.

Hobbs, C.E. *Botanical Handbook.* Boston: 1876.

"Injection of Ammonia for Snake-bites." *Pacific Medical and Surgical Journal,* Vol. 16, No. 10 (March 1875): 507.

Jackson, Dudley. "Treatment of Snake Bite." *Southern Medical Journal,* Vol. XXII, No. 7 (July 1929): 605–607.

"Justin's Rattlesnake Bite Story." Rattlesnakebite.org.

Kirkpatrick, J.A. "Ammonia for a Rattlesnake Bite." *Southern Journal of Homoeopathy,* Vol. 11, No. 3 (1893): 117–118.

Kulcyzk, David. "The Snake Woman—Cypress Orange Country." 20 July 1948. Posted 25 June 2012, http://www.dkulczyk.com/.

Lewis, Danny. "Controversial Texas Rattlesnake Roundup Nets Largest Catch to Date." Smithsonianmag.com, 25 March 2016.

_____. "Why a Single Vial of Antivenom Can Cost $14,000." Smithsonian.com, 11 September 2015.

May, Roger. "Looking Back at Russell Lee's Appalachia—1946." Walkyourcamera.com, 2 January 2013.

McCollough, Newton C., and Joseph F. Gennaro. "Treatment of Venomous Snakebite in the United States." *Clinical Toxicology,* 3(3) (1970): 483–500.

McCreary, Thomas, and Harold Wurzel. "Poisonous Snake Bites: Report of a Case." *Journal of the American Medical Association,* Volume 170, Issue 3 (May 1959): 268–272.

McVicar, Michael J. "Take Away the Serpents from Us: The Sign of Serpent Handling and the Development of Southern Pentecostalism." *Journal of Southern Religion* 15 (2013). http://jsr.fsu.edu/issues/vol15/mcvicar.html.

A Methodist Preacher (no real name given). "Saliva as an Antidote to Poison." *Southern Cultivator,* Vol. 11, No. 1 (1853): 91.

Nochughi, Hideyo. "Snake Venoms." *Modern Medicine,* Vol. 1 (1907): 247–265.

"Ophidians, No. 3—Their Evils." *The Dublin University Magazine,* Vol. LXXXVII (March 1876): 344–360.

Palmer, Jesse T. "The Banana in Caribbean Trade." *Economic Geography,* Vol. 8, No. 3 (July 1932): 262–273.

Parham, Charles F. "The Latter Rain: The Story of the Original Apostolic or Pentecostal Movements." In *The Life of Charles F. Parham, Founder of the Apostolic Faith Movement,* ed. Sarah E. Parham (1930; New York: Garland, 1985), 51–52.

Parks, William J. "Venomous Reptiles." *Medical Council: A Practical Journal for the General Practitioner,* Vol. 27 (1912): 228.

Parrish, Henry M., James Dikroeger, and Homer Hall. "Counting California's Snakebites." *California Medicine,* Vol. 101, Issue 5 (10 November 1964): 352–357.

Pennsylvania State Department of Agriculture, *The Monthly Bulletin of the Division of Zoology,* Vol. 11, No. 3 (July 1904).

Pizon, Anthony F. "Snakebites: Prehospital Assessment & Treatment of Envenomations."

Journal of Emergency Medical Services, 31 March 2007. http://www.jems.com/articles/2007/03/snakebites.html.

Prairie Illinois Farmer. "Snakes." *The Working Farmer,* Vol. 9 (1858): 165.

"Rasche Hall: A Plain Monument to a Colorful Character." *Virginia Tech Magazine* (Winter 2006). www.vtmagazine.vt.edu/winter2006/retrospect.html.

"Rattlesnakes." *Eclectic Magazine of Foreign Literature, Science, and Art,* Vol. 16 (1872): 723–728.

Reid, H.A., and R.D. Theakston. "The Management of Snake Bite." *Bulletin of the World Health Organization,* 61 (6) (1983): 885–895.

"Remedy for Hydrophobia." *Scientific American,* Vol. XLII, No. 1 (3 January 1880): 264.

Rice, Morris R. "Snake Poison and Its Treatment." *Medical Brief,* Vol. 32, Issue 2: 795–796.

Schraum, Brian. "100 Years of Homecomers: Changes and Constants." *Southeast Missourian,* 20 July 2008. www.semissourian.com/story/1446177.html.

Shipman, George. *The United States Medical and Surgical Journal,* Vol. 3 (1867–8).

Simonds, P.L. *The Journal of the Society of Arts,* No. 216, Vol. V (9 January 1857): 101–105.

Smith, Frances Gow. "Snakes Are Safe If You Know." *Popular Science Monthly,* Vol. 108, No. 1 (January 1926): 20–21, 136–38.

Smith, Sidney, Jr. "Snake Bite." *American Veterinary Review* Vol. 44 (1911–1912): 162.

"Snake Bite." *Animaland,* Staten Island Zoological Society, Vol. XI, No. 3 (July-August 1944): 3–4.

"Snake-bites and Their Treatment." *American Medico-surgical Bulletin,* Vol. 12, No. 21 (10 November 1898): 1031.

"Something About Snake-Root—The First Legislative Grant for a Medical Discovery, North Carolina." *North Carolina Medical Journal,* Vol. XV and XVI (1885): 185–186.

Watts, W.H. "The Bite of the Rattlesnake." *Monthly Homeopathic Review,* Vol. 17, No. 7 (1 July 1870): 442–43.

Webb, Clive E. "Snake-Bite in Horses." *Journal of Comparative Pathology and Therapeutics,* Vol. 20 (1907): 100–104.

Willson, Prentiss. "Snake Poisoning in the United States: A Study Based on an Analysis of Seven Hundred and Forty Cases," *Archives of Internal Medicine,* No. 1 (January 1908): 516–570.

Books

Anthony, Leslie. *Snakebit: Confessions of a Herpetologist.* Vancouver: Greystone Books, 2008.

Beard, Lina, and Adelia Belle Beard. *On the Trail: An Outdoor Book for Girls.* New York: Charles Scribner's Sons, 1915.

Breslaw, Elaine. *Lotions, Potions, Pills and Magic: Health Care in Early America.* New York: New York University Press, 2012.

Cameron, Jenks. *The Bureau of Biological Survey: Its History, Activities and Organization.* Baltimore: Johns Hopkins University Press, 1929.

Chalmers Da Costa, John. *Modern Surgery, General and Operative,* Fifth edition. Philadelphia: W.B. Saunders and Co. 1908.

Chase, A.W. *Dr. Chase's Recipes or Information for Everybody: An Invaluable Collection of about Eight Hundred Practical Recipes.* Ann Arbor: Published by the Author, 1864.

Chen Yuan-Lee, ed. *Snake Venoms.* New York: Springer-Verlag Berlin Heidelberg, 1979.

Chippaux, Jean-Phillipe. *Snake Venoms and Envenomations.* Malabar, FL: Krieger Publishing, 2006.

Christy, Bryan. *The Lizard King: True Crimes and Passions of the World's Greatest Reptile Smugglers.* New York: The Hachette Book Group, 2008.

Conant, Roger, and Joseph T. Collins. *Reptiles and Amphibians: Eastern/Central North America*. Boston: Houghton Mifflin, 1998.

Conn, Charles W. *Like a Mighty Army: A History of the Church of God, 1886–1995*. Cleveland, TN: Pathway Press, 1996.

Detroit Zoological Society. *Wonders Among Us: Celebrating 75 Years of the Detroit Zoo*. Detroit: Detroit Zoological Society, 2003.

Ditmars, Raymond L. *Confessions of a Scientist*. New York: Macmillan, 1934.

_____. *Strange Animals I Have Known*. New York: Harcourt, Brace and Company, 1931.

Ellzey, M.G., in H.H. Soule. *Hints and Points for Sportsmen*. New York: Forest and Stream Publishing Co., 1889.

Findlay, Russell E. *Snake Venom Poisoning*. Great Neck, NY: Scholium International, 1983.

Fleisher, Moyer S., and Leo Loeb. "Action of Calmett's Cobra Antivenin upon the Venom of Heloderma." In Leo Loeb and Carl Alsberg, eds., *The Venom of Heloderma*: 201–203. Washington, D.C.: Carnegie Institute of Washington, 1913.

Galambos, Louis, and Jane Eliot Sewell. *Networks of Innovation: Vaccine Development at Merck, Sharp & Dohme, and Mulford, 1895–1995*. Melbourne: Cambridge University Press, 1995.

Gambin, Lee. *Massacred by Mother Nature: Exploring the Natural Horror Film*. Baltimore: Midnight Marquee Press, 2012.

Green, Harry. *Snakes: The Evolution of Mystery in Nature*. Berkeley: University of California Press, 1997.

Gregersdotter, Katarina, Johan Hoglund, and Nicklas Hallen. "Introduction." In Katarina Gregersdotter, Johan Hoglund, and Nicklas Hallen, eds., *Animal Horror Cinema: Genre, History and Criticism*: 1–18. New York: Palgrave Macmillan, 2015.

Haraway, Donna. *When Species Meet*. Minneapolis: University of Minnesota Press, 2008.

Harger, Wilson G., and Edmond Bonney. *Handbook for Highway Engineers*, 3rd Edition. New York: McGraw-Hill, 1919.

Hoag, R.J., and William A. Deiss, eds. *New Worlds New Animals: From Menagerie to Zoological Park in the Nineteenth Century*. Baltimore: Johns Hopkins University Press, 1996.

Hopley, Catherine C. *Snakes: Curiosities and Wonders of Serpent Life*. London: Griffith and Farran; New York: E.P. Dutton & Co., 1882.

Horowitz, Helen Lefkowitz. "The National Zoological Park: 'City of Refuge or Zoo?'" In R.J. Hoage and William A. Deiss, eds. *New Worlds New Animals: From Menagerie to Zoological Park in the Nineteenth Century*: 126–135. Baltimore: Johns Hopkins University Press, 1996.

James, Jamie. *The Snake Charmer: A Life and Death in Pursuit of Knowledge*. New York: Hyperion, 2000.

King, John, and Robert Newton. *The Eclectic Dispensatory of the United States of America*. Cincinnati: H.W. Derby, 1852.

King, W.A., Jr. *Rattlingly Yours ... Snake King*. Brownsville, TX: Springman-King Lithograph Company, 1964.

Klauber, Laurence M. *Rattlesnake: Their Habits, Life Histories, and Influence on Mankind*. Berkeley: University of California Press, 1997.

Lapidus, Richard. *Snake Hunting on Devil's Highway: Humorous Tales from the Glory Days of Snake Hunting*. Indianapolis: Dog Ear Publishing, 2006.

Levin, Ted. *America's Snake: The Rise and Fall of the Timber Rattlesnake*. Chicago: University of Chicago Press, 2016.

Loeb, Leo, and Carl Alsberg, eds. *The Venom of Heloderma*. Washington, D.C.: Carnegie Institute of Washington, 1913.

Lynch, Charles. *American Red Cross Abridged Text-Book on First Aid, Police and Firemen's Edition*. Philadelphia: P. Blakiston's Son & Co., 1914.

McFarland, Joseph. *A Text-Book Upon the Pathogenic Bacteria and Protozoa*, Seventh Edition. Philadelphia: W.B. Saunders Co., 1912.

Means, Bruce D. *Stalking the Plumed Serpent and Other Adventures in Herpetology.* Sarasota, FL: Pineapple Press, 2008.

New Oxford Annotated Bible, with Apocrypha. New York: Oxford University Press, 1991.

O'Shea, Mark. *Boas and Pythons of the World.* Princeton, NJ: Princeton University Press, 2007.

Otis, George A. *A Report of Surgical Cases: Army of the United States from 1865 to 1871.* War Department, Surgeon General's Office, Circular No. 3, 1871.

Parrish, Henry. *Poisonous Snakebites in the United States.* New York: Vantage Press, 1980.

Peck, H.T. *The International Cyclopaedia*, Vol. 13. New York: Dodd, Mead & Co., 1900.

Potts, James Henry. *Black and White or the Saloon Versus Temperance: The Greatest Problem Facing Our Nation Today.* Detroit: F.B. Dickerson and Co., 1908.

Robins, R.G. *A.J. Tomlinson: Plainfolk Modernist.* New York: Oxford University Press, 2004

Roosevelt, Theodore. *Through the Brazilian Wilderness.* New York: Charles Scribner's Sons, 1914.

Seton, Ernest Thompson. *The Woodcraft Manual for Boys.* Garden City, NY: Doubleday, Page & Co., 1917.

Singer, Peter. *Animal Liberation.* New York: Random House, 1975.

Stutesman, Drake. *Snake.* London: Reaktion Books, 2005.

Swainhardt, Blanche, Ray Cyrus Yeoman, Carlos Grant Williams, Leo Leavitt Rummell, Zeno Payne Metcalf, George Colvin Humphrey, and Florence Forbes. *The Rural Efficiency Guide.* Cleveland: The People's Efficiency Publishing Co., 1918.

Thomson, Rosemarie Garland. *Freakery: Cultural Spectacles of the Extraordinary Body.* New York: New York University Press, 1996.

Warren, John Collins. *Surgical Pathology and Therapeutics.* Philadelphia: W.B. Saunders, 1894.

Wood, George Bacon, and Franklin Bache. *The Dispensatory of the United States of America*, Eleventh Edition. Philadelphia: J.B. Lippincott and Co., 1858.

Television Shows, Documentaries, Movies and Podcasts

Adair, Peter. *Holy Ghost People* (1967).

Anaconda (1997).

Bartley, Larry. *Texas Snake Man.* Rising Star Entertainment Network. Good Ol' Boy Videos.

Big Ass Spiders (2013).

Clayton, Al. *In Jesus' Name: Taking Up Serpents* (1991).

Curse II: The Bite (1981).

Hell Frog Warrior (2002).

Jaws (1975).

Killer Tomatoes Eat France (1981).

Knighton, Ryan. "You're So Screwed." *The Moth Stories Told Live* podcast.

Man Who Injects Venom—Steve Ludwin (2013).

Python Hunters, National Geographic.

Rattlesnake Republic, National Geographic Documentary.

Rattlesnake Roundup, National Geographic.

Robinson, Gretchen, and Stan Woodward. *People Who Take Up Serpents* (1974).

Snake Salvation, National Geographic Channel (2013).

Snakes on a Plane (2006).

Venom Hunters, The Discovery Channel.

Venom Man Lets Deadliest Snake Bite Him (2016). Bancroft T.V.

ZomBeavers (2014).

Index

www.ingramcontent.com/pod-product-compliance
Lightning Source LLC
Chambersburg PA
CBHW031130270326
41929CB00011B/1565

* 9 7 8 1 4 7 6 6 6 2 6 5 7 *